PHILOSOPHY AND RHETORIC IN DIALOGUE

PHILOSOPHY AND RHETORIC IN DIALOGUE: REDRAWING THEIR INTELLECTUAL LANDSCAPE

Edited by
Gerard A. Hauser

The Pennsylvania State University Press
University Park, Pennsylvania

Library of Congress Cataloging-in-Publication Data

Philosophy and rhetoric in dialogue :
redrawing their intellectual landscape / edited by Gerard Hauser.
p. cm.
Includes bibliographical references.
ISBN 978-0-271-02768-5 (pbk. : alk. paper)
1. Philosophy.
2. Rhetoric.
I. Hauser, Gerard A.

B53.P497 2007
100—dc22
2007034945

Printed in the United States of America
Published by The Pennsylvania State University Press,
University Park, PA 16802-1003

It is the policy of The Pennsylvania State University Press to use acid-free paper. This book is printed on Natures Natural, containing 50% post-consumer waste, and meets the minimum requirements of American National Standard for Information Sciences—Permanence of Paper for Printed Library Material,
ANSI Z39.48–1992.

Contents

Philosophy and Rhetoric: An Abbreviated History of an Evolving Identity

Gerard A. Hauser

With this volume, *Philosophy and Rhetoric* begins its fortieth year of publication. As a milestone of longevity, it is both a mark of its youth and its maturity. Most disciplines have flagship journals with considerably longer spans of continuous publication, in some cases exceeding 100 years. *Philosophy and Rhetoric,* however, has no professional society as its sponsor. Its survival has and continues to rest on maintaining a level of intellectual excellence that attracts sufficient subscribers to make it viable. That creates an imperative to publish articles that both sustain a dialogue among an international audience with a focused set of concerns and engage intellectual issues that emerge from a dialogue among scholars who find the relationship between philosophy and rhetoric mutually informing. The intersections, new roads, and cul-de-sacs along the way have been discoveries among authors who often travel in different disciplinary company and write mainly to different disciplinary audiences, but who share in common the view that they cannot fully understand their disciplinary issues without taking their sometimes irreconcilable differences and/or their reciprocal inflections into account.

As the journal begins its fortieth year of publication, it seems fitting to look back at how it started and how it has changed over its course. I must admit that having been associated from its outset, publishing my first scholarly article in the first volume of *P&R* and serving in one editorial capacity or another since its second year of publication, a brief and selective account of how it started and how its path has continued to open new discursive arenas also seems an appropriate way for me to acknowledge its founders and contextualize the papers in this volume. Of course tracing the journal's path, in one respect, cannot help but fall short of the mark. The concerns and issues its authors have addressed are broad, technical, and fraught with disparate interpretations beyond the ken of any single person, not to mention the consequences of space limitations. Nevertheless, there are a few fixed moments along its historical path that offer a sense of how it has evolved and that are worth recording.

Philosophy and Rhetoric was born from a small conference on philosophy and rhetoric held in 1963 under co-sponsorship by the Philosophy and the then Speech departments at Penn State University. The conference itself was the brainchild of the happy union of minds and spirits shared by Carroll Arnold and Henry Johnstone. Shortly after Arnold joined the Penn State faculty in 1961, he and Johnstone became interlocutors on their common passion for the study of argumentation, an enjoyment of intellectual give and take, and an afternoon martini shared among friends. Their bond lasted for the remainder of their lives—nearly forty years.

The journal's founding was one of three significant developments in the 1960s, the others being the Western world's experience of student unrest and rhetoric studies' appropriation of Kenneth Burke's dramatistic theory as paradigmatic, that altered the face of rhetoric studies and also opened philosophy to reconsider the dismissal of rhetoric initiated by the work of René Descartes and continued unabated, if at times challenged, into the middle of the twentieth century.[1] The twentieth-century renaissance of rhetoric studies was a multidisciplinary phenomenon. It commenced with the exodus of public speaking teachers from English departments at the beginning of the century to found departments of speech; broadened its base by mid-century through the research of scholars of antiquity, American and British history, literature, political science, sociology, and speech; saw a return to prominence during the last quarter of the century in writing theory and instruction; and emerged by century's end in the form of new rhetorics that burgeoned as fruitful paradigms in intellectual and social histories, literary and social criticism, and a variety of theoretical works across the humanities and interpretive social sciences. This movement included revival of the ancient dialogue between philosophy and rhetoric that had lain moribund since the Enlightenment. This renewal of philosophy's discussion with rhetoric was particularly important.

From its inception as an area of inquiry at the beginning of the last century, rhetorical theory had been largely confined to investigation of historically significant works. Its manifestations were in the form of intellectual histories, such as W. S. Howell's *Logic and Rhetoric in England, 1500–1700* (1956) and Walter Ong's *Ramus, Method, and the Decay of Dialogue* (1958), or in commentaries on specific doctrines of historically important systems and theories of rhetoric. However, by mid-century philosophers such as Richard McKeon (e.g., 1942, 1957, 1966, 1969, 1970, 1971, 1973) and Ch. Perelman (1969) were turning to rhetoric as a mode of thought and analysis that could address basic questions of knowledge and action in an age lacking a dominant set of shared assumptions. During the last third of the century these important but relatively isolated initial statements exploded into a flurry of intellectual work aimed at theorizing rhetoric in new terms. Henry Johnstone was a leading figure—both as participant and facilitator—in this renewed dialogue.

Among rhetoricians during the middle of the last century, Johnstone was known for his incisive analysis of the nature of philosophical argument. His papers and books on this subject were especially important for their careful consideration of the communicative dimension of philosophical argumentation. He was most centrally identified with the thesis that a philosophical argument relies on its capacity to make a valid assertion within the framework of ones' interlocutor. Quite unlike his Belgian counterparts Ch. Perelman and Lucie Olbrechts-Tyteca (1969), who advocated that philosophical validity resided in appeals that could gain the adherence of a universal audience, Johnstone maintained that philosophical arguments were valid only insofar as they were deemed valid by those to whom they were addressed (1952). For Johnstone, all arguments were bounded by the system of presuppositions in which they were situated. In his view, a proposition without an underlying system of presuppositions was open to the charge of being an arbitrary assertion. One justified one's claims, including alterations in one's assertions, with an eye to achieving consistency with the presuppositions on which the system rested. Indeed, six years before Toulmin's *The Uses of Argument* (1958) appeared, in which he advanced his much-acclaimed theory of field-dependent argument, Johnstone's article on the *argumentum ad hominem* (1952) and subsequent elaborations on and from this thesis (1954a, 1954b) were articulating a position that cut across the grain of universality as the benchmark of validity.

Johnstone and Arnold were founders of the journal in 1968 and its editor and co-editor until 1977. *P&R* heralded a new era in which rhetorical theory itself was reconfigured from elaborations with an almost universally accepted Aristotelian paradigm and studies in the history of ideas to original formulations that marked rhetoric as having its own theoretical domain.[2]

Johnstone's invaluable editorial contribution to the journal's founding and continuing purpose was informed by his own career as a prolific scholar whose philosophical analysis of rhetoric as a mode of argument and philosophical argument as a mode of communication made an important contribution to our understanding of their intertwined character and possibilities. His *oeuvre* of more than 170 scholarly papers, books, and reviews across the last half of the twentieth century provides a legacy that exemplifies the *raison d'étre* of scholarly inquiry and of the journal.[3] Its function as a meeting place for scholarly inquiry of interest and value to both philosophers and rhetoricians was advanced by his relationship with Arnold.

Arnold was equally prominent in the scholarly community of American rhetoricians. He was a generalist who had command of what were then the subareas of the discipline, which was not uncommon, although it was becoming increasingly rare among leading rhetoric scholars of his generation. Within the discipline, his texts on public address (Wilson and Arnold 1964), which had six editions, group discussion (Wagner and Arnold 1950), which had two, and criticism (Arnold 1974), as well as his argued position in several articles, exemplified his vision of the domain of inquiry formerly known as speech. It was a study of discourse, not situations or contexts of communication, in which A communicated with B for some purpose and, therefore, an examination of communication practices that were rhetorical all the way down. His theoretical breadth was expressed in his essay "Oral Rhetoric, Rhetoric, and Literature" (1968), which is reprinted as the concluding contribution to this edition. Arnold was best known as an editor's editor. He possessed an unparalleled eye for the seam of an argument, and insight into how to improve it so that the argument itself became clearer and stronger in revision, even when he was in deep disagreement with its thesis.

Both he and Johnstone had the hallmark trait of the accomplished philosopher and rhetorician to consider without prejudice the possibilities of any serious claim. From the journal's inception until they stepped down as editor and associate editor in 1977, they made joint decisions on every article published by the journal. Their collaboration established a foundation that has supported *P&R's* continuing role as a leading voice in the ongoing discussion of rhetoric's philosophical dimensions and philosophy's concern with, as Maurice Natanson expressed it, "the dialectical possibility of argument with the intent to persuade" (1965, 15). Argument with this intent brings a risk; the arguer may become open "to the viable possibility that the consequences of an argument may be to make (one) see something of the structure of my immediate world" that it calls into question (15).

The topics addressed in the journal have evolved in harness with the issues of the times and, to some extent, those that were associated with its editors. The journal's first issue, published in 1968, announced its purpose as follows:

> *Philosophy and Rhetoric* concerns itself with rhetoric as a philosophical concept. It will publish definitive articles on the nature, scope, and limits of rhetoric, as well as incisive answers to the question whether man [sic] necessarily engages in rhetoric or, on the contrary, can ideally dispense with it. It will encourage explorations of the relations between rhetoric and other human activities, and phenomenological studies of the rhetorical transaction. It will concern itself with the role of rhetoric in philosophical argumentation, and with historical accounts of rhetorical theories insofar as the theories are presented as genuine philosophical views. It also will publish psychological and sociological studies of rhetoric with a strong philosophical component.

At its inception, the editors of *Philosophy and Rhetoric* considered it important to sketch a scholarly horizon that, in their judgment, would frame rapprochement between philosophy and rhetoric. Its concern with examining basic epistemological, ontological, and ethical assumptions underlying human symbol use radically altered the relationship between philosophy and rhetoric from irreconcilable antagonists to interlocutors in a shared inquiry into the constitutive powers of discourse for human experience and the formation of social will. Its framing of the terms of engagement also reflected Johnstone's abiding concern for validity, which attracted papers concerned with the relationship of formal and informal logic to rhetoric, the nature of philosophical argument, and his own position on all philosophical argument being *ad hominem*.

For rhetoricians, the journal marked the beginning of an interdisciplinary, international dialogue on their subject. For philosophers, it called for consideration of pragmatic discourse on subjectivity, agency, and the intersection of a dialectically secured position with human experience and ethical choice.[4] Perhaps as a reflection on the nature and quality of the papers it was publishing as indicating subscribers and readers had a good sense of its intellectual terrain, Johnstone and Arnold loosened the specificity of *P&R's* purpose statement. The publication of its twenty-fifth anniversary issue in 1974 carried a more general expression of the scholarly submissions it sought:

> The editors of this journal believe that the nature and scope of rhetorical activity are philosophically unsettled matters. Papers which explore rhetorical action, rhetorical art, or rhetorical experience without presupposing a priori conceptions of rhetoric are solicited. (7:1)

With the change of editorial responsibilities in 1977 to Donald Verene, the call for articles borrowed from its original statement while expanding its scope to include cultural concerns and to specify particular interest in the *rhetorical* views of historical figures and periods.

> *Philosophy and Rhetoric* publishes papers on theoretical issues involving the relationship between philosophy and rhetoric, studies of rhetorical views of historical figures and periods, analysis of rhetoric to other areas of human culture and thought, and psychological and sociological studies of rhetoric with a strong philosophical emphasis. (10:1)

Verene's concerns with the humanist tradition, and most particularly with the thought of Giambattista Vico, attracted papers that addressed rhetoric's pre-philosophical status. These articles were addressed to the nature and role of *fantasia* and *ingenium* as Vico and the Italian humanists had conceptualized them.

Importantly, during Verene's editorship, the philosophical thought of Ernesto Grassi on rhetoric and philosophy was first introduced to English speakers. Grassi published original papers in the journal (1976, 1978) that sparked rethinking rhetoric and invention in performative terms associated to poetics.

When Johnstone reassumed the editorship in 1987, he kept Verene's call but modified it, in his words, to make a "mid-course correction" as reflected in the policy statement.

> The difference between this (revised) statement and the one it amends are that this statement refers to argumentation and logic and that it repeats, perhaps pleonastically, the adjective "philosophical." (20:3)

He does not mention that the call for papers dealing with "rhetorical views of historical figures and periods" was changed to "philosophical views on the nature of rhetoric of historical figures and during historical periods" for "rhetorical views of historical figures and periods," which reflected his view that philosophy precedes rhetoric and underwrites philosophically interesting rhetorical theory.[5]

In the early 1990s, Johnstone invited others to be his co-editors. First I served in that role. After I accepted an appointment at the University of Colorado at Boulder, Stephen Browne and Marie Secor were his co-editors. Doubtless Secor and Brown prevailed on Johnstone to alter the call to smooth out the revision he had made to announce an added interest in the differences between Western and non-Western rhetorics. It substituted the relationship of rhetoric to "other areas of human experience" for "other areas of human culture and thought," and added literature and scientific inquiry to those areas of study that might have a strong interest for their philosophical emphasis. When Johnstone retired at the completion of volume 30, the co-editorship model continued with Stephen Browne, Richard Doyle, and Pierre Kerzberg serving in that capacity until 2003, when I became editor. During this period, Browne acted as the lead editor and his tenure was marked by the appearance of essays concerned with the implications of postmodern thought for rhetoric and with the character of philosophically informed critique of rhetoric, which he reflects in his contribution to this issue.

Each of these additions and emendations has remained as part of its publication purpose, as has the continuing interest throughout *P&R*'s history with the arguments of significant thinkers and dimensions of language related to its mission. The 1995 revision remains in place today.

The broad concerns that have defined *P&R*'s purpose are represented in the papers that appear in this anniversary issue and are captured by the contributions of Johnstone and Arnold republished here. The opening paper is a lecture presented by Henry Johnstone as his contribution to a colloquium on rhetoric at Marquette University in 1967. It appeared shortly thereafter in *Validity and Rhetoric in Philosophical Argument: An Outlook in Transition* (1978), which was a collection of his essays published by The Dialogue Press of Man & World. Dialogue Press was stillborn, and the paper remains uncirculated and relatively unknown, except to the few who own one of the rare extant copies of *Validity and Rhetoric in Philosophical Argument.* The paper, however, is distinctive in that Johnstone claims he has seen nothing to alter his position on the relationship of philosophy and rhetoric and that this represents his thought at that time. It both advances previous themes and foreshadows others. In Johnstone's view, the mere attempt to persuade was not of philosophic interest. Rhetoric became philosophically interesting only insofar as it was evocative of consciousness. In his words, "*Rhetoric is the evocation and maintenance of the consciousness necessary for communication*" (italics his). His definition of rhetoric as discourse that evokes consciousness was one he continued to maintain, as Donald Verene discusses in his paper. From this perspective, he regarded communication as maintaining an interface between a person and the data of experience. It is a bridge between the two and drives a wedge that brings the person to consciousness of the data calling for reflection. Rhetoric, for Johnstone, is the technique of driving the wedge.

Johnstone's thesis is repeated, built upon, and challenged throughout this volume. A series of papers by Donald Verene, Jean Goodwin, and Frans van Eemeren and Peter Houtlosser center on Johnstone's theory of philosophical argument and its rhetorical dimensions. His view opens to the way rhetoric varies the tone of philosophical formulations in the traditions of *inventio* with respect to human experience, argumentation theory, and argumentation pedagogy.

Verene considers the relationship his conception of philosophical rhetoric bears to Johnstone's and Ernesto Grassi's. Whereas Johnstone kept the two distinct but in relationship—philosophy and rhetoric—that led to consciousness of the self as that which is at risk when engaged in sincere argument, Grassi (1980) fused them when he maintained that rhetoric served a pre-philosophic function wherein it is the inventional tool for producing an idea with signifiance that could be subjected to philosopical analysis. Against these, Verene argues for his own position of *philosophical rhetoric*. Verene maintains that literal-minded constructions of philosophical arguments inevitably misconstrue their nature and function. Verene contends that philosophical arguments are narratives; they are the speech of meaning whose function is to act against forgetting.

Jean Goodwin takes Johnstone's positions on the *ad hominem* and self-risk in a different direction to consider how they illumine the student experience of arguing. Although *P&R* has not published articles dealing directly with pedagogical practices, many of those that have appeared have had deep pedagogical implications, and some have become standard reading assignments. Lloyd Bitzer's paper on the rhetorical situation (1968), Ernesto Grassi's paper on rhetoric and philosophy (1976), and the debate between Edward Schiappa and John Poulakos on the origins of the term "rhetoric" in Greek antiquity (1990a, 1990b, 1990c) are among the many. Goodwin's "Rhetorical Pieties, Johnstone's Impiety, and Ordinary Views of Argument" contends, however, that students have exerted a significant influence on rhetorical theory and its companion theory of argumentation as they are presented in the classroom. She regards this influence, for the most part, to have had unfortunate consequences. Docile students cram for exams and offer little resistance to the intellectual hobby horses of their instructors, while others seem to regard these subjects as either removed from their lives or bring negative attitudes and resist them, which can shut down learning. Meanwhile instructors, sensing this semester's class will be like its predecessors, commonly offer students a defensive piety about their subject: "the first day defense of the dignity of argument." Her article develops a reading of Johnstone's position as an impious acceptance of student critique of argument as conflict ridden, as a challenge to accept its conflictive nature, and as theorizing argument as a search for truth that has conflict at its core. She develops her thesis by examining how students in a course structured around Johnstone's premises experienced argument. Implicit in her analysis is a reciprocity between a student's living through the making, hearing, and answering of arguments and that student's reflection at the level of performance, as Johnstone defended it in his analytic consideration of the a prioris for arguing in the first place. That is, her students encountered making arguments as evoking their sense of the self-risk that Johnstone positioned at the center of a commitment to argue.

Frans van Eemeren and Peter Houtlosser share Goodwin's concern for the way arguments are experienced. Their "Kinship: The Relationship between Johnstone's Ideas about Philosophical Argument and the Pragma-Dialectical Theory of Argumentation" agrees with Johnstone that "only *ex consessis* arguments, whether they are philosophical or not, are considered potentially sound." However, they take issue with the regulative norms on which his position rests. Specifically, they reject his view that all valid philosophical argument is *ad hominem* and adopts the attitude of *con amore*. They contend that these criteria ultimately rest on psychological conditions that are difficult to verify and fail to satisfy the meta-theoretical requirement of externalization. From their pragma-dialectical perspective, the convincing argument combines reasonableness with a pragmatic view of strategic maneuvering, or the moves made in argumentation to achieve a specific aim.

Phillipe Salazar also addresses the pragmatic intersections of philosophy and rhetoric in his analysis of rhetoric's struggle for a place in France's curricular domain, a domain regulated by the state and over which philosophy reigns. It is a meditation on how "the vexed situation of 'argument' in relation to rhetoric and philosophy, and politics, presents itself" in France. In the French curriculum, in which philosophy is regarded as the source of the student's formation as a citizen, rhetoric is considered to be deeply problematic. Philosophy stands in opposition to it because it regards rhetoric as preparing students for a life of "administering oppression." At the same time, how does one form the citizen without attention to his or her ability to be an "efficient speaker"? Salazar traces the varied arguments for dismissing rhetoric from the curriculum, until the debate seems to be resolved by the *Vocabulaire européen des philosphies,* in which rhetoric is denied its own entry while gaining inclusion in discussions of concepts considered part of rhetoric, such as voice and sublimity, and more pointed notions, such as dialectic and sophistic. In Salazar's view, there is a maneuvering around rhetoric to present a philosophical account of rhetorical reasoning acceptable to philosophy as it appears in the French curriculum.

Marilee Mifsud leads us away from the pragmatic to the ontological in her study of rhetoric as gift-giving. Her article brings us into contact with ancient Greek experience of thought and action through its analysis of the tension between gift giving in the Homeric culture and that of the fifth and fourth centuries BCE polis—bestowing gifts to honor the recipient and for calculation of advantage to the gift giver. This difference forms a productive tension, in her view, that takes advantage of rhetoric's power to generate a surplus of meaning. Insofar as creative communication can only occur among persons who, in turn, require creative communication, Mifsud maintains that the tension between the Homeric and the ancient polis cultures of the gift creates the experience of alterity. Drawing on the thought of Hélène Cixous, she proposes that experience of the in-between is "generative of new theoretical directions for rhetoric, so as to get out of the trapping of both the gift and polis economies." Her argument, which seems to be at odds with the emphasis on strategic maneuvering found in pragma-dialectics as advanced by van Eemeren and Houtslosser, ultimately asserts that rhetoric is a form of hospitality, a sumptuous expenditure of its surplus meaning freed from exchangist terms.

The final set of essays is concerned with the disclosive power of philosophical considerations that underwrite criticism and of philosophically informed criticism on the intersections of philosophy and rhetoric. Stephen Browne ruminates on his experiences as a critic and a past editor of *P&R* to argue for the necessity of informed criticism to adhere to meta-critical considerations of a philosophically informed act. He regards criticism, at its core, as an argument. It is a form of bilateral communication and, as such, requires a reader capable of joining the discussion of its subject. As with all arguments, criticism makes commitments, which are, themselves, open to critique. Browne strikes a chord reminiscent of Johnstone's concern over those who want "philosophy without tears" and thus offer analysis that exhibits an interest in a philosophical issue but failure to have engaged in the hard thinking necessary to make a sound philosophical argument (1987, xvii). The norm of bilaterality is violated, he contends, whenever critics write their critiques in ways that make them inaccessible to critical engagement themselves.

The essays by Erik Doxtader and Barbara Biesecker are illustrative of philosophically informed critical inquiry that raises basic questions about the relationship of conceptual frames to practice. Using the case of post-Apartheid reconciliation in South Africa as his object of study, Doxtader explores how the difference between identity and identification complicates the relationship between recognition and reconciliation. Inspired in part by Hegel's discussion of recognition and reconciliation in *Phenomenology of the Spirit,* he considers how, on one hand, the ontology of identity is at risk, if not stripped of meaning, by the relational terms of reconciliation. Reconciliation denies meaning in and of itself and replaces it with meaning in terms of the other. If reconciliation and identity form a circle of otherness that causes friction between the world of sovereignty and the word of rhetorical invention, on the other side, the world of identity alone can be one of violence. The risk self without reflection on costs betrays failure to find sovereignty without (self)sacrifice. Recognition and reconciliation form a constellation of meanings. He finds their relationship clarifies the problem of identity for the form(ation) of human relationship and the problem of movement between the world of (self)sacrifice and the world that "discovers sovereignty only in the acceptance of its own (self)sacrifice." His exploration intensifies both understanding the consequences of recognition versus reconciliation in reconstructing South Africa as a democracy and insight into the risks underlying tension between identity and community when viewed through the South African experience.

(Self)sacrifice rings in a quite different and more ominous tone in Barbara Biesecker's paper, "No Time for Mourning: The Rhetorical Production of the Melancholic Citizen-Subject in the War on Terror." This paper continues her reflections on the relationship between the assumptions underlying psychiatric construction of collective identity in the social imaginary and performances of social will (e.g., Biesecker 1998, 2002). In this case, she explores how the conceptual transformation of melancholia from a Freudian mechanism of "failure" to one of "resistance," as framed by radical cultural and social theorists, is itself challenged by Slavoj Žižek, who argues that those who figure melancholy as resistance have failed to go far enough and, consequently, aid and abet global capitalism and its devastating effects. Drawing on his argument that contrary to the prevailing view of melancholy as loss, it is rather lack, she raises the provocative question of source of "modulation or particularization of forms" when confronted by "the irremedial gap between symbolization and the Real." Her analysis of how the Bush Administration's rhetoric following the 9/11 attack on the World Trade Center induces confusion of loss with lack is a demonstration of the philosophically informed criticism called for by Browne and by the journal's statement of purpose.

The concluding paper by Carroll Arnold was, he wrote, "his final struggle with the conventional categories used in discussing prose." In subtle ways, Arnold's argument was ahead of its time. His exploration of oral rhetoric's ontological conditions, written just as the influence of thinkers such as Habermas, Derrida, Foucault, Benhabib, Cixous, and others were beginning to reframe the terms of engagement for philosophy with rhetoric and push theorizing in new directions, is prescient. For him, rhetoric was definitively performative, in which "something resembling the speaker's script is to be played ensemble despite the fact that no one engaged in the personalized, rhetorical situation can be cast as a minor actor within *his* (sic, italics his) dramatic world." The stakes of this performance are sovereignty of the self, which entails the ethical norm of respecting the soverignty of those addressed. His concerns and commitments in this paper, expressed from different starting points and for different ends, are resonant with the arguments raised by Verene on narrative as the speech of memory, of the bounds van Eemeren and Houtlosser place on strategic maneuvering, on Doxtader's exploration of the problematic of recognition and reconciliation, and the stripping of sovereignty Biesecker finds in the melancholia of presidential discourse on 9/11.

***

Writing an introduction to a collection of papers assembled to celebrate the journal's fortieth year of continuous publication offers no easy conclusion; the dialogue between philosophy and rhetoric continues, both are indelibly if at times illegibly in and of the human condition. There can be no stopping point. The topics continue to change, the guiding ideas change with them, as they have over its past thirty-nine years. These are the necessities of thought that is alive and evolving.

It was my privilege to be colleague and friend of Johnstone and Arnold. In private conversation, Henry once distinguished between academicians who engage in an activity and those who study its practitioners: the former engage in the discipline's intellectual practices to generate new statements about a set of intellectual concerns; the latter engage in the discipline's professional practices to transmit and comment on what others have produced. Writing in the discipline's specialized vocabulary, adhering to its professional norms, producing evidence that allows for continual certification of professional standing but without going through the slow and painful process of intellectual work necessary to produce an original contribution has become increasingly commonplace in the contemporary academy. As a young academician who asked Arnold to critique his papers, I learned first hand that he lived by the same credo. For both men, the allure of professional standing meant far less than their passion for engaging a serious question on its own terms as an intellectual problem worth consideration and of following the argument with open-mindedness, wherever it may lead. They set the guidelines for what *P&R* has been and what it might become.

Department of Communication
University of Colorado at Boulder

Notes

1. This is not to say that other developments, albeit less directly influential on a rapprochement between philosophy and rhetoric, did not also change the face of rhetoric studies, including the work of Edward P. J. Corbett, whose *Classical Rhetoric for the Modern Student* (1965) revived rhetoric as central to the writing process, Wayne Booth, whose *The Rhetoric of Fiction* (1961) made a case for the centrality of rhetoric to literary criticism, and the founding of the Rhetoric Society of America, which has become the umbrella organization for the many traditions of teaching and research within the discipline.

2. Rhetorical theory, in significant ways, is a historicized subject with roots in Greek antiquity that continue to inflect it as a domain of inquiry. The breadth of this frame, however slavish to ancient models it may have been up to 1968, was still significantly challenged by a conceptualization of methodology set forth in Duhamel's significant paper (1949), in which he argued for multiple rhetorics that could only be explicated in terms of the epistemological, psychological, and metaphysical assumptions they employed. The controversy over the explanatory power of Greco-Roman antiquity on rhetorical thought is captured in the exchanges between Ehninger (1955, 1963) and Douglas McDermott (1963), with Ehninger's paper, "On Systems of Rhetoric" (1968), published in *Philosophy and Rhetoric,* becoming a standard that influenced the next generation of historical studies. This view, in turn, has been challenged by post-structural, deconstructionist, psychiatric, and other frames in which rhetoric is conceptualized as a historicized subject and by the ways past thought is both appropriated and challenged. A representative example is the paper by Barbara Biesecker in this volume.

3. For a complete bibliography of Johnstone's publications, see Hauser (2001).

4. The novelty of *P&R*'s purpose and relevance to philosophy and rhetoric studies is exemplified by Arnold and Johnstone, along with their wives, Bie and Marjorie, passing out pamphlets in the lobby and outside the hotels where their respective scholarly associations were holding their annual meetings. This "hawking our wares," as Arnold put it, to penetrate the awareness of one discipline

that had dismissed the relevance of rhetoric or, at best, held it at arms length, and the other tied to a conception of theory as the study of historically significant treatises, continued through the first three years of *P&R*'s existence.

5. Johnstone expresses his view in the foreword to *Rhetoric and Philosophy* (1990), edited by Richard Cherwitz.

Works Cited

Arnold, Carroll C. 1968. "Oral Rhetoric, Rhetoric, and Literature." *Philosophy and Rhetoric* 1:191–210.

———. 1974. *Criticism of Oral Rhetoric*. Columbus, OH: Charles E. Merrill.

Biesecker, Barbara A. 1998. "Rhetorical Studies and the 'New Psychoanalysis: What's the Real Problem? or Framing the Problem of the Real." *Quarterly Journal of Speech* 84:222–38.

———. 2002. "Remembering World War II: The Rhetoric and Politics of National Commemoration at the Turn of the 21st Century." *Quarterly Journal of Speech* 88:393–409.

Bitzer, Lloyd. 1968. "The Rhetorical Situation." *Philosophy and Rhetoric* 1:1–14.

Booth, Wayne. 1961. *The Rhetoric of Fiction*. Chicago: U of Chicago P.

Burke, Kenneth. 1950. *A Rhetoric of Motives*. New York: Prentice-Hall.

Corbett, Edward P. J. 1965. *Classical Rhetoric for the Modern Student*. New York: Oxford UP.

Duhamel, P. Albert. 1949. "The Function of Rhetoric as Effective Expression." *Journal of the History of Ideas* 10:344–56.

Ehninger, Douglas. 1955. "Campbell, Blair, and Whately: Old Friends in a New Light." *Western Speech* 19:263–69.

———. 1963. "Campbell, Blair, and Whately Revisited." *Southern Speech Journal* 28:168–82.

———. 1968. "On Systems of Rhetoric." *Philosophy and Rhetoric* 1:131–44.

Grassi, Ernesto. 1976. "Rhetoric and Philosophy." *Philosophy and Rhetoric* 9:200–216.

———. 1978. "Can Rhetoric Provide a New Basis for Philosophizing? The Philosophical Tradition." *Philosophy and Rhetoric* 11:1–18, 75–97.

———. 1980. *Rhetoric as Philosophy*. University Park: Pennsylvania State UP.

Hauser, Gerard A. 2001. "Henry W. Johnstone Jr.: Reviving the Dialogue of Philosophy and Rhetoric." *Communication Review* 1:1–25.

Howell, Wilber Samuel. 1956. *Logic and Rhetoric in England, 1500–1700*. Princeton: Princeton UP.

Johnstone, Henry W. 1952. "Philosophy and *Argumentum ad Hominem*." *Journal of Philosophy* 49:489–98.

———. 1954a. "The Nature of Philosophical Controversy." *Journal of Philosophy* 51:294–300.

———. 1954b. "A New Theory of Philosophical Argumentation." *Philosophy and Phenomenological Research* 15:244–52.

———. 1978. *Validity and Rhetoric in Philosophical Argument: An Outlook in Transition*. University Park, PA: The Dialogue Press of Man & World.

———. 1990. "Foreword." In *Rhetoric and Philosophy*, ed. Richard Cherwitz, xv–xviii. Hillside, NJ: Lawrence Erlbaum Associates.

McDermott, Douglas. 1963. "George Campbell and the Classical Tradition." *Quarterly Journal of Speech* 49:403–9.

McKeon, Richard. 1942. "Rhetoric in the Middle Ages." *Speculum* 17:1–32.

———. 1957. "Communication, Truth, and Society." *Ethics* 67:89–99.

———. 1966. "The Methods of Rhetoric and Philosophy: Invention and Judgment." In *The Classical Tradition: Literary and Historical Studies in Honor of Harry Caplan*, ed. Luitpold Wallach, 365–73. Ithaca: Cornell UP.

———. 1969. "Discourse, Demonstration, Verification, and Justification." In *Discourse, Demonstration, Verification*, 37–55. Louvain: Nauwelearts.

———. 1970. "Philosophy of Communication and the Arts." In *Perspectives in Education, Religion and the Arts*, ed. H. Keifer and M. Munitz. Albany: SUNY P.

———. 1971. "The Uses of Rhetoric in a Technological Age: Architectonic Productive Arts." In *Prospect of Rhetoric*, ed. Edwin Black and Lloyd Bitzer, 44–63. Englewood Cliffs, NJ: Prentice-Hall.

———. 1973. "Creativity and the Commonplace." *Philosophy and Rhetoric* 6:199–210.

Natanson, Maurice. 1965. "The Claims of Immediacy." In *Philosophy, Rhetoric, and Argumentation,* ed. Maurice Natanson and Henry W. Johnstone Jr., 10–19. University Park: Pennsylvania State UP.

Ong, Walter. 1958. *Ramus, Method, and the Decay of Dialogue*. Cambridge, MA: Harvard UP.

Perelman, Ch., and L. Olbrechts-Tyteca. 1969. *The New Rhetoric: A Treatise on Argumentation,* trans. John Wilkinson and Purcell Weaver. Notre Dame, IN: Notre Dame UP.

Poulakos, John. 1990. "Interpreting Sophistical Rhetoric: A Reply to Schiappa." *Philosophy and Rhetoric* 23:218–28.

Schiappa, Edward. 1990a. "Neo-Sophistic Rhetorical Criticism or the Historical Reconstruction of Sophistic Doctrines." *Philosophy and Rhetoric* 23:192–217.

———. 1990b. "History and Neo-Sophistic Criticism: A Reply to Poulakos." *Philosophy and Rhetoric* 23:307–15.

Toulmin, Stephen. 1958. *The Uses of Argument.* Cambridge: Cambridge UP.

Wagner, Russell H., and Carroll C. Arnold. 1950. *Handbook of Group Discussion.* Boston: Houghton Mifflin.

Wilson, John F., and Carroll C. Arnold. 1964. *Public Speaking as a Liberal Art.* Boston: Allyn and Bacon.

The Philosophical Basis of Rhetoric

Henry W. Johnstone Jr.

I want to begin by distinguishing between what has a philosophical basis at all and what has none. Science, history, morals, and art have a philosophical basis. Fishing, tennis, needlecraft, and carpentry do not. The criterion that determines membership in each list is simple: an activity has a philosophical basis if, and only if, the practice of it distinguishes man from the animals. It must be disqualified on the ground that some animals, as well as men, fish. It might be argued, however, that there is an art of fishing requiring tools utilizable by man alone, and that the ability to fish in this way distinguishes man form the animal. To be sure, in some cultures fishing with appropriate tools is necessary. In others, carpentry is. But if we came across a culture in which fishing did not occur, we would not say, "This creature does not fish; hence he is not a man'; and the same for carpentry. It may seem that the same question arises for science and history. Not all cultures are scientific. If science is indeed, as I maintain, necessary for men, what then prevents us from visiting some primitive tribe and saying, "These creatures have no science; hence they are not men"? The answer is that the culture we have encountered is prescientific. Even though its participants have at the moment no science, science is somehow "in the cards" for them. We would not characterize the nomads of Afghanistan as being in a pre-fishing era. We would not say that fishing was in the cards for them. Of course if the desert should become a sea, they will become fishermen, and there will have been a pre-fishing era. But it is not *necessary* to the character or status of the nomad that he represent either a pre-fishing or a fishing, or, for that matter, a post-fishing era. It is not necessary for man, however, that he be either prescientific man or scientific man or postscientific man. I add the last rubric to accommodate not only the tragic possibility of a cataclysm that could wipe out all humans capable of maintaining the tradition of science but also the ironic possibility that man might some day simply turn away from science. In either eventuality, man would be essentially characterized as a being living in a postscientific era; that is, not merely as a being bereft of science, but as a being living a life either oriented to the cataclysm that had shattered the tradition of science or else oriented to the conviction that science is a thing of the past. The non-fishing nomad, on the other hand, need not take any position at all with regard to the nature or value of fishing. The possibility of fishing need receive no mention in any characterization of him.

The principle I have roughly stated and exemplified implies that if rhetoric has a philosophical basis, it is necessary to man, in the sense that all men live in either a pre-rhetorical culture, or a rhetorical culture, or a post-rhetorical culture. Each of these cultures is characterized by a disposition toward rhetoric. In the pre-rhetorical era, even though man does not engage in any form of rhetoric that we can recognize, we can see rhetorical activity as in the cards for him. Perhaps someone will object that there never has been such an era; as long as man has existed, he has engaged in rhetoric. So much the better for my argument; for then it is all the more clearly the case that rhetoric is necessary to man. But if man has gone through a pre-rhetorical phase, he is distinguished form all nonhuman creatures in this respect. No one would say of rats, cats, or cows that they are not yet engaged in rhetoric, but that once the idea occurs to them they will be. But man is either rhetorical from the outset or fated to become so once a certain idea dawns upon him—this, at any rate, is what anyone would be claiming who asserted that rhetoric has a philosophical basis. The assertion also implies that if man ever ceases to be rhetorical, his cessation will not be a mere turning of attention from rhetoric to some other activity—as a primitive tribe might turn from fishing to hunting—but will take the form of a positive attitude; the belief, for example, that rhetorical activity is out of date or is immoral.

Although there is some *prima facie* plausibility in the thesis that rhetoric is necessary to man, the thesis is not easy to prove. The two main attempts to prove it have been those made by naturalists and pragmatists. According to the naturalists, man is by nature a bellicose being, and rhetoric arises as a substitute for his warlike propensities—a temporary transfer of hostility from the battlefield to the halls of disputation. This theory seems doubtful at best; I am sure that a careful reading of history would show that most wars are caused by rhetoric rather than the other way around. Even if the theory were true, furthermore, it would not establish that rhetoric is necessary to man—it would simply show that rhetoric is an expedient sometimes tried out in the attempt to gain a surcease from fighting, but in principle doomed to failure.

The pragmatic view defines rhetoric in terms of the fundamental category of action. Action, on this view, is intrinsically fraught with risk. We cannot know what the ultimate consequences of our acts will be. Our estimates are at best probable, and rhetoric is argumentation over the probabilities. Personally, I prefer this view to the naturalistic one, because it seems to me to reflect a sounder judgment concerning what it is to be a man; but in the last analysis I cannot accept it. The pragmatic view is unable to show the necessity of rhetoric to man, and this is for a very simple reason: it cannot show the necessity of anything other than statements that are trivially true. Where all nontrivial statements are at best probable, it can hardly be necessary for a man to use rhetoric.

My own argument for the necessity of rhetoric to man is that rhetoric is implied in the very activity which is supposed to supersede it; to wit, the communication of objective fact. In attempting to spell out this argument, I may seem at times to be moving rather far afield; much of what I want to say I find I can most conveniently say by discussing computers. But having disposed of computers, I will eventually turn to rhetoric as such, and I hope my readers will then agree that what appeared to be a digression was not a digression at all.

What, then, can we say of a situation in which rhetoric has been totally suppressed in favor of communication? In such a situation there would be no need for persuasion. Information would replace argument. Instead of attempting to convince me of the truth of a certain proposition or the correctness of a certain course of action, my interlocutor would simply tell me. My readers may feel that this situation is already familiar to them, in the writings of Orwell if not in accounts of past and existing monolithic states. But these are not situations without rhetoric; they are rather situations which ironically must be sustained by rhetoric. Only through the official rhetoric can private and deviant uses of rhetoric be rigorously suppressed. A situation totally devoid of rhetoric would be more appropriately exemplified by a system of devices designed to receive, store, manipulate, and transmit information. Certainly rhetoric could have no effect on such a system. One can't argue with a machine—one can only control it. The question I want to ask is whether a machine of this kind or a system of them does in fact represent a situation in which we have succeeded in suppressing rhetoric in favor of communication.

It might be supposed that no more perfect vehicle of communication could be imagined than a deck of punched cards constituting a computer program. There is no ambiguity whatever about the information conveyed to the machine. Nor would it make sense to suppose the machine in any way reluctant to receive the information. A rhetoric of belief would be absolutely gratuitous even if it were possible. Nor is there any need for a rhetoric of action. Some of the cards in this deck formulate commands to the machine. For example, if a certain statement is true, the machine is told to go to another statement designated as "200" and execute the command therein expressed; otherwise, it is to go to "300." The machine does not need to be convinced of the correctness of this course of action. Indeed, the very notion that a course of action would be correct for it is tenuous, to say the least.

Using a deck of punched cards, or some other input device like a magnetic tape or a light-pen, I establish absolute communication with the computer. Is it not obvious, though, that this absolute communication is identical with absolute noncommunication? I "tell" the computer that the initial value of the variable N is 15. But have I really communicated anything to it? It has no choice but to accept 15 as the value of N. Perfect communication, and hence noncommunication, characterizes the transmission of messages from man to machine and from the machine to other machines. In order to show why it amounts to noncommunication, let us contrast it with the transmission of a message from machine to man. Suppose that "N = 15" is not the initial datum of a problem, but rather the solution to the problem that a user has programmed a computer to solve. Accordingly, the user in question will receive from the machine a sheet of paper on which is printed the expression "N = 15." One might suppose that this, too, is perfect communication. Certainly there is no ambiguity about it. But the fact remains that the user need not accept it. He may say, "Hey! Wait a minute! That can't be right!" Anyone who has had experience with computes will recognize this situation. Computers do not always tell the truth; they do so only when they are correctly programmed and given data that are correct. Even if "N = 15" is actually the correct answer, the user need not accept it; his past dealings with the machine may have made a doubting Thomas of him. And even if the user does not reject "N = 15" as the solution to the problem, he need not accept it, either. His mind may simply be on something else. Perfect communication presupposes a perfect listener. But, as I will try to show, a perfect listener would hear nothing.

The question before us is whether we can replace rhetoric by communication. A likely instrument for carrying out the replacement is the computer. It turns out, however, that in the process of getting rid of rhetoric, we have gotten rid of communication as well. For we can actually communicate nothing to the machine; we can at best get it to accept. The issue here is not whether the datum is true or false; it is only whether the recipient can judge it false, or ignore it altogether. Hence, in our dealings with a computer, we have not suppressed rhetoric in favor of communication; we have simply been discussing a situation to which rhetoric and communication are alike irrelevant.

The machine in the version we were just considering failed to serve as an appropriate model of a kind of communication with no rhetorical component because it did not engage in communication at all. It might be thought, however, that by modifying the machine we could create the needed model. If the fault lies in the perfection of perfect communication, let us undo that perfection. Receiving communications imperfectly, the modified machine will, we hope, at least receive them. Rhetoric, however, will still play no part in the message we address to the machine. We can address it rhetorically no more than we can preach to the waves—at least, success in the one enterprise is an unlikely as it is in the other.

Accordingly, let us try to construct a machine to which we cannot communicate perfectly. In fact, we may feel that we do not need to devote much effort to this task. We have merely to shift our perspective on existing machines. When we avowed that we could communicate perfectly to them, what we really had in mind were ideal machines. For it is only in theory that a computer would always and of necessity accept, say, the information that N is 15. Now, shifting our perspective slightly, we acknowledge that existing machines are fallible; mechanical parts wear out, short circuits occur, unexpected "bugs" develop. One cannot at all be sure that an existing machine will accept the information that N is 15.

It does not follow, however, that we are able to communicate with it. For the explanation of its failure is nothing at all like the explanation of human failure. The man fails to accept the datum that N = 15 either because he refuses to believe it or because his mind is not on the printed sheet before him. We could communicate with him if his mind were on what we told him and he believed it. The machine, however, can neither have its mind on what is being transmitted to it nor receive this datum absent-mindedly; and it can neither believe nor disbelieve what it is told.

Conversely, we may ask whether we would regard the ability on the part of the human to accept or reject information as the machine accepts or rejects it as evidence that we could communicate with him or her. The machine accepts information by passing into a certain state—a certain piece of iron in the machine, for example, is magnetized. Perhaps the closest parallel in the case of a person is post-hypnotic suggestion. If the hypnotist succeeds in putting me in a state in which my nose itches whenever I hear the word "freight," he has stimulated me in exactly the way in which a punched card bearing the message "N = 15" stimulates a computer. But no one would say that he had communicated anything to me—indeed, the very point of post-hypnotic suggestion is that I be unaware of suggestion.

We have failed to communicate with the machine because our communication is still perfect. The computer had to accept whatever it *did* accept. Suppose that instead of accepting the datum that N is 15, the computer stores the value 14 in the location identified with the variable N. This malfunction can undoubtedly be explained. And to explain it is to show why the machine *had* to accept 14 as the value. This value is thus perfectly communicated to it by errant features of the situation (for example, by a card reader with a short circuit), even though it is not the value the user intended to communicate to it. The machine's failure, furthermore, is not like the failure of a human to accept a datum. It is not *either* because the machine believes that 15 is not the correct value *or* because its mind is not on what it is doing that it stores 14 as the value. But it is only when communication can fail in ways like these that it can occur at all.

It might be supposed that a computer could simulate theses human failings. Computers do in fact comment on the programs that are given to them, pointing out syntactical errors and inconsistencies. Why could not a machine be designed to criticize the data fed into it, rejecting those which, on one criterion or another, were unacceptable? For example, if N has already been assigned the value 14, it may be inconsistent to assign it the value 15. The machine I am envisaging would say, in effect (and could say quite explicitly, if we wanted it to), "Hey! Wait a minute! That can't be right!"

When we tell the machine we have just constructed that N = 15, we run a risk. Perhaps it will accept the datum. But it need not, and if it does not it will print out the error message that I have just phrased in a colloquial form. In view of this risk, have we not at last managed to avoid perfect communication with the machine and thus managed to engage in genuine communication with it? If so, we have communication without rhetoric, for, short of magic, we cannot persuade the machine.

There is a difference, however, between the machine's refusal to accept 15 as a datum and a similar refusal on the part of a person. The machine's refusal consists in *telling the user* that 15 is not an acceptable value for N, and in not storing 15 in the appropriate location. The person's refusal, on the other hand, involves *telling himself* that 15 can't be right. (He may also tell others, but he need not.) The machine does not tell *itself* anything. In other words, it is not *conscious* of anything. An individual incapable of telling himself, in images if not in words, whatever he is claimed to be conscious of, is not conscious of it. The mere ability to blurt it out is no criterion of consciousness. Now if the computer cannot be said to be conscious that 15 is not an acceptable value of N, even though it tells *us* that it is not acceptable, then it cannot be conscious that a datum *is* acceptable when it *is*. But we do not succeed in communicating. To say that he must be conscious of what we are communication is just another way of saying something I said before—that he must be free to accept or reject the datum. The nature of consciousness is the root of the paradox of perfect communication. The communication of a datum could be perfect only if it were in principle impossible for the recipient to tell himself otherwise. But in this case, he would be unconscious, and no communication at all would have taken place.

My argument so far has been that we cannot use machines, or systems of them, to illustrate the thesis that there are cases of communication requiring no rhetoric, because machines do not exemplify communication in the first place. As soon as we approach genuine communication, we depart form the world of the machine, and we set foot in a domain requiring rhetoric as an inextricable adjunct or aspect of communication. But this point I have so far made only in a negative way. It cries out for positive argumentation and illustration. Why is rhetoric necessary? What is the indispensable role it plays?

I have just claimed that communication entails consciousness. Without further ado, let me state my main thesis: *Rhetoric is the evocation and maintenance of the consciousness required for communication.* The reason rhetoric does not work when applied to a machine is that the latter cannot be conscious of anything. But it is required whenever there is genuine communication. Let us recall the computer user who received the printed statement "N = 15" from the computer. We might be tempted to wonder what role rhetoric could possible have in this act of straightforward communication. But it was just the fact that the man could have failed to accept the statement that certified his acceptance as the consummation of a genuine act of communication. And rhetoric, whatever else it is, is certainly concerned with the acceptance of refusal to accept statements. There is a rhetoric of factual communication as well as a rhetoric of exhortation. The facts never speak for themselves; they are always spoken for or against by the rhetorical ambiance of the situation in which they are asserted—an ambiance that is the suppressed premise of the rhetorical enthymeme. Even computer output has rhetorical force, the source of which is in the user himself. If I trust the machine, and feel competent to handle it, and am familiar in addition with the general range of values within which the solution of my problem must fall, I endow the machine's output only if I am not completely under the spell of the machine. Most programmers are not; they know that the computer is not more than a device for confronting them with the consequences of their own thinking, exposing its shoddiness to the full light of day when it has been shoddy.

Supposing that all genuine communication does require rhetoric, what does all this have to do with the evocation and maintenance of consciousness? The machine is once again a handy model to serve as the basis of the discussion. Let me begin my mentioning the concept of an *interface.* And interface is the point at which a message passes from one form into another. For example, the card-reader, which converts holes in punched cards into electrical impulses, is an interface. So is the output printer, and so is a cathode-ray tube into which output might be fed. Now if the phenomenon if *being conscious of* is something that is to occur, or is to have an analogue, in the machine, it seems plausible to look for it in the relation between what lies on one side of an interface and what lies on the other. If there is to be consciousness anywhere in the machine, for example, one might expect to find it in the machine's acceptance, in terms of an electrical response, of the datum of which he is conscious. But in face, the analogy does not hold; for, as we have seen there is in fact a radical difference between a person's acceptance of a datum and a machine's acceptance of it. I want to argue that the analogy collapses because, in the sense of "interface" in which interfaces are actually involved in communication, there are really no interfaces at all in the machine; or, alternatively, if we insist on maintaining a sense of "interface" in which there are interfaces in the machine, these latter separate activities that are not separated from each other by any distance of a relevant kind. The relevant kind of distance is that between a person and what is communicated to him. It is this distance that permits him to accept or reject the proffered datum. The only reason why such distance is not available to the machine is that it is impossible to maintain the distinction between the two sides of the interface. For if the card-reader is an interface between punched card and computer, why can we not say, with equal justice, that whatever connects any two elements of the computer is an interface between them? We thus immediately push the concept to triviality. Conversely, we can show that there are in principle no interfaces at all in the system in which the machine is involved. For we can regard the printer as the interface between the output and all of the earlier parts of the train taken together. But if we take these parts together, what is there to prevent us from taking the printer along with them? It seems altogether arbitrary to call the printer an "interface."

Yet even if the concept of an interface cannot be consistently applied to the machine, for the benefit of which it was invented, it can be applied to the reception of messages by people, even though not invented for this purpose. If we elect to say that consciousness is an interface between the computer's output and a person's acceptance or rejection of this output, this statement is not obviously trivial or false in the way that the statement on which it is modeled is. The interface in this case can be neither endlessly proliferated nor eliminated. There is a distance between the person and the datum, but this distance is not to be found everywhere.

We can imagine, furthermore, what it would be like if the interface between the person and the datum were eliminated. One is very often confronted with data of which one is not conscious—the weather report one is not listening to, the striking of the clock; for that matter, any background sound (which is always a datum of *something*). To say that one is not conscious of such data is just to say that there is no distance between oneself and the data—one accepts the data only in a sense in which one could not reject them. Who is to say in this case which is the interface? Is it the vibrating body, the sound waves, the vibrating eardrum, or the cochlea, which converts mechanical into electrical energy? Or is there no interface at all to interrupt the unity of this seamless fabric? Whichever way we look at the activity in question, it is one in which the person is sometimes engaged and in which the machine is always engaged.

It now becomes evident what would be required if we were to succeed in communication with the machine. We would have to introduce a genuine interface between the machine and the datum we wished to communicate to it. Is it not clear, however, that in the entire world of physical things, of which the machine is a part, there is no genuine interface? Nothing is sufficiently *other* than a person can be communicated to him.

To be conscious of something is always to interrupt the unity of the transaction between subject and object. Consciousness confronts the person with something radically other than himself. I have the power to accept or reject a datum only because I am not the datum. The question that now seems most imperative to deal with is "How can two beings that are radically different be brought into relation to each other at all?" I myself believe that no consistent answer to this question is possible. Consciousness is a contradiction which consists in bringing together the poles of a contradiction. But without consciousness there could be no distinction between the person and a datum other than the person; no interface could ultimately be maintained. For that matter, without the distinction between person and datum there could be no consciousness of anything. If consciousness is a contradiction, let us not presume that it accordingly does not exist; it is only in a world in which all problems have been swept under the rug that there are no contradictions.

To get back to rhetoric, I have so far characterized it as the evoking and maintaining of consciousness insofar as consciousness is involved in communication. This characterization distinguishes rhetoric both from suggestion and from the aesthetic experience. The former is specifically not an evocation of consciousness, but a technique of getting a person to accept data in just the way that a machine accepts them. Suggestion attempts to dissolve the interface between person and datum. Aesthetic experience, on the other hand, does invite consciousness, but it is not consciousness arising *a propos* of an attempt to communicate.

An interface is a kind of wedge as well as a kind of bridge, and rhetoric is the technique of driving the wedge between a person and the data of his immediate experience. We have seen how the rhetoric of factual communication can drive it. Just as the data of sensuous experience can constitute a background from which the person is not separated, so can data in a more technical sense. The computer operator sits idly by while the machine spews forth page after page of numbers arranged in columns. To him, this flow of printed paper is just an aspect of the metabolism of a healthy machine. He takes it in, just as the machine itself has taken in the data on the punched cards fed to it. The user to whom the printed sheets are eventually handed may also merely take in the numbers. He may simply accept them as the machine accepts data. But he need not. A distance may be interposed between him and the numbers. The force that interposes it is the rhetoric of objective communication. The source of the rhetoric, as we have already seen, is in the user himself. He has an idea what the numbers ought to be like, and if they fail to conform to his idea, he suddenly begins to view them with suspicion. If he does, his consciousness of the numbers has been evoked by his own previous state; he has moved himself. Objective data are communicated, of course, by other persons as well as by machines. In both cases, the sole source of the rhetoric required to evoke consciousness in the recipient is the recipient himself. The fact that the person who communicates the data does not engage in rhetoric in the act of communicating them—or at least does not properly do so if the communication is objective—has made it appear that no rhetoric at all is involved in objective communication. If it were not, however, communication would collapse into the mere acceptance of data *à la* machine.

A reflexive rhetoric of objective communication has not generally been recognized. It is perhaps more plausible, however, to characterize the irreflexive rhetoric that applies to the other domains of discourse in the same terms as those in which we have characterized the reflexive rhetoric. It, too, seeks to evoke and maintain consciousness—in this case, consciousness on the part of someone other than the user of the rhetoric. What is attacked by both the irreflexive rhetoric of belief and the irreflexive rhetoric of action is just unconsciousness in all its forms: unawareness, naive acceptance, shortsightedness, complacency, blind confidence, unquestioning conformity to habits of thought and action, or lack of appreciation of the personal qualities of a distinguished man. The senses have long been held to dull the mind, and the rhetoric of the Puritan is once again intended to evoke a heightened consciousness. Of course consciousness is a matter of relativity; he who is conscious of some things will perforce be unconscious of others. This is precisely why the use of rhetoric generates controversy. If I take the position that you are unconscious of the suffering and the waste of human lives in Viet Nam, you may find me unconscious of the moral issues that account for our county's being there.

I have neither the space nor the inclination to compare my conception of the nature of rhetoric with all the others that have been widely adopted. But it is surely incumbent upon me to compare it with the conception of rhetoric as the art of persuasion, since this has been by far most widely held. One of the shoals on which this conception continually threatens to founder is the distinction between the persuasion that is the legitimate concern of rhetoric and the persuasion that is not. Where shall we draw the line between subliminal stimulation, coercion at gunpoint, and brainwashing, on the one hand, and rhetorical persuasion, on the on the other? I would argue that it is natural to draw the line in terms of the evocation of consciousness for purposes of communication. Subliminal stimulation deliberately avoids consciousness. The armed bandit evokes fear, not consciousness, although perhaps he incidentally communicates something in the process. Brainwashing depends upon a physiological deprivation. Although we may say that it *causes* a state of consciousness, it would be incorrect to hold that it *evokes* the state. Unless we are taking poetic liberties we do not say that A evokes B when A merely causes B. The wind does not evoke the slamming of the door.

If rhetoric is no more than the art of persuasion, we will have a difficult time convincing the rationalists and positivists that it is really necessary—we will have and indeed have had such difficulty throughout the centuries. When men see the truth, say the rationalists and positivists, they do not need to be persuaded of anything. Persuasion holds sway only in the twilight zone in which there is neither formal truth nor objective fact. But that zone will some day be abolished.

I think I have indicated how I would reply to the rationalist and the positivist. Rhetoric, in my view, permeates even formal truth and objective fact. Even in the utopian world envisaged by my interlocutors, people must still manage to remain conscious. If they do not, communication will become perfect and collapse into noncommunication, and there will no longer be a world at all—only a system comparable to a machine or system of machines.

This reply serves also to show why I regard rhetoric as an activity distinguishing man from the animals, and hence why it has a philosophical basis. Any effort to prove rhetoric unnecessary would already involve rhetoric—the rhetoric of factual communication, if not of exhortation. Another way of indicating the necessity of rhetoric is to point out that without it there can be no consciousness of fact or value, and hence no human experience at all. Rhetoric is necessary to man, and is unnecessary only if man is unnecessary.

Having shown *that* rhetoric has a philosophical basis, I turn to the question of *what* that basis is. I think that question can be disposed of quite briefly. For what could the philosophical basis of anything be, over and above the manner in which it is shown to have such a basis? The philosophical basis of rhetoric would be required to make us conscious of this very situation. In philosophy, content is expressed by the very argument for the existence of the content. In arguing for the existence of a philosophical basis of rhetoric, I think I have revealed what that basis is, and I know no other way to reveal it.

Department of Philosophy
The Pennsylvania State University

Philosophical Rhetoric

Donald Phillip Verene

I knew Henry Johnstone as a colleague and friend for nearly three decades, one of which was the decade (1976–87) during which I served as editor of *Philosophy and Rhetoric.* My editorship fell between Johnstone's first tenure as founder and editor and his second period of editorship, during his retirement. Johnstone introduced me to the importance of rhetoric while we were colleagues at Penn State. Before that time, I had the usual prejudice of philosophers against rhetoric, deriving from Descartes' exclusion of rhetoric from truth in the *Discourse,* Locke's designation of rhetorical statements as "perfect cheats" in the *Essay,* and Kant's nasty claim in the third *Critique* that *ars oratoria* "*ist gar keiner Achtung würdig,*" that it deserves no respect whatsoever.

Johnstone was from beginning to end a logician. He made his initial reputation in philosophy as the author of a logic textbook. Because he took logic seriously, as the heart of philosophy, he was led to write *Philosophy and Argument* (1959). It became one of three widely read books on philosophical argumentation and reasoning published within a few years, the others being Stephen Toulmin's *The Uses of Argument* (1958) and John Passmore's *Philosophical Reasoning* (1961). These works came at a time when many professional philosophers were claiming, to each other and in their classrooms, that to philosophize is to argue, and that the validity of all arguments could be assessed by the application of symbolic logic to what was said. Johnstone, Toulmin, and Passmore showed that more was involved in the evaluation of philosophical arguments than could be gotten from formal logic.

Johnstone's *Philosophy and Argument* begins with the problem of disagreement in philosophical argument and claims that something more than the principles of formal validity is required for its resolution, and concludes with the sense in which argumentation is rooted in selfhood. This feature of argumentation led Johnstone to publish, just over a decade later, *The Problem of the Self* (1970), and a little less than a decade after that to recapitulate his own philosophical development in the collection of his essays, *Validity and Rhetoric in Philosophical Argument* (1978).

What is Johnstone's approach to rhetoric as connected to philosophy? To what extent is his approach complete, that is, to what extent does it require supplementation and development? Johnstone's views have been commented on by many. It is not my intention to explain his conception of rhetoric and philosophy in its complexity. My aim is to elicit the inner form of Johnstone's thought as a philosopher, to describe the problem that originates and drives his position, to see the woods instead of the trees.

Johnstone's problem was as follows: Philosophers make claims about the nature of things, the nature of knowledge, the nature of human existence, and so forth. These claims must be tested by argument. In argument, philosophers aim at validity. The principles of validity are determined in logic. Philosophy is about controversy; it is a critical activity. When there is disagreement in philosophy, formally valid arguments can be produced by both sides. How are philosophical disputes to be resolved?

In disputes occurring in fields of empirical and scientific knowledge there are open avenues for their resolution. Such fields contain methods of experimentation and investigation that allow for the production of evidence and facts that can settle such disputes. But, in philosophical reasoning, what can count as evidence or as a fact is itself in dispute. A fact is a fact only in accord with a specific theory. In philosophical controversy it is the theory that is in dispute.

The standards of empirical objectivity in scientific investigation make possible the use of *argumentum ad rem* to resolve a dispute. The thing to which thought can appeal is not itself in question. In philosophical dispute, as Johnstone claims, *argumentum ad rem* can go nowhere, because the nature of the thing appealed to is itself at the basis of the dispute. Philosophical *argumenta ad rem* can all be valid if properly formulated. The standard of objectivity of thought that logic can supply cannot resolve the controversy. This leads Johnstone to his doctrine of *argumentum ad hominem,* the definition of which he takes from Whately. Whately says that such argument does not show "that 'such and such is the fact,' but that '*this* man is bound to admit it, in conformity to his principles of reasoning, or consistency with his own conduct, situation,' etc."[1]

Johnstone expands the idea of validity from its meaning in formal logic, that the argument is formed so as to have the premise justify the assertion of the conclusion, to the meaning that the argument is formed not only as formally valid but also so as to have it accepted by the person to whom it is directed. A proper philosophical argument must be both formally and informally valid, in Johnstone's terms. By incorporating *argumentum ad hominem* into the meaning of validity, Johnstone has taken the name for an informal fallacy in standard Aristotelian logic and made it a principle of correct reasoning in philosophical matters.

Informal fallacies are committed in ordinary arguments that are subjectively or psychologically persuasive but that do not contain objective grounds for their conclusions. Johnstone wishes the appeal *ad hominem* to have an objective character, at least in terms of philosophical exchange. Philosophers are committed to consistency in thought. For a philosophical position to stand requires the attempt, not simply to avoid formal, logical self-contradiction, but to avoid resting the position on principles that are in any sense in opposition to themselves.

For example, a problem that exists for the Leibnizian conception of monadology is how God can act in the world as a causal force. If all monads are "windowless," meaning that all causal action is immanent within the self-movement of each monad (each monad acting upon its own prior states), how can God act upon the world? God's causal power would affect the monads as an external force on their being. A similar problem may remain in Whitehead's cosmology of "actual entities," even though he attempted to solve it through his doctrine of "prehension" of one actual entity by another. God is still a special kind of actual entity.[2]

On Johnstone's view, a valid philosophical argument, directed to a Leibnizian or a Whiteheadian, might bring out this metaphysical inconsistency. The holder of such a metaphysical position would be moved by an attachment to consistency to take steps to modify or abandon this position. Because of this dimension of *argumentum ad hominem,* philosophical dispute can accomplish something rather than remaining as a spectacle of two sides, each holding its own.

So far as I can see, Johnstone's position is essentially Socratic. All Socratic arguments are *ad hominem* in this sense; they all follow the pattern of bringing the person Socrates is questioning to a point where two or more of that person's beliefs are in conflict. The resolution of controversy, for Johnstone, is a modern version of Socratic midwifery. In Socratic *elenchos,* one philosophical position is not simply pitted against another, instead, some one position is brought into opposition with itself.

Johnstone holds that one feature of his approach, for communication, is that philosophical reasoning of this type increases morale. Good thinking builds morale in human affairs (1978, 69– 72). I think Johnstone is right in this. Good thinking is good for human beings. But his comments on this miss the irritating and dangerous affect the demand for consistency and distinctions can have on a person, which is evident in the Socratic version, namely, that of the gadfly. Ultimately the Socratic approach is the only one to pursue, but it is not always smooth. In Johnstone's world we are all rational selves.

Johnstone's connection of his conception of argumentation with selfhood is also Socratic. Johnstone's *argumentum ad hominem* is not simply an appeal to the particular circumstances of a person to gain acceptance, as such an argument does when it functions as an informal fallacy. The power of Johnstone's conception of *argumentum ad hominem* is its appeal to the person's sense of selfhood. We attempt to construct our existence as a self by bringing the facets of our experience together into a consistent pattern. The philosopher's philosophical position is an extension of this aim at consistency. Johnstone's appeal is to this basic process by which we achieve character. This is of a piece with the Socratic aim of self-knowledge. Johnstone's conception of morale is part of the larger aim of self-knowledge and the sense that philosophy is rooted in the self's drive toward a knowledge of itself.

Johnstone developed his views of argumentation and the self largely in terms of the tradition of Anglo-American philosophy, the analytic philosophy of his day. But to believe this was his source would be wrong. The epigraphs to both *Philosophy and Argument* and *The Problem of the Self* are from Hegel, quoted in the original German. Each states eloquently the thesis of the book. The first makes the point that the fundamental refutation of a principle must be accomplished by a development of it in terms of itself rather than by opposing it to some other. The second makes the point that the goal of actuality is movement and the unfolding of becoming and that this restlessness extends to the self.

In his introduction to the essays in *Validity and Rhetoric in Philosophical Argument,* Johnstone said that few readers other than his former colleagues at Williams College, who were schooled in absolute idealism, "have noticed the idealistic character of my writings on philosophical argumentation." He says his readers "have not seemed to be aware, for example, that when I said that I thought that philosophical arguments were *sui generis*—not be to judged by the standards of argumentation in everyday discourse—I was expressing much the same idea that can be expressed by saying that Hegelian dialectic is not to be judged by the standards of argumentation in science and everyday discourse" (1978, 2). It was no accident that, when Johnstone decided to disband a substantial portion of his personal library and pass works on to graduate students at Penn State, one of the prizes therein was a complete set of *Jubiläumsausgabe* of Hegel's works.

What Johnstone had discovered in his concern for the role of argumentation in philosophical controversy was the relationship, stated in the first sentence of Aristotle's *Rhetoric,* that "Rhetoric is the counterpart of dialectic." Dialectic is that part of logic that concerns argumentation involved in reasoning from commonly held views (*endoxa*). As Aristotle says, "dialectic is a process of criticism wherein lies the path to the principles of all inquiries" (*Topics* 101b3). Johnstone's conception of philosophy and argument is in fact a conception of dialectic applied to philosophical disagreement. Having started with a version of dialectic, Johnstone was naturally led to the counterpart of dialectic, that is, to rhetoric. His conception of *ad hominem* is a theory of persuasion.

Johnstone's conception of persuasion in philosophical dispute as essentially self-persuasion forms a bridge between Aristotle's conception of dialectic and Hegel's. Hegel grounds his dialectic of opposites in the life of the self or spirit (*Geist*). Hegel's *Phenomenology of Spirit,* which is the schema of movement of the categories in his *Science of Logic,* is the science of the experience of consciousness. Hegel's *Phenomenology* has been called a *Bildungsroman,* in which the self moves from one stage of consciousness to the next, in a grand process of self-knowledge. Like Johnstone's *argumentum ad hominem,* human consciousness at each stage discourses with itself realizing the inconsistency of its position at that stage and thereby moving to a new standpoint, only to repeat the process. Consciousness is continually restless in its movement, arguing, so to speak, with the oppositions within itself and moving to a greater comprehension of experience through a process of self-refutation. Consciousness as the general form of selfhood is always its own opponent. Johnstone's Hegelianism lies in his grounding of argumentation in the self.

How complete is Johnstone's attempt at making rhetoric the counterpart of dialectic? In the end, Johnstone's position is a version of the *ars critica.* Philosophy, for Johnstone, is criticism, and hence argumentation is the means to conduct the critical evaluation of ideas. Instead of a doctrine of *ars topica,* Johnstone develops his theory of the self as the locus of arguments. He begins his account of philosophy and rhetoric with philosophical claims as *given*. The problem is to test such claims and to find a way to move ahead in the controversy that ensues. But how do we come to formulate such philosophical claims in the first place? For an answer to this we must turn to the work of Ernesto Grassi.

My association and friendship with Grassi was of almost as many years as that with Johnstone. The many conversations I had with Grassi, both here and in Europe, opened up new dimensions for me of the relation of rhetoric to poetic and to philosophy. Although I introduced them to each other, and Grassi's first essay on rhetoric to be published in English appeared in the first issue I edited of *Philosophy and Rhetoric,* I think Johnstone and Grassi remained largely in separate worlds (Grassi 1976, 200–216). Johnstone was the humane rationalist; Grassi was the rhetorical humanist. In his above-mentioned essay, Grassi first stated his thesis that rhetoric is not exterior to philosophical thought but at its very center—that rhetoric is what makes philosophy possible. This thesis became his book title, *Rhetoric as Philosophy* (1980), now recently reprinted.

Grassi raises the question of the starting points of logic, of the process of rational argument. Rhetoric as the speech of the emotions, as the instrument of persuasion of an audience, the discipline of preachers and orators, is traditionally regarded as external to the establishment of philosophical truths. Philosophical truth is understood as arrived at by a process of rational thought, investigation, and speech, which, once formulated, may be communicated to others through rhetorical forms of language. But, as Grassi points out, it is a scandal to logic that logic cannot provide its own starting points. Once an argument is stated, once a philosophical claim is made, we can evaluate its validity, even extending the principle of validity as far as does Johnstone, to include the factor of *ad hominem*. This depends upon our power to use language rationally to develop ideas.

But how do we originally come to an idea, a claim that is then subject to criticism? This requires another sense of speech, one not *demonstrative* or critical but *indicative,* or one that can simply produce a significance. Such speech "leads before the eyes" (*phainesthai*). It is metaphorical speech or imaginative speech. The speech that produces *archai* has a prophetic (*prophainesthai*) character that cannot be comprehended from a rational point of view, yet it is required for the formulation of any beginning from which reason can act. Grassi ties rhetoric to this originating power of language. He says: "Thus the term 'rhetoric' assumes a fundamentally new significance; 'rhetoric' is not, nor can it be the art, the technique of an exterior persuasion; it is rather the speech which is the basis of the rational thought" (1980, 20).

Grassi has developed this view in a wide number of works, running from his first statement in *Rhetoric as Philosophy* to his demonstration of how rhetoric functions as philosophy for Renaissance thinkers in *Renaissance Humanism* (1988), to the collection of his essays in *Vico and Humanism*, in which he shows the importance of Vico's imaginative universal (*universale fantastico*) and Heidegger's notion of the "clearing" (*Lichtung*) for this view (1988; see also Grassi 1990). Grassi, like the Latins, joins rhetoric and poetic. To initiate a thought in a fundamental sense, to make a beginning point, we require an image, a metaphor. The power of the metaphor is to bring together a similarity in dissimilars, which requires *ingenium*. As Aristotle says: "the greatest thing by far is to be a master of metaphor. It is the one thing that cannot be learnt from others; and is also a sign of genius" (*Poetics* 1459a5–7).

The art of cultivating this power of ingenuity has been lost since the Renaissance. Since Descartes, the focus of thought and education has turned from *ars topica* to *ars critica.* Grassi wishes to revive *ars topica* and make it the centerpiece of rhetorical study. Philosophies depend upon metaphors, what the American contextualist Stephen Pepper (1942) called "root metaphors" in his *World Hypotheses,* or what the French feminist philosopher Michèle Le Doeuff (1989) calls *The Philosophical Imaginary.* When Grassi's perspective is brought to bear on Johnstone's conception of argumentation, we can see that what we are attacking in a philosophical controversy is not only a rational claim that must be tested against itself, but also, behind it, a metaphor, an image of the world upon which it depends. For example, this image could be the root metaphor that the world is a machine, or that the world is an organism, or other metaphors that derive from these.

The self confronts itself not only in terms of the consistency of the claims it wishes to hold but also in terms of the images of itself that form the imaginative reality on which its existence depends, as rooted in human culture. A rational conception of selfhood is insufficient to grasp the poetic and rhetorical basis of human consciousness. Rational senses of communication presuppose and depend upon the imaginative forms of the self that are expressed in myths, religions, and poetry, which function as *topoi* from which the self "draws forth" its significance. The self, as Cassirer shows, is connected to all the symbolic forms of human culture, and they are its nature writ large. Cassirer says: "That self-knowledge is the highest aim of philosophical inquiry appears to be generally acknowledged" (1944, 1).

We might describe Johnstone's position as *philosophy and rhetoric,* the conjunction of the two, and Grassi's position as *rhetoric as philosophy,* the placing of rhetoric as prior to philosophy and the moving of philosophy back to its roots in rhetoric. The position I wish to suggest might be called *philosophical rhetoric,* which presupposes the other two. I attempted to explain this in my essay in *Philosophy and Rhetoric,* "The Limits of Argument: Argument and Autobiography" (1993) and in my book, *Philosophy and the Return to Self-Knowledge* (1997). This position is a stand against "literal-mindedness" in philosophy; Hegel called such philosophers "*unsere Buchstabenphilosophen.*" What the approach of philosophical rhetoric adds to Johnstone's logical approach, joined to Grassi's humanist insights, is the importance of narrative. Johnstone has expanded the philosophical notion of validity into its rhetorical dimension. Grassi has advanced metaphor from its role as a literary device to its status as the form of philosophical *archai,* tying rhetorical speech to primordial speech. Both of these require narrative.

Narrative is the speech of memory. Philosophies are essentially narratives. All great works of philosophy simply tell the reader what is the nature of things.

The arguments we find within such works are meaningful within the structure of the narrative they contain. The narration confers meaning. Questions of meaning always precede questions of truth. Philosophical arguments do not stand on their own. They cannot profitably be removed from the narrative that informs them and evaluated as though they had independent value and truth.

Philosophies, like all narratives, act against forgetting. To forget is to leave something out, to omit or overlook a feature of a subject matter or of the world. Philosophical speech is memorial speech because it reminds us of what we have already forgotten or nearly forgotten about experience. The speech of philosophical narrative can never become literal-minded because to act against forgetting is to attempt to hold opposites together. The narrative is always based on a metaphor; a metaphor is always a narrative in brief. The narrative is also the means to overcome controversy, because for the self to overcome an inconsistency of its thoughts it must develop not simply a new argument but a new position, a new narrative in which to contain any new argument.

The self makes itself by speaking to itself, not in the sense of introspection but in the sense of the art of conversation, which is tied to the original meaning of dialectic. On this view, philosophy is not rhetorical simply in its need to resolve controversy, nor is it rhetorical simply in terms of its starting points for rational demonstration. Philosophy is rhetorical in these senses, but it is further rhetorical in its total expression. Any philosophy commands its truth by the way it speaks. Great philosophies speak in a powerful manner that affects both mind and heart. It is common, in the *Dialogues,* that, after engaging in the *elenchos,* Socrates says he is unsure whether a claim that seems to be true really is true. His answer is to offer a "likely story." All philosophies, on my view, are likely stories, which originate in the philosopher's own autobiography and are attempts to move from this to the autobiography of humanity, to formulate the narrative of human existence in the world and to speak of things human and divine.

These are not narratives in the fictional sense because they purport to have more than a temporal structure; they purport to show the necessary connections between things, to be able to say what was, is, and must be the case, to offer a knowledge *per causas*. To accomplish such a speech, we find the philosopher in fact using all the tropes, from metaphor to irony, and all the principles of rhetoric, including the ethos of the speaker. Philosophies viewed in this way are already rhetorical. Those that are deficient in this regard tend to be or are paltry things. The great philosophies of the tradition convince and remain because their language is by nature rhetorical and continues to communicate to those who will encounter it.

In the end, another way to say what I have said is that all the great philosophies of the canon, whether they claim to or not, and whether or not they openly dismiss rhetoric, do employ rhetoric. The great philosophies gain their authority not simply from what they say, but from how they say it, including those of Descartes, Locke, and Kant. They serve as models for philosophical speech. The great philosophies tend toward Hegel's principle that "the true is the whole" (*Das Wahre ist das Ganze*), and to express this they aim, consciously or unconsciously, at the Renaissance principle to be "wisdom that speaks" (*la sapienza che parla*). To speak of the whole forces language toward eloquence. There seems to me every reason to say, of such philosophies, what Horace (*Ars poetica* 333) says of poetry and Cicero (*Brutus* 185) says of rhetoric: that they instruct, delight, and move.

Department of Philosophy
Emory University

Notes

1. Quoted in Johnstone (1959, 73); see also (1978, 8, 53).
2. Johnstone's examples are Norman Malcolm's "Ordinary language is correct language"; see (1978, 53–61) and Socrates' argument with Thrasymachus in the *Republic*; see (1959, 50–51).

Works Cited

Cassirer, Ernst. 1944. *An Essay on Man: An Introduction to a Philosophy of Human Culture*. New Haven: Yale UP.
Grassi, Ernesto. 1976. "Rhetoric and Philosophy." *Philosophy and Rhetoric* 9:200–16.
———. 1980. *Rhetoric as Philosophy: The Humanist Tradition*. University Park: Pennsylvania State UP; reprint, 2000, Southern Illinois UP.
———. 1988. *Renaissance Humanism: Studies in Philosophy and Poetics*. Center for Medieval and Early Renaissance Studies. Binghamton, NY: Medieval & Renaissance Texts & Studies.
———. 1990. *Vico and Humanism: Essays on Vico, Heidegger, and Rhetoric*. Ed. Donald Phillip Verene. New York: Lang.
Johnstone, Henry W., Jr. 1959. *Philosophy and Argument*. University Park: Pennsylvania State UP.
———. 1970. *The Problem of the Self*. University Park: Pennsylvania State UP.
———. 1978. *Validity and Rhetoric in Philosophical Argument: An Outlook in Transition*. University Park, PA: The Dialogue Press of *Man and World*.
Le Doeuff, Michèle. 1989. *The Philosophical Imaginary*. Trans. Colin Gordon. Stanford: Stanford UP.
Passmore, John. 1961. *Philosophical Reasoning*. London: Duckworth.
Pepper, Stephen. 1942. *World Hypotheses: A Study in Evidence*. Berkeley and Los Angeles: U of California P.
Toulmin, Stephen Edelston. 1958. *The Uses of Argument*. Cambridge: Cambridge UP.
Verene, Donald Phillip. 1993. "The Limits of Argument: Argument and Autobiography." *Philosophy and Rhetoric* 26:1–8.
———. 1997. *Philosophy and the Return to Self-Knowledge*. New Haven: Yale UP.

Theoretical Pieties, Johnstone's Impiety, and Ordinary Views of Argumentation

Jean Goodwin

The greatest single influence on rhetorical theory throughout its long history, and likewise on its daughter or sister enterprise, the theory of argument, has without doubt been students.

In part, the influence has been bad. Docile students have (it seems) offered little resistance to their teachers' theoretical hobbyhorses, being willing to cram for the exam, or the speech, fantastical systems of staseis, topoi, figurae and five or seven part formulae for developing arguments. Even the more realistic bits of lore have proved so eminently learnable that as Sperber and Wilson (1990) have pointed out, students have not pressed us, teachers and theorists, to elaborate them further over eighty generations of basic courses.

Recalcitrant students have also caused us problems, and it is this bad influence that I want to examine here. Some students, we think, resist argument. They bring negative attitudes to our classrooms. Their misconceptions shut down learning; they are wrong; moreover, they are somewhat insulting. So we have in response been tempted to a sort of preachiness, an apologetic stance—a piety about our subject. I suppose we've all caught ourselves doing it; I know I have: the first day of class defense of the dignity of argument.

Like most defensiveness, this reaction feels unsatisfactory. We seem to be prisoners of what we take to be our students' limited views. In this essay, I am going to enlist the aid of Henry W. Johnstone Jr. to help show us an escape. Impiously, Johnstone accepts and even elaborates some of our students' common critiques of argument. He challenges us, teachers and theorists of argument, not to resist these critiques, but to acknowledge and embrace them. And in this way he invites us to a more complex understanding of our subject and to a deeper conversation with our students.

I want to close this essay by opening such a conversation, listening to what students actually say about their experiences with argument. To begin, however, let us recall the conversation we open with our students in our textbooks, starting with chapter one, page one.

1

> We frequently say things such as "Yesterday, Rhonda and Janice had a terrible argument" or "those two are always arguing." Much of our ordinary usage of the term *argument* implies two people engaged in interpersonal conflict. *Argument* thus becomes a synonym for verbal hostility. (Rybacki and Rybacki 2004, 1)

Argument is conflict: this is what we think many students come to the basic argument class thinking. The idea turns up even in the earliest works of the American debate tradition—for example, in George Pierce Baker's recognition that "many people" believe argument to be mere "contentiousness" (Baker and Huntington 1905, 2). Our best textbooks ever since have opened by constructing an ordinary student/reader who takes argument to be "a kind of (usually unpleasant) interpersonal exchange," like "quarrels" or "squabbles" (Inch and Warnick 2002, 6, 7), "angry," involving a "desire to win" (Rieke, Sillars, and Peterson 2005, 11), "unhealthy, destructive of human relationships and thus [to] be avoided" (Hollihan and Baaske 2005, 7), "futile" (Foster 1908, 280), and "aggressive, hostile, and stubborn" (Patterson and Zarefsky 1983, 6). And at least some textbooks from the tradition of teaching written argument in English departments project a similar reader, one for whom "that word"—argument—"sets off alarm bells ... because it evokes images of quarreling or worse" (Williams and Colomb 2001, xxviii).[1]

Our textbooks propose a variety of sources from which students could have picked up this view. The debate process itself, with its attack and defense, its victory and defeat, Ehninger and Brockriede admit, may "understandably" induce "the casual observer" to regard it "as a species of competition or conflict" (1963, 19). Some textbooks go on to blame "the traditional model for teaching argumentation and debate" (Inch and Warnick 2002, 68)—that is, other textbooks—for actually promoting the idea. More broadly, the negative conception of argument can be traced back to the associations of argument and war "entrenched even in our language" (Williams and Colomb 2001, 3) and pervading "the conceptual system of western culture" (Rieke, Sillars, and Peterson 2005, 52).

So it seems our students, being like "many people," come to our classes ready to say that argument is conflict. What do we reply? Emphatically, "no." "That is not the sort of argument with which this book is concerned" Inch and Warnick declare (2002, 7). Or as Rybacki and Rybacke put it bluntly, "if ... your definition of *argument* or *having an argument* is based on verbal hostility and escalating emotions, it is our intention to change your perception. In this textbook, we want to open your eyes" (2004, 1).

In some sense this denial is a laudable attempt to carve out a space for learning. Every teacher has to say "no" to some things students bring with them. But I want to question whether we can maintain our denial of students' ordinary views of argument. Our textbooks adopt three "eye-opening" strategies—three ways of distinguishing argument as we teach it from the hostile and futile argument of the "many people." But Johnstone, we will see, has warned us against the limitations of each.

Take a first approach to "eye opening." Perhaps the conflict apparent in so many arguments is merely that: an appearance. In this view, the disagreements that occur on the surface of argument can only proceed because they rest on deeper agreements. Argument may look like conflict, but as Ehninger and Brockriede assert in their classic articulation of this thesis, "considered as a whole" debate is "clearly a co-operative endeavor" (1963, 20, 22).

Our textbooks identify several types of agreement underpinning argument. James Herrick offers a particularly sophisticated discussion of the possibilities. Arguers may agree about the starting points, premises, or "*evidence*" for their arguments; they may agree about "*procedures,* the rules or guidelines according to which the argumentation will take place," including "the most basic agreement . . . *to enter into argumentation*" at all; and they may agree about the "*goals*" of the dispute (2004, 14, 15). This final possibility has been the one most frequently taken up. One early textbook declares that "adversaries in debate should have at least this common purpose,—the search after truth" (Foster 1908, 310). Ehninger and Brockriede elaborate the same theme:

> Every debate that ever has occurred or ever will occur must be dominated by a basic harmony of aim. Unless the opposing debaters hold the same goal in view—peace, prosperity, social welfare, national security, or whatever it may be—no debate is possible. There is no ground upon which they may come together in argument, no area where the thrusts of proof and the counterthrusts of refutation may meet and interact. Interpretations, inferences, and values may vary; on the ultimate goal itself, there can be no disagreement. (1963, 20)

In this view, argument begins in apparent disagreement, but ideally ends by revealing the consensus that was implicitly present all along. As Herrick puts it succinctly, "argumentation depends on *agreements* that permit resolution of the disagreements that led to argumentation" (2004, 15).

Johnstone acknowledges that this pious attempt "to reduce philosophical disagreement to appearance" has its attractions (1959, 15). But he intransigently reminds us that this answer does not stay true to our experience of argument. As we well know, there may be no agreements about evidence, since each arguer's position "has in advance stipulated what is to constitute evidence" in such a way that the opponent's attempts at proof are ruled out even before they are made (1967, 52).[2] There may be no agreements about rules or procedures, either, since the dispute, "rather than being governed by fixed rules, represents the effort of each disputant to enforce his own rules" (1959, 12). And there may be no agreements about ultimate ideals, since the ends we observe emerging in discussion are often diverse (1959, 15).[3]

In Johnstone's view, "hopeful theories" of controversy such as those put forward in our textbooks try to avoid admitting that "philosophical antagonism may be so radical as to preclude any but the most trivial reconciliation" (1959, 132). Philosophical argument begins when we encounter someone who disagrees, and although we can try to evade the argument by seeking some agreement in which to rest, if the controversy is truly philosophical we will find no such common ground. There is no deeper "level" (Ehninger and Brockriede 1963, 20) of agreement; disagreement is not merely a "stage of an activity destined to eventuate in unanimity" (Johnstone 1962, 118). Johnstone rather invites us to acknowledge the "abyss," "impassible gulf," or even "intergalactic spaces" between opposing philosophical positions (1959, 3; 1967, 50; 1978a, 56). Philosophical disagreement is therefore "radical" (e.g., 1959, 3, 19; 1962, 118), and "controversy," not agreement, "ultimately real" (1978a, 86).

Now, the textbooks might defend their "hopeful" assertions by noting that Johnstone is only talking about *philosophical* controversy, not the garden-variety kind we invite our students to enter. And there do seem to be some non-radical disagreements: Johnstone gives the example of a dispute over the date of the first atomic bomb (1967, 48). But it will be impossible to protect our students entirely from philosophical controversy in Johnstone's sense. "Philosophers are by no means the only ones who experience [philosophical] confrontations," Johnstone explains; "we all do. . . . All of our fundamental commitments are philosophical" (1967, 56). And we all *have* fundamental commitments, however "unsophisticated, undeliberate, and even altogether unconscious" (1959, 127) they may be. So many civic and interpersonal issues seem painful and irresolvable because even the smallest can implicate the deepest conflicts between worldviews. One suspects that Johnstone's dispute over dates could reveal some new epistemological "intergalactic space," since "the most innocent statements are sometimes, in fact, violently controversial" (1959, 36).

If we cannot rest with the idea that conflict is merely apparent, we might adopt a second strategy for "opening the eyes" of our students: admitting that the deep disagreement in argument is real, but asserting that we can distinguish a good, argumentative way of handling it from a bad, non-argumentative approach. Although "the situations that spark conflict will never disappear," nevertheless "the potential for conflict and even war" can be avoided through "*arguing*—the process of resolving differences of opinion through communication" (Hollihan and Baaske 2005, 4). Argument is in specific preferable to "*coercion* . . . the threat or use of force" (Freeley and Steinberg 2000, 11) and to "violence or coercion" (Herrick 2004, 51) as a way of managing disagreement.

Hitler probably remains the paradigmatic case of the alternative to argument, for example:

> Critical choices and decisions are ... the ideal toward which wise men strive. For though they fall short in the attainment, the striving itself sets them in the proper direction. Hitler bellowed, "Wir denken mit unserem Blut" ("We think with our blood"), and led the world into war. Adlai Stevenson speaks for a saner and happier society when he emphasizes the importance of critical decision-making in our own democratic culture. (Ehninger and Brockriede, 1963, 5)

But more contemporary examples can also be cited. Hollihan and Baaske juxtapose "effective argumentative dialogue" against "the alternative: terrorist assaults, the bulldozing of homes, and other acts of violence that could potentially escalate to a full-scale war that might kill thousands of people" in the Middle East (2005, 12). Inch and Warnick, possibly remembering events in Seattle, contrast argument with "extralegal protest ... because violating the law and being violent ... use force as opposed to argument to compel a decision" (2002, 70).

Argument (or indeed communication generally) is our most promising alternative to war. That pious thought runs deep in the rhetorical tradition, so it comes as a surprise to see Johnstone dismiss it almost off-hand. "Throughout recorded time," Johnstone reminds us, "men have always based their conflicts upon arguments. Every war has been preceded by the search for an excuse for fighting." Argument is therefore not the opposite of war, except in the trivial sense that it is hard to both fight and argue at the same time; otherwise, Johnstone remarks, the best argument would be the one that puts everyone to sleep (1963, 36).

Argument is implicated in war; war, or at least some force, is also implicated in argument. Johnstone persistently urges us to be curious about modes of persuasion "that on other theories would be dismissed as uses of force" (1990, 334): extralegal protests such as "shouts, obscenities, sit-ins, and interruptions of lectures" (1971, 80), the "psych-out" (1982), commands (1963, 1990), and most frequently, threats (e.g., 1963, 1980, 1990). "A threat is a form of argument," Johnstone asserts, albeit a "degenerate" one (1963, 31). Threats and arguments both break into an ordinary existence in which the self is simply taken for granted. Both require a person to pay attention to her limits: in the case of physical threats, to death, the limit of her life; in the case of arguments, to the limits of her deepest commitments, marked off by their now-conspicuous conflict with the equally deep commitments of others. Both thus open—wedge open, Johnstone says—a space for the person to recognize the nature of the risk, to consider it, and to choose a response in which she freely chooses limits for herself. On the bright side, this means that both threats and arguments are deeply human modes of address, as contrasted with the stimuli we direct to animals, or the input we feed into machines (1990). But there is another side, too: in both threats and arguments we experience a demandingness that is reasonable to call *force*.[4]

A final approach to "opening the eyes" of our students might be to admit that disagreement in argument is real, and that the argumentative way of proceeding cannot be distinguished cleanly from other uses of force, but still to assert that argumentative conflict can be contained if argument is done right. "The problem, as we see it, is not that arguments per se are unhealthy," one textbook insists; "rather, too many people have never learned how to argue in a constructive and socially beneficial fashion" (Hollihan and Baaske 2005, 7). Or as another puts it, "we hope to rehabilitate that [negative] image of argument by focusing not on its tone but on its form and intention. We'll show you how we use argument not to upset social relationships, but to establish and strengthen them" (Williams and Colomb 2001, xxviii). What "fashion" or "form" is appropriate? To keep their arguments contained, our textbooks advise students to contain *themselves*; to not take or make argument personal, but to maintain "disinterestedness" (Ehninger and Brockriede 1963, 6). "Ego" is a common cause of painful argument, Fahnestock and Secor point out, at least in face-to-face encounters:

> We often defend our positions the way a bird defends its territory—fiercely, automatically, without stopping to think. We often fail to see when ego is involved in any position we hold. After all, if we hold it, we undoubtedly have good reasons. Ego also forces us to defend positions just because someone else holds the opposite, and we cannot see that our attitude toward our audience or opponent is crippling our judgment. … All of us find it difficult to "give points" to the people we resist, for whatever reasons we resist them, deep-seated or trivial, temporary or long-standing. (1990, 8)

To transact argument well, the arguer must therefore give up a bit on her own ego. She also must refrain from involving others' egos in the way that's ordinarily called *ad hominem*. A "destructive use of argument" occurs when the "self-concept of another person" is attacked "instead of, or in addition to, the person's position on a topic," an attack that "has the effect of inflicting … psychological pain" (Rieke, Sillars, and Peterson 2005, 210). We can manage argumentative conflict, in this pious view, if we avoid such personalisms.

Johnstone is of course best known for his challenge to this position. In his view, all valid arguments are *argumenta ad hominem*—that is, they possess force because they show the addressee the self-contradictions within his own commitments. After all, once we accept that controversy is radical, there seems to be no other way of proceeding; there are no facts external to the dispute. We might hope to distinguish such Johnstonian *ad hominem* arguments from the personal attacks that our textbooks term fallacies. Unfortunately, this distinction too will prove difficult to maintain. The belief that an *ad hominem* argument draws upon is not just "a whim, prejudice, or dogma that any given individual is free to choose or reject, as he may choose or reject a brand of cigarettes" (1959, 17). Rather, the relevant belief is his *own*: he has an interest in it (1963, 33), it counts among the commitments that define him as a person. When the person finds that he is out of accord with such a commitment, he must take it personally in order to maintain his sense of being a person at all. Indeed, "it is precisely the aim of the *argumentum ad hominem* to force, or at least invite, an interlocutor to apply this epithet ["unwitting asserter of a contradiction"] to himself; i.e., to "*admit* ... assume responsibility for," and "take the blame for" being "caught up" in a contradiction (1989, 258–59). Thus in a Johnstonian *ad hominem,* "the argument is addressed to the man" (1978a, 54).

Self-recognition in these circumstances is almost inevitably going to hurt. Johnstone may be drawing on his own experience here. In the autobiographical introduction to *Validity and Rhetoric* (1978b) he recounts how he encountered from colleagues at his first teaching job an unexpected challenge to his whole way of philosophizing. Not only was he unable to overcome the challenge, he began to realize that while his colleagues were granting a partial legitimacy to his position, he was unable to respect theirs in turn. He was not being generous. The result of this self-recognition was he says "a painful period during which it was nearly impossible for me to carry forward any intellectual project at all." What emerged from this silence and "desperation" (1978b, 2) were some of Johnstone's earliest words on argument: "To become aware for the first time of the existence of philosophical disagreement is surely one of life's darkest moments" (1954, 245).

We now find ourselves in a painful moment somewhat like that Johnstone experienced. Facing our students on the first day of a basic argument course, or addressing them on the first page of a basic argument textbook, we realize that some are recalcitrant. They seem to think argument is angry and futile. We try to deny that argument is like that, saying "that's not what we teach," and attempt to alter their perceptions and "open their eyes" to our perspective. We build a case in support of our view: we argue that conflict is merely apparent, that managing conflict with arguments is an alternative to using force, and that argumentative force can be acceptable when it is impersonal. Our students may not resist such pieties, but, as we've seen, Johnstone does. He reminds us impiously that controversies are real, that arguments have force, and that their force is inevitably personal. Argument can indeed be painful, never-ending, and conflict-ridden. What then can we say to our students in defense of the dignity of our subject? Are we reduced to silence?

2

We can begin by accepting recalcitrance as a legitimate response to argument. We can try to remain true to the full range of our experience, and attempt a reply that takes up the insights that even our recalcitrant students offer. Here is what Johnstone might have us say.

We argue because we have to. "The individual who attempts to speak and act in such a way as to remain true to himself must come into radical conflict with others no less true to themselves but according to different beliefs" (1959, 19). In such a conflict, we are obligated to defend our ground; to do anything less would be demeaning. Indeed, it is only because we encounter others who disagree that we become aware of and able to articulate the contours of our own commitments. The meaning of our position is dependent on the arguments that support it, and those arguments arise in real controversies.

We argue, then, to own up to the responsibilities of our positions. But in arguing we also have to answer back to the other. Inevitably, we must reply to them *ad hominem,* imagining their position with "tolerance, intellectual generosity, or respect," from the inside, in order to demonstrate to them its inadequacy (1963, 34).

Arguing thus requires us to endure a contradiction, holding at once both our own and others' positions within the embrace of what can only be called the self (1967, 54). "A person who chooses argument does in fact choose himself," and from the argument earns a perspective that "tells the self who it is and where it stands." In Johnstone's terms, "philosophical arguments ... have a morale function" (1963, 35, 38, 39):

> Philosophy is the articulation of morale. Good morale is not associated with a dull or confused person. It belongs only to those who have to some extent broken out from illusion and confusion. They know what they are about, and they have a sense of their own competence. Morale is thus a certain rather explicit self-confidence. (1978b, 69)

Now, I doubt that we could look at our students and tell them that argument has a "morale function," or explain that argument constitutes a self as the locus of responsibility and transcendence. But as I will try to show, there are resonances of Johnstone's ideas in the ordinary views of argument students bring with them to class.

It's useful to take one of the more commonplace terms in Johnstone's account as a starting point. I began to notice a few years ago how many students were telling me that they enrolled in argumentation classes to gain "self-confidence." That was surprising. I wasn't sure what they meant. So in the 2004 fall term I decided to explore this question with the twenty students enrolled in one Argumentation and Debate course. Throughout the course, I ask students to commit to their goals, to reflect on their performances, and to articulate their views of what argument is and why it should (or should not) be cultivated. In the following I untangle some of the themes evident in their work.

Even at the very beginning of the course students were interested in where argument would place them. For example, at the end of the first week, half the class listed the ability to argue impromptu among their main learning goals. Some students expressed this in temporal terms: they wanted to learn to argue "fast." But more stressed a disposition in space: arguing "on the spot," "on their feet," or even "on their toes." This vocabulary of posture was elaborated later in the semester by talk of "standing" to argue. At times, the students' references to "standing" seem literal, since I do make them rise to debate. The following student, for example, may be speaking just of that physical act when he/she says:

> I thought standing up in front of class speaking and giving our side was a good experience, but was kind of frustrating because we needed more evidence and proof to stand behind us.[5]

Notice though that even here the physical standing up is coupled with a figurative "standing behind." Most frequently in the students' reflections references to "standing" and arguing have a wider significance, whether they evaluate it positively or negatively. For example:

> Having skills as a debater would help me stand up for things I want or am passionate about in general [14].

> I dislike conflict because I am forced to stand up for my own views and I tend to feel that my self-worth is under attack. I don't feel conflicts are worth my feeling bad about myself or my views so I just avoid them [3].

In addition to talk of the upness of "standing" we find also talk of its outness, as when one student noted that in a democracy,

> anyone can come out in public and take a stand for anything they believe in. Whoever takes a stand must be ready to defend doubts and objections, but all reasonable arguments are valid [1].

It is notable that in all these passages, what arguers are "standing up" or "out" for are quite personal—"things I … am passionate about," "my *own* views," what "they believe in." More radically, students sometime speak of argument as a disposing "out" of the *self:*

> I think that if you are arguing you are putting yourself out there in a way [5].

> I personally prefer the research part of the debate because if I do eventually have to put myself out there to be attacked I want to have as strong a defense as possible, to protect myself from humiliation [3].

As the two passages quoted from student [3] suggest, some experience the self-revelation of argument as decidedly risky. Being "on the spot" or "on your toes" is of course an unstable position. Further, the ground on which students are "standing" turns out to be a terrain of disagreement. Indeed, the basic act of argument may be a "standing up *against,*" as observed by one student:

> In order for my generation to make a change we must stand up against what we don't believe in and inevitably that will entail debate and argument [2].

This means that arguing opens one to attack, as many students commented:

> I felt sort of trapped and I needed to explain myself which I'm not used to.

> I felt nervous as if I were in front of a firing squad. I was worried that when it came to my turn I wouldn't have anything to say. Arguing values also leaves people vulnerable. To argue your values leaves you open to scorn and ridicule from people who don't agree with you [13].

The "vulnerability" mentioned in this last passage was expanded upon by student [19], who had had considerable experience in public speaking prior to the course:

> Standing before a [large] audience … creates an incredible sense of vulnerability. As a speaker, offering yourself so wholly to an audience creates a human interaction whereas you are judged and examined for your ability to communicate but also the speaker experiences acceptance or rejection from the audience.… Opinions about you are quickly formed by the other person. Debating puts a person in the position to be examined by another [19].

If one fails to meet the challenges of the argument, the consequences to the self can be severe. Student [3]'s negative views have been quoted twice above—his/her feeling of having "self-worth" under "attack," and being faced with "humiliation;" these reactions appear well-justified.

Success in facing such risks of argument gives students an immediate sense of "accomplishment and competency" [2]. One put it simply: "I truly felt empowered by the debate" [16]. And there are other rewards of arguing that help outweigh the risks. In part, students speak of "standing" as an opportunity—or compulsion—to consider more deeply where they stand. Another student with extensive prior experience articulated his/her view thus:

> The more you're forced to defend an idea, the more you really grow to understand and gain a better view of your own opinion. I spend a lot of time defending [a topic]. Each time I find myself defending that issue, I just become that much more passionate about it and understand better why I believe what I do. Being challenged, and being forced to defend my own view only creates better understanding of where I stand. It gets to the point where I welcome a challenge because I always grow stronger as a result [9].

And again, what can grow stronger through argument is not only one's "own *view*" but one's *self.* "Being forced to define your ideas also forces you to define yourself ," as one student explained. Others similarly pointed out the "self-discovery" [7] that can come from argument. For example:

> I think arguing creates personal growth in everyone. It does make you listen to the other side of arguments and if nothing else, makes your arguments stronger. As your

arguments become stronger, so do you as a person as does your knowledge of the subject and others' views. I think arguing helps us learn about others, but we also learn about ourselves [16].

I think argumentation and debate have helped me define who I am as a person. It forces me to examine the facts and decide for myself what is important to me. People who choose not to take a stand on an issue would have a hard time defining their beliefs and values [7].

The themes in this last passage were picked up by other students who noted the negative effects of *not* "standing" for things. For student [16], the alternative to "standing up" was to "sit silently where no one can judge your ability to communicate, interact, think, or passions." Several other students commented on the personal costs of "sitting" the argument out, or of "sitting back, being passive." One recounted this experience:

There exists a girl in [an organization the student belongs to] that holds a very high position.... I see her as a giant pushover because she never expresses her views on anything; she simply lets people tell her what to think and how to feel about something.... If this girl would stand up and vocalize what she believes in, then I would have more respect for her in such a leadership role. A person should never be ashamed to voice something they believe in. I think that some people don't stick up for something they think is right because either they don't think it's that big of a deal or they so desperately want to avoid conflict that they won't say anything so they don't make anybody angry with them [6].

So "self-definition" through argument may be painful, but it also seems necessary.

As this last passage suggests, "standing up" has effects on more than just the self; it also gives the self a place or "voice" among others. As one student put it, "I believe that debate is about getting my voice heard and gaining respect" [14]. Student [9] articulated a similar thought, writing, "there are many reasons to argue, but to me, it's a way to voice opinions and be heard." Having a "voice" is here portrayed as a way of gaining "respect" from others. In another reflection, student [9] added that it is also a way of gaining "respect" *for* them.

I never changed my stance [when arguing one year] but I started to see things from another angle, and after being challenged I also developed respect for the other side. Having respect for the other side only makes you stronger [9].

Yet other students spoke of the "respect" as *mutual.* "Argument (debate) brings on respect for one another" [2] one said; or again: "Even when you don't agree with others on key issues listening to them can lead to a mutual respect and understanding of the fundamental differences between humans" [13]. Still another wrote of a significant experience he/she had had:

> I started out by thinking that arguing involves and frustration (I think) because I often argued with my parents and felt the emotions of anger and frustration. Then, I moved to [the city] my senior year of high school to work in the legislature and my views of arguing shifted. I saw people who would "argue" over a particular piece of legislation and still remain respectful and friends afterwards (and during I suppose). Even I would get into arguments with the legislators and it generally strengthened our respect for each other. I learned, by observing and by doing, that arguing can actually be very positive.

To summarize: it seems that for some students personal ontogeny indeed reduplicates Johnstonian phyllogeny; they experience their initiation to argument as a moment in the constitution of a self. These students articulate their experience by talking of their stance. In taking a stand, a student makes a place for herself in the world. She makes her location visible, creating the conditions in which understanding, including self-understanding, is possible. Standing up is an uncomfortable position to be in, and dangerous, since there is no guarantee that she will be able to maintain her upright posture. But in taking this risk, she gains assurance in the stability of her self and her commitments. In putting herself out there, she earns respect and finds the grounds to respect others as well. This disposition of the self, achieved through argument, is as Johnstone put it, "a certain rather explicit self-confidence." In the words of one student, folding together many of these themes:

> To get up and speak and be respected for what I was saying, even if others did not agree, was truly, as is explained in [one course reading] exhilarating. There is no other way to describe the feeling when you're in an argument and you're stating your opinion and you know that you're winning. I would like to feel like that again: confident and knowledgeable and eloquent [12].

What, then, if we adopted a defense of argument along these lines, stressing that in argument, even never-resolving, painful argument, we come to stand more solidly in the world? Rhetorically speaking, we could hope that by invoking students' ordinary views of argument, our attempts to persuade them to buckle down and work would be more effective. In accord with Johnstone's theory we would also be exhibiting a praiseworthy generosity in addressing students from within their own positions, instead of trying to preach from our own. And finally, we might be defending argument in a way that makes evident its true dignity.

Argument is not fragile. It doesn't make us wait until we find ourselves in agreement. It doesn't need to be deferred until we transform social relations, based as they now unhappily are on coercion. It doesn't have to be put off until we transform ourselves also, into people who are above giving or taking slights. We can start where we are, following Johnstone's essentially tragic view with a cheerful confidence. When we take up our responsibility to argue, the worst will happen. The space we create in defending our deepest commitments will give to our friends, those who most disagree, the opening to end them.

English Department
Iowa State University

Notes

1. It is interesting to note that argumentation and informal logic textbooks from the tradition of teaching argument in philosophy departments appear to be remarkably unapologetic. I found none that projected onto readers the view that argument in philosophy might be taken too personally or get out of hand.

2. Johnstone elsewhere offers this amusing elaboration of the inadequacy of "facts": "You don't get a man to change his position in philosophy by beating him over the head with facts. You 'refute' him by pointing to hard evidence, but his mind will be unchanged. Having myself often been 'refuted' in this way, I would characterize it as a very confusing experience. Your interlocutor is yelling that such-and-such a fact proves you completely wrong, and insinuating that you are a fool unworthy of the attention of the roomful of people who came to hear you, but somehow you can't see where his words put pressure on your position" (1978a, 53–54).

3. Indeed, Johnstone became pessimistic that arguers could even make charges of inconsistency stick, since each could have a different conception of consistency constituted within his philosophical position; see the epilogue to *Validity and Rhetoric* (1978b) for an account of his struggle with this problem.

4. In remarks that appear just as impious as his examination of threats, Johnstone is also consistently willing to view argument as a use of power and an attempt to control an interlocutor. "Philosophical controversy is one of the channels through which a person may seek power," Johnstone asserts (1959, 133)—although paradoxically, it is a power gained only by a thoroughgoing sympathy with the position the person wants to remove (135), and that grants the opponent "the option of resisting us" (1963, 30).

5. Where the response was not anonymous, I identify the author by number. Spelling errors are corrected silently.

Works Cited

Baker, George, Pierce and Henry Barrett Huntington. 1905. *The Principles of Argumentation, Revised and Augmented.* Boston: Ginn and Company.

Ehninger, Douglas, and Wayne Brockriede. 1963. *Decision by Debate.* New York: Dodd, Mead.

Fahnestock, Jeanne, and Marie Secor. 1990. *A Rhetoric of Argument,* 2nd ed. New York: McGraw-Hill.

Foster, William Trufant. 1908. *Argumentation and Debating.* Boston: Houghton Mifflin.

Freeley, Austin J., and David L. Steinberg. 2000. *Argumentation and Debate,* 10th ed. Belmont, CA: Wadsworth.

Herrick, James A. 2004. *Argumentation: Understanding and Shaping Arguments,* updated ed. State College, PA: Strata Publishing.

Hollihan, Thomas A., and Kevin T. Baaske. 2005. *Arguments and Arguing: The Products and Process of Human Decision Making,* 2nd ed. Long Grove, IL: Waveland Press.

Inch, Edward S., and Barbara Warnick. 2002. *Critical Thinking and Communication: The Use of Reason in Argument.* Boston: Allyn and Bacon.

Johnstone, Henry W., Jr. 1954. "Some Aspects of Philosophical Disagreement." *Dialectica* 8:245–57.

———. 1959. *Philosophy and Argument.* University Park: Pennsylvania State UP.

———. 1962. "Reason Limited." In *Essays in Philosophy,* 115–32. University Park: Pennsylvania State UP.

———. 1963. "Some Reflections on Argumentation." *Logique et Analyse* 6.21–24:30–39.

———. 1967. "Controversy and Selfhood." *Journal of General Education* 19:48–56.

———. 1971. "Some Trends in Rhetorical Theory." In *The Prospect of Rhetoric,* ed. Lloyd Bitzer and Edwin Black, 78–89. Englewood Cliffs, NJ: Prentice-Hall

———. 1978a. "From Philosophy to Rhetoric and Back." In *Rhetoric, Philosophy, and Literature: An Exploration,* ed. Don M. Burks, 49–66. Lafayette, IN: Purdue UP.

———. 1978b. *Validity and Rhetoric in Philosophical Argument: An Outlook in Transition.* University Park: Pennsylvania State UP.

———. 1980. "Rhetoric and Death." In *Rhetoric in Transition,* ed. Eugene E. White, 61–70. University Park: Pennsylvania State UP.

———. 1982. "Communication: Technology and Ethics." In *Communication, Philosophy, and the Technological Age,* ed. Michael Hyde, 38–53. Tuscaloosa: U of Alabama P.

———. 1989. "Self-Application in Philosophical Argumentation." *Metaphilosophy* 20:247–61.

———. 1990. "Rhetoric as a Wedge: A Reformulation." *Rhetoric Society Quarterly* 20:333–38.

Patterson, J. W., and David Zarefsky. 1983. *Contemporary Debate.* Boston: Houghton Mifflin.

Rieke, Richard D., Malcolm O. Sillars, and Tarla Rai Peterson. 2005. *Argumentation and Critical Decision Making,* 6th ed. Boston: Pearson.

Rybacki, Karyn Charles, and Donald Jay Rybacki. 2004. *Advocacy and Opposition: An Introduction to Argumentation,* 5th ed. Boston: Pearson.

Sperber, Dan, and Deirdre Wilson. 1990. "Rhetoric and Relevance." In *The Ends of Rhetoric: History, Theory, Practice,* ed. David Wellbery and John Bender, 140–55. Stanford: Stanford UP.

Williams, Joseph M., and Gregory G. Colomb. 2001. *The Craft of Argument.* New York: Longman.

Kinship: The Relationship Between Johnstone's Ideas About Philosophical Argument and the Pragma-Dialectical Theory of Argumentation

Frans H. van Eemeren and Peter Houtlosser

1. Johnstone on the Nature of Philosophical Argument

As he himself declared in *Validity and Rhetoric in Philosophical Argument* (1978, 1), the late philosopher Henry W. Johnstone Jr. devoted a long period of his professional life to clarifying the nature of philosophical argument. His well-known view was that philosophical arguments are *sui generis,* i.e., not to be judged by the standards of argumentation in science or everyday discourse. Philosophical arguments are not *ad rem,* but are based on premises that are expressed or implied commitments of a party in dialogue. This is why philosophical argumentation is, according to Johnstone, always *ad hominem*. In philosophical argumentation, every *ad rem* argument begs the question.

Usually, *ad hominem* argumentation is dismissed as invalid. Johnstone, however, maintains that making use of *argumentum ad hominem* is the only way to establish a philosophical conclusion. In an *argumentum ad hominem,* inferences are drawn from propositions stated or implied by the other party and critical questions are raised about the conclusions that were drawn, so that it can be used to refute a philosophical position by showing that this position is inconsistent. As Walton (2001) rightly observes, this type of *ad hominem* argumentation boils down to arguing from commitments of the other party, i.e., *ex concessis*.

The use of *ad hominem* argumentation as the criticism of a position in terms of its own presuppositions is, in Johnstone's view, the only valid argument in philosophy, if any philosophical argument is indeed valid. All philosophical polemic is in this perspective in fact addressed *ad hominem*. This applies not only to philosophical argumentation that concerns self-referential refutation but also to other *ad hominem* types of philosophical argumentation, including the *tu quoque* argument (1978, 11–12).

According to Johnstone, there is no objective criterion for determining the validity of *ad hominem* argumentation. Validity must, says Johnstone in the epilogue of his collected essays on philosophical argument, be viewed as "a regulative ideal" (135). Much earlier, Johnstone had already come to the conclusion that "the valid argument is the one that maintains philosophical discussion" (38). It is this self-perpetuating feature that is the distinctive rationality of philosophy. By forcing the interlocutor to elaborate his philosophical position rather than just repeat it, the gap between the interlocutors is bridged.

In order to distinguish between constructive persuasive argumentation and mere repetition or other forms of paralyzing the discourse, the line must be drawn between responsible and irresponsible persuasion. This is a problem for Johnstone. Where the Ancients solved the problem by insisting that the persuader be virtuous, Johnstone proposed to base the distinction between responsible and irresponsible persuasion on the attitude of the philosopher and his interest in maintaining the philosophical enterprise. The philosopher is a critic who criticizes *con amore*. His intention to do so, however, is revealed "only in the way he goes about his work" (84).

A more down to earth criterion for responsible persuasion that Johnstone proposed is that the discourse should not tend to degenerate. Logic, as the discipline concerned with reason, serves to prevent the discussion from degenerating, but it can do so only if the parties concerned have jointly committed themselves to certain logical principles. If in philosophical argument a defendant is under no obligation to acknowledge an inconsistency when the other party points out an inconsistency in his position, then the other party's criticism cannot count as valid. According to Johnstone, however, it will depend on the parties' presuppositions whether or not they consider two statements as being inconsistent. In other words, what is inconsistent for the one party may not be inconsistent for the other party.

Few obligations are imposed on everyone; most obligations arise from commitments made by specific individuals or groups of individuals. As Johnstone says, "Even the cogent philosophical argument is not, of course, absolutely cogent; it is cogent only relatively to interlocutors who maintain the premises on which it depends" (27). Once we abandon the search for objective conditions under which philosophical arguments can be valid, according to Johnstone, rhetoric has a legitimate role to play. Although in his early work he depicts rhetoric in a bad light, his later position is "just the opposite" (3). In "Persuasion and Validity in Philosophy," which was first published in 1965, Johnstone still maintains that the "*actual* commitments of the speaker do not enter into the analysis of his rhetorical success.... His task is to *manipulate* his audience so as to secure agreement" (1978, 19, our italics). Later on he takes a completely different view of rhetoric. He then considers that argumentation may be a kind of rhetoric, so that philosophers *ipso facto* engage in rhetoric. The reason why rhetoric applies to argumentation is that argumentation is communication. The communication of argumentation amounts to getting the position defended in the argumentation accepted with the help of rhetorical techniques. Traditionally, rhetoric is concerned with the acceptance of statements or the refusal to accept statements in the rhetorical ambiance of the situation in which they are asserted. When Johnstone came to see the necessity of rhetoric, he embraced "'evocation' in communication"—invoking and maintaining consciousness—as the proper function of rhetoric. He declared *argumentum ad hominem* the exercise of precisely that function in philosophical communication: it "evokes the man where he lives" (137). Because "he who is conscious of some things will perforce be unconscious of others," consciousness, too, is "a matter of relativity" (132).

Persuasive argumentation is, according to Johnstone, pointless unless there is an initial disagreement between the parties as well as an initial area of agreement (18–19). This fundamental observation is—we readily note—in perfect accordance with the way in which argumentation is envisioned to be functioning in the pragma-dialectical approach. There are still more pertinent connections between Johnstone's views and our views.

In order to clarify in which ways the pragma-dialectical position connects with or deviates from Johnstone's views, we shall in this paper describe the principles of pragma-dialectics more precisely and make a comparison with Johnstone's views. First we discuss, in section 2, the pragma-dialectical "standard theory," with its ideal model of a "critical discussion" and the rules that constitute the norms for conducting a critical discussion. Next we discuss, in section 3, the way in which rhetorical insights have been integrated into the pragma-dialectical framework for analysis and evaluation in order to account for the strategic maneuvering inherent in argumentative discourse aimed at overcoming the tension between getting things one's own way and being reasonable. Then, in section 4, we focus on the way in which fallacies can be viewed as derailments of otherwise perfectly legitimate ways of strategic maneuvering. Finally, in section 5, we concentrate on the *tu quoque* fallacy as a derailment of pointing out inconsistencies, which connects the pragma-dialectical approach directly to Johnstone's approach.

2. The Pragma-Dialectical Standard Theory

The pragma-dialectical perspective on argumentation combines a dialectical view of argumentative reasonableness with a pragmatic view of the moves made in argumentative discourse (van Eemeren and Grootendorst 1984, 2004). The dialectical conception of argumentative reasonableness is inspired by critical rationalists such as Popper, Albert, and Naess and by formal dialectical logicians such as Hamblin, Lorenzen *cum suis,* and Barth and Krabbe. It is manifested in the pragma-dialectical ideal model of a "critical discussion." In this model argumentative discourse is conceived as aimed at resolving disagreements by putting the acceptability of the "standpoints" at issue critically to the test. The pragmatic conception of argumentative moves is firmly rooted in Austin and Searle's philosophy of verbal communication, Grice's theory of conversational rationality, and other studies of verbal communication by discourse and conversation analysts. This conception is manifested in the definition of the moves made in the various stages of the resolution process as speech acts such as "presenting a standpoint," "casting doubt on a standpoint," "advancing arguments in favor of a standpoint," and "concluding what the result of a discussion is."

The meta-theoretical starting-points of the pragma-dialectical theory of argumentation are "functionalization," "externalization," "socialization," and "dialectification." Functionalization means that argumentation is not to be studied as just a structure of logical derivations or syntactic patterns, but as a complex of linguistic (and sometimes also non-linguistic) acts with a specific communicative ("illocutionary") function in a discursive context. Externalization involves concentrating on the public commitments that arguers undertake—and the consequences of these commitments—in their performance of argumentative speech acts, rather than speculating on their internal motives or psychological attitudes when assuming a certain argumentative position. Socialization amounts to the recognition that argumentative speech acts are not performed in a social vacuum, but between two or more parties who are having a disagreement and interact with each other in an attempt to resolve this disagreement. Dialectification, finally, aims at transcending a merely descriptive stance in studying argumentation by taking account of the critical standards to which reasonable arguers appeal and to which they hold each other accountable when engaging in a regulated critical exchange.

When viewed analytically, a critical discussion consists of four different stages. There is a confrontation stage in which a difference of opinion manifests itself. There is an opening stage, in which the procedural and material points of departure for the discussion are established. In the argumentation stage the standpoints at issue are defended and their defense may be challenged. In the concluding stage the results of the discussion are determined.[1] In order to comply with the dialectical standards of reasonableness, in all four stages the speech acts performed in the discourse have to be in agreement with the rules for critical discussion (van Eemeren and Grootendorst 1984, 2004). These rules range from the prohibition to prevent each other from advancing a particular position in the confrontation stage of the discussion to the prohibition to unduly generalize the result of the discussion in the concluding stage. Any move made in the discourse that does not comply with any of the rules can be seen as an obstruction to achieving the critical aim of the discussion and may therefore (and in this particular sense) be considered "fallacious." The validity of the rules for critical discussion depends on their problem-solving capacity ("problem-validity") and their intersubjective acceptability ("conventional validity").[2]

This approach to the fallacies is intended as an alternative to the Standard Treatment of the fallacies so severely criticized by Hamblin (1970) and is fleshed out in van Eemeren and Grootendorst (1992). Instead of viewing the fallacies in the pre-Hamblin fashion as arguments that seem (logically) valid but are not (logically) valid, the fallacies are now defined as discussion moves that violate a particular rule that applies to a particular stage of a critical discussion. The single norm of logical validity is thus replaced by a collection of different norms that argumentative discourse has to comply with and that are expressed in the rules for critical discussion. In this way, many of the traditional fallacies can be characterized more clearly and more consistently, while "new" fallacies that went earlier unnoticed are detected. When identifying fallacies in argumentative discourse, however, it should be borne in mind that judgments concerning fallaciousness only apply if the relevant higher-order conditions are fulfilled.[3]

Although the critical evaluation of argumentative discourse (and the improvement of argumentative procedures and skills) is often considered the main goal of argumentation studies, this goal can only be realized if the appropriate analytic tools are available for carrying out a methodical reconstruction of the discourse that bridges the gap between the theoretical ideal of critical discussion and argumentative discourse as it occurs in practice. In the pragma-dialectical theory such tools have been developed. The reconstruction that can be achieved by applying these tools results in an *analytic overview* of the resolution process—a representation of the discourse in terms of a critical discussion (van Eemeren and Grootendorst 2004, 95–122). The analytic overview clarifies the difference of opinion at issue and the positions of the participants. It identifies the procedural and substantive premises that serve as the starting point of the discussion. It surveys the arguments and criticisms that are—explicitly or implicitly—advanced, the argument schemes that are used, and the argumentation structures that are developed, and determines the conclusion that is reached.

Unlike Johnstone's, the pragma-dialectical analysis and evaluation of argumentative discourse are not limited to philosophical argument. The insights developed in pragma-dialectics are supposed to apply to argumentation of every kind. We think that the difference of principle between philosophical argument and all other kinds of argument that Johnstone assumed in reality does not exist. Although Johnstone regards the *argumentum ad hominem* in its *ex concessis* variant as characteristic of philosophical argument, this does not mean that it does not occur in other domains as well. In pragma-dialectics it is claimed that the *ex concessis argumentum ad hominem* is in fact used in all domains because the premises of *ad rem* argumentation too must be accepted by the other party if the difference of opinion between the parties is to be resolved in the sense that the difference is no longer there because one of the two positions has been given up on reasonable grounds, just like Johnstone would like a philosophical discussion to be completed. Johnstone suggests that *ad rem* arguments are "objective" in the sense that they refer in one way or another to empirical reality, but eventually this is true only for those practitioners of a certain discipline who do indeed accept these arguments. In a critical discussion in the pragma-dialectical sense such acceptance is explicitly expressed in the opening stage, which is the discussion stage that provides the locus for a mutual acceptance of material premises. As Crawshay-Williams (1957) taught us—Johnstone as well as pragma-dialecticians—in order to reach agreement the discussants must also share certain procedural presuppositions—concerning validity, for instance—that can serve as joint starting-points in the discussion.

According to Johnstone, a philosopher wants to test his assertions against the criticisms of his colleagues. The critical testing process Johnstone had in mind is similar to the pragma-dialectical process of refuting a thesis by exposing an inconsistency between this thesis and its presuppositions, which we regard as primarily a dialectical process rather than a rhetorical process. The latter explains why it does not come as a surprise to us that Johnstone eventually, in spite of his earlier loose use of the term *dialectic,* stated that the "final account of philosophical argumentation will have to be given by a philosophy which endorses *dialectic*" (1978, 92, our italics). Johnstone also makes clear that he fully realizes that one cannot have a constructive argumentative exchange without the kind of disagreement that is in a critical discussion situated in the confrontation stage and the prior agreement that is situated in the opening stage. In addition, he shows a certain awareness of the need for the meta-theoretical starting points that are so emphatically articulated in pragma-dialectics; in particular the need for functionalization and socialization appear to be understood. The onset of Johnstone's functionalization, for instance, shows in his essay "Self-Refutation and Validity," when he emphasizes that in order to identify a contradiction we first have to know "in what manner a sentence is being used": "we must ascertain … that [the speaker] is asserting the sentence; for to assert is to intend to convey something" (33). Whereas Johnstone's inclination toward socialization is clear throughout his work, from his discussion-minded approach to philosophical argument, his efforts at what we call externalization do not go that far because Johnstone tends to concentrate on the psychological attitudes of the arguers rather than on their public commitments.

As far as dialectification is concerned, which brings validity in pragma-dialectics at the same time on a broader and on a more varied and more specific plane, Johnstone initially starts with restricting validity to formal logical validity and widens his concept of validity later on, albeit not in such a specific fashion as happens in pragma-dialectics. A commonality, again, is that "validity" is both for Johnstone and for the pragma-dialecticians a "regulative ideal." In the pragma-dialectical theory of argumentation, however, compliance with this ideal (which was in the first place inspired by Popper) is not connected with the speaker's attitudes: those who enter a discussion must commit themselves in the opening stage explicitly to the (first order) validity norms involved in the set of procedural rules for critical discussion, which in some institutionalized contexts may be slightly amended for the purposes of a specific activity type, such as conducting a law case. What it means to be a person who wants to conduct the discussion in this critical way is postulated in the higher order conditions.

3. Strategic Maneuvering in Resolving Disagreements

Initially, the pragma-dialectical method of analysis concentrated solely on the dialectical aspect of argumentative discourse; meanwhile the tools for reconstructing argumentative discourse have been strengthened by incorporating rhetorical considerations in the analysis and its justification (van Eemeren and Houtlosser 2002a). Although people engaged in argumentative discourse are characteristically oriented toward resolving a difference of opinion and may be regarded as committed to norms instrumental in achieving this purpose—maintaining certain standards of reasonableness and expecting others to comply with the same critical standards—these people are at the same time also interested in resolving the difference to their own advantage. Their argumentative speech acts may even be assumed to be designed to achieve precisely this effect. In other words, there is not only a dialectical, but also a rhetorical aspect to argumentative discourse.[4]

The combination of rhetorical and dialectical lines of analysis brought about in pragma-dialectics amounts to a systematic integration of rhetorical considerations in a (pragma-)dialectical framework of analysis, which means that the attempts made by the arguers to have things their way must be realized in accordance with the proper standards for a critical discussion. This implies in practice that in every stage of the resolution process, irrespective of whether it is the confrontation stage, the opening stage, the argumentation stage or the concluding stage, the parties may, while being out for the optimal rhetorical result at that point in the discussion, be presumed to hold also to the dialectical objective of the discussion stage concerned. In their efforts to reconcile the simultaneous pursuit of a dialectical as well as a rhetorical aim, which may at times even seem to go against each other, the arguers make use of *strategic maneuvering* directed at diminishing the potential tension between pursuing the two different aims (van Eemeren and Houtlosser 2002a).[5]

An understanding of the role of strategic maneuvering in resolving differences of opinion can be gained by examining how the opportunities available in a certain dialectical situation are used to handle that situation for a given party in the most favorable way. Each of the four stages in the resolution process is characterized by a specific dialectical aim. Because the parties involved want to realize this aim to their best advantage, they can be expected to make the strategic moves that serve their interests best. In this way, the dialectical objective of a particular discussion stage always has a rhetorical analogue and the presumed rhetorical objectives of the participants must be specified according to stage: it depends on the dialectical stage one is in what kind of advantages can be gained.

In the confrontation stage, the dialectical objective of the parties is to achieve clarity concerning the specific issues that are at stake in the difference of opinion and the positions that each of the parties assumes. Viewed rhetorically, the parties will aim to direct the confrontation in the way most beneficial from their own perspective. This means that each party will attempt to achieve a definition of the disagreement that favors the issues that party wants to discuss and the position he or she would like to assume. In the opening stage, each party's strategic maneuvering will be aimed at establishing the most workable starting points and the most opportune allocation of the burden of proof. In the argumentation stage, both parties' strategic maneuvering will be directed at making the strongest case for themselves in the actual testing process. In the concluding stage, their strategic maneuvering will be designed to reach the best outcome that can be achieved in the light of the preceding discussion.

In all cases, strategic maneuvering consists of making an expedient choice from the options available at a particular discussion stage ("topical potential"), adapting responsively to the other party's perspective ("audience demand"), and exploiting the appropriate stylistic means ("presentational devices"). As regards choosing from the topical potential,[6] strategic maneuvering in the confrontation stage, for instance, will aim for the most effective choice among the potential issues for discussion—restricting the "disagreement space"[7] in such a way that the confrontation is defined in accordance with the party's preferences—and strategic maneuvering in the opening stage will be directed at creating the most advantageous starting point by calling to mind, or eliciting, helpful "concessions" from the other party. Adaptation to audience demand will generally consist in an attempt to create in each stage the required "communion." In the argumentation stage, for instance, the adaptation may consist in quoting arguments the other party is supposed to agree with or in referring to argumentative principles the other party adheres to. Putting presentational devices to good use means that the phrasing and stylistic framing of the moves is systematically attuned to their discursive effectiveness in order to "diriger le discours dans une certaine direction," as Anscombre (1994, 30) put it. Among the rhetorical figures that can serve argumentative purposes are, of course, classical ones such as the rhetorical question, *praeteritio*—drawing attention to something by saying that you will refrain from dealing with it—and *conciliatio*—in one interpretation: adopting the opponent's premises to support one's own position. Although the three aspects of strategic maneuvering, which run roughly parallel with important classical areas of interest (topics, audience orientation and stylistics), can be distinguished analytically, in actual practice they will as a rule work together.[8]

Disregarding that Johnstone concentrated solely on philosophical argument, which he proclaimed to be unique, our taking account of rhetorical considerations in the argumentative testing process is fully in line with Johnstone's view that the philosopher "naturally wants his point of view to prevail" (1978, 16). And like Johnstone, who recognized that a point of view should never prevail if its author had silenced criticism in an irrational way, we also think that *mere* rhetoric will not do: for reasonableness to be maintained, rhetorical considerations should be counterbalanced by considerations of a dialectical nature. Cases in which such dialectical considerations are abandoned, as in Johnstone's example of the defense lawyer who, having just succeeded in getting his client acquitted, "does not ... pause to consider whether the jury reached the verdict for the right reasons" (24), are not reasonable in the dialectical sense. Only when a judgment is reached that is based on criteria that are open for inspection and mutually acceptable to the parties involved in the argumentative process a reasonable resolution can be reached.

In a similar vein, Johnstone has it that an attack on a philosophical position by pointing out an inconsistency in the other party's position can only be rational if the appropriate criteria are used, i.e., "criteria that are or ought to be acknowledged by the partisans under attack" (52). Johnstone's interest in intersubjectively accepted criteria for judging argumentation is explicitly responded to in the pragma-dialectical theory of argumentation: in the model of a critical discussion the opening stage enables—and forces—the participants to make their procedural criteria explicit and to commit themselves explicitly to these criteria.

Obviously, Johnstone and the pragma-dialecticians share an interest in arguments that are at the same time sound and persuasive. In pragma-dialectics, however, rhetorical insight is systematically incorporated in a dialectical framework of reasonable argument and it is explicitly recognized that the tensions between rhetorical and dialectical demands can only be resolved by strategic maneuvering on the part of the arguer. For the four stages of a critical discussion it is specified what such maneuvering may amount to. In this way, pragma-dialectics constructively elaborates on Johnstone's idea that reasonable discussion necessarily involves rhetoric. Remarkably, the pragma-dialectical view that, analytically, there are three aspects (or "dimensions") to be distinguished in strategic maneuvering agrees with Johnstone's tripartite view of rhetoric as always involving the arguer's attitude, the audience to whom the argument is directed, and the way in which the argument is presented. The audience dimension and the presentational dimension are virtually the same as in pragma-dialectics. The fact, however, that Johnstone emphasizes the arguer's attitude whereas pragma-dialecticians concentrate on the functional topical choices an arguer can make at every stage of the discussion, points to a significant difference in view concerning the way in which rhetoric is to be constrained in order to be considered reasonable. We shall now turn to the problem of what this difference in view amounts to.

4. Fallacies as Derailments of Strategic Maneuvering

In pragma-dialectics, argumentative moves are only considered sound if they are in agreement with the rules for critical discussion. Clear criteria are required to determine methodically for all the moves in all the stages of the resolution process whether or not the move concerned involves a violation of a certain rule and must thus be regarded fallacious. The concept of strategic maneuvering as an attempt to alleviate the potential tension between arguing reasonably and having things one's own way can be of help in clarifying the problems involved in identifying such criteria.

The two aims involved in strategic maneuvering are not always in perfect balance. Not only may arguers neglect their persuasive interests for fear of being perceived as unreasonable, but also, and more important, in their assiduity to win the other party over to their side, they may neglect their commitment to the critical ideal. Neglect of persuasiveness comes down to bad strategy—or even a blunder (Walton and Krabbe 1995). It harms the arguer but not the adversary and is therefore not "condemnable" in the sense of being fallacious. A party, however, whose strategic proceedings allow its commitment to a reasonable exchange of argumentative moves to be overruled by the aim of persuading the opponent, may victimize the other party. Then the strategic maneuvering has got "derailed," and is condemnable for being fallacious. All derailments of strategic maneuvering are fallacious.[9]

The view of fallacies as derailments of strategic maneuvering can be of help in developing criteria for identifying fallacious argumentative behavior because each form of strategic maneuvering has, as it were, its own continuum of sound and fallacious acting.[10] In the multi-varied practice of argumentative discourse particular categories or "types" of strategic maneuvering can be identified, and for each of these types specific conditions can be formulated that must be fulfilled if the maneuvering is to be dialectically sound because they serve as criteria for determining whether or not a certain specimen of strategic maneuvering is indeed in agreement with the specific dialectical norm of reasonableness incorporated in the relevant rule for critical discussion. Certain instances of strategic maneuvering can then be recognized as sound while other instances can be pinned down as fallacious because the relevant conditions have not been met.[11] It should be borne in mind, however, that fallacy judgments concerning specific instances of strategic maneuvering are in principle always context-dependent because the exact way in which the soundness criteria for strategic maneuvering are defined may in the end vary according to the type of interactional background ("activity type") in which the maneuvering occurs and the turn in the argumentative development ("dialectical situation") where it takes place.[12]

The criteria for identifying fallacies can only be fully developed in a systematic way if first a well-considered classification is available of the diverse types of strategic maneuvering. Such a classification is to be based on a systematic specification of both the critical aims and the persuasive aims that the parties may be supposed to attempt to achieve at the various stages of an argumentative exchange. In this endeavor the pragma-dialectical model of a critical discussion can serve as the point of departure because it specifies the critical objectives of the parties in the four discussion stages as well as their complementary "rhetorical" aims. At all stages of the discussion, strategic maneuvering will be aimed at making the argumentative moves that optimally further one's own case in such a way that the critical objective of the stage concerned is not ignored—at least not openly. Therefore, the critical objectives of a particular discussion stage determine what the strategic maneuvering may be aimed at. This fundamental insight enables us to identify for each stage the potential discrepancy between the dialectical and the rhetorical aims, the types of strategic maneuvering relevant for dissolving this discrepancy, and the soundness conditions of each type of strategic maneuvering.[13]

Johnstone clearly did not go into the concept of strategic maneuvering. It is just as clear, however, that he was aware of the fact that rhetorical persuasion, even when it is viewed as contributing to a reasonable discussion, may "degenerate" (1978, 43). In this connection he loosely mentions "logic" as the force that can keep rhetoric under control (110). Also, and much more emphatically, he mentions the "attitude" of the discussants as the main constraint on a "responsible" pursuit of rhetorical aims: these discussants need to discuss things "con amore." The (first order) pragma-dialectical rules, however, which govern a critical discussion, do not stipulate that the discussants need to discuss things "con amore." That the discussants should have the right attitude for conducting a critical discussion is, as it were, presupposed in the (second order) higher order conditions that need to be fulfilled.

An unexpected pointer to a commonality between the pragma-dialectical approach to argumentation and "the vast majority of members of American philosophy departments" at the time when Johnson started his philosophical career comes to the fore when Johnstone speaks critically about a notable tendency, at the time, among these philosophers "to draw a sharp distinction between philosophy and rhetoric, denigrating the latter." Johnstone observed that these philosophers saw the standard fallacies as "violations of rules ignored by rhetoric" (1993, 379). Remarkably, the pragma-dialectical position resembles the position Johnstone ascribed to the philosophers in the sense that the (standard and other) fallacies are viewed as discussion rule violations that are ignored because rhetorical considerations prevail in the strategic maneuvering in which the fallacies occur. Contrary to how the philosophers' position is portrayed by Johnstone, we think that their position is, just like our own position, "problem-valid." Connecting the constraints on rhetoric with the rules for critical discussion and the conditions for sound strategic maneuvering is, in our view, more practical than resorting to the attitudes of the discussants, if only because it is hard to decide whether or not a "critic" is indeed criticizing "con amore." The latter is a psychological issue, which cannot be determined from an analysis of the critic's criticisms as such but only from the way in which he goes about delivering theses criticisms, "lovingly or viciously" (1978, 84).

5. The *Tu Quoque* Fallacy as a Derailment of Pointing Out Inconsistencies

As a case in point, we shall discuss the demarcation of non-fallacious and fallacious instances of a specific type of strategic maneuvering in which a party attacks the other party by pointing out a logical or pragmatic inconsistency between a starting point proposed by the other party and a starting point this party assumed on a different occasion. Pointing out such an inconsistency can be a perfectly sound—and even very strong—strategic maneuver, but it may also derail and result in a *tu quoque* fallacy, violating the rule that parties may not prevent each other from advancing or criticizing any position (van Eemeren and Grootendorst 2004, 190).

When we are talking about inconsistencies between starting points we must distinguish between two kinds of starting points. First, in a proper critical discussion there are always (explicit or implicit) *procedural* starting points. Second, there are also *material* starting points. Ideally, at the opening stage both kinds of starting points are fully clear, so that the parties involved in the disagreement not only know *how* the discussion is going to be conducted but also *what* propositions they can safely bring to bear once the discussion has come off the ground. In argumentative practice, there are indeed certain institutional contexts, such as parliamentary debates, in which an agreement on particular procedural starting points is presupposed. It may also be the case that some material starting points are established beforehand. In non-institutionalized argumentative discourse, however, there are usually no explicit agreements as to the facts that are pertinent to the points at issue. It would in fact be highly inefficient and superfluous if each and every discussion had to begin by listing all the relevant propositions on which the parties agree. Generally, the parties use certain propositions as their starting points and take the other party's consent, rightly or wrongly, for granted. All the same, there are a lot of cases in which it is first negotiated whether or not particular propositions may serve as a common starting point. When such negotiations occur, they can be viewed as sub-discussions about the acceptability of a sub-standpoint that has emerged in the opening stage of the main discussion. Characteristically, such a sub-discussion results in a conclusion as to whether or not the proposition can be used as a common starting point.

The "dialectical profile" of the initial exchange of moves in such negotiations is as follows. The protagonist, aiming at securing a basis for his defense, initiates the negotiation process by proposing to consider a specific proposition as a common starting point. The antagonist may accept the protagonist's proposal, so that the negotiation comes to an end, but he can also reject the proposal. Viewed dialectically, the antagonist is under no obligation to provide a reason for not admitting a proposition as a common starting point (see van Eemeren and Grootendorst 2004). Viewed rhetorically, however, it may be better if he does. After all, it is generally regarded of no use to start a discussion with people who refuse, without reason, to commit themselves to any common starting point. Explaining why a certain proposition is denied the status of a common starting point can thus be regarded as a germane form of strategic maneuvering. This type of maneuvering is aimed at reconciling the rhetorical aim of admitting only starting points that are agreeable to the antagonist's own position and the dialectical objective of achieving sufficient common ground for a critical discussion.

Giving reasons for a refusal to admit a proposition as a common starting point can be a perfectly sound way of strategic maneuvering, but it can also derail into a fallacy, e.g., the fallacy of *tu quoque*. In the *tu quoque* case, the reason-giving amounts to saying that the protagonist's proposal to treat a proposition as a starting point is not acceptable because the proposition is inconsistent with something the protagonist has said or implied (by what he said or did) on a different occasion.

What soundness conditions make it possible to decide whether or not an antagonist maneuvers in an admissible way when refusing to admit a proposition as a starting point because of a proclaimed inconsistency between the proposed proposition and the protagonist's (verbal or nonverbal) behavior on a different occasion? The soundness of the strategic maneuvering hinges on three points. The first point is one of a logico-pragmatic nature: how is "inconsistency" to be defined so that it is possible to determine whether two propositions are logically or pragmatically inconsistent? The second point is how an accusation by the antagonist that pertains to an inconsistency between the proposition that the protagonist presently proposes as a starting point and something the protagonist has earlier *done* can be incorporated in the analysis. The third point is to find out what in practice is to be understood by "on a different occasion," so that it can be determined in a specific case whether, viewed dialectically, pointing at an inconsistency makes sense.

An adequate argumentation theory should make clear how the parties engaged in an argumentative exchange can make use of logical and pragmatic insight to arrive at a common understanding of (undesired) inconsistency. Because logical as well as pragmatic insight may be derived from a variety of logical systems and theories of language use, it would be helpful if a coherent choice could be made that is based on a well-considered and mutually agreed upon philosophy of reasonableness and rationality. The pragma-dialectical theory of argumentation offers such an opportunity because it is externalized in the model for conducting a critical discussion. If the parties engaged in a critical discussion have come to an agreement about which logical and pragmatic views of inconsistency they will rely on, a decision about whether or not two propositions are actually logically or pragmatically inconsistent depends eventually on the result of the "intersubjective inference procedure" they need to go through (van Eemeren and Grootendorst 2004).

Strictly speaking, the question of how a person who has performed a certain action can be held committed to a certain proposition falls within the domain of action theory. The current state of affairs in action theory, however, is such that no decisive criteria are available for determining univocally in all cases whether or not a certain action implies a commitment to a particular proposition (see, e.g., Walton 1998, 31). Our earlier contribution (van Eemeren and Houtlosser 2002b, 20) to resolving this problem consisted of making a distinction between "avowed commitments" and "contextual commitments." Avowed commitments are propositional commitments that are explicitly assumed by the performance of speech acts of the assertive type and they resemble the commitments that Walton and Krabbe (1995) call "concessions." Contextual commitments are, in our conception, commitments that are assumed to be inherent in the discussion situation at hand. Obviously, the propositional commitments that might be implied by the protagonist's actions belong to the latter category. Because contextual commitments are open to rejection and can eventually only be of real consequence for the discussion if they stand up to an appropriate intersubjective identification procedure, having performed a certain action can commit a party to a certain proposition only if the parties engaged in the dialogue agree that the action implies, or can be "translated in," the proposition concerned. This may not seem to be very helpful, but it should be borne in mind that in practical discussion situations all kinds of agreements are presupposed that admit certain actions but prohibit others because they imply a particular propositional commitment that is at odds with an "external" agreement. Examples of such external agreements are legal (or semi-legal) contracts, legal (or semi-legal) procedures, and even engaging in particular institutional or semi-institutional practices (see, e.g., Walton 1998, 285).[14]

We still have to address the issue of what is to be understood by "on a different occasion," which seems an empirical issue but is not entirely so from a pragma-dialectical point of view. In pragma-dialectics, "on a different occasion" is defined as meaning "in a different critical discussion than the present one." Therefore, from a pragma-dialectical point of view, an inconsistency between something that is presently said and something that was said on a different occasion matters only if it involves an inconsistency in *one and the same critical discussion*. This point is particularly important when we are dealing with a proclaimed inconsistency between a party's starting points. The starting points that are assumed in a critical discussion are assumed *for the sake of having a constructive critical discussion in a specific argumentative situation* and this implies that the participants in such a discussion cannot automatically be held committed to having accepted these starting points in their own right and for their own sake. In a different critical discussion they are fully entitled to assume starting points that are precisely the opposite. The only thing they are not allowed to do is to accept *and* deny one and the same starting point in one and the same critical discussion.

This insight may seem hard to apply to a practical argumentative situation because a critical discussion in the pragma-dialectical sense is an idealization of a resolution-oriented argumentative exchange and not a real-life discussion. It is, however, precisely this discrepancy that makes it possible to resolve the problem of what is to be understood by "on a different occasion" in a primarily theoretical way, instead of purely empirically. Because real-life discussions never fully coincide with a critical discussion, an evaluation of a piece of actual argumentative discourse with the help of the model of critical discussion always requires a certain amount of methodical reconstruction which takes those and only those (explicit and implicit) elements of the discourse into account that can have a function in the process of resolving a difference of opinion. Such a reconstruction may assign contributions to the resolution process to one and the same critical discussion that are in practice temporally or locally distributed. If, for instance, a letter to the editor reacts to a newspaper article that was published a week earlier, the article and the letter will be reconstructed as two contributions to the same critical discussion. In some cases, pieces of argumentative discourse can only be properly understood if they are first reconstructed as one critical discussion. This implies that the answer to the question of what should count as "one and the same critical discussion" ultimately depends on whether it is theoretically as well as empirically *justified to reconstruct* particular pieces of argumentative discourse as being part of one and the same critical discussion.

A reconstruction of two or more pieces of argumentative discourse as being part of one and the same critical discussion is justified only if the following conditions are fulfilled: (1) All pieces are aimed at resolving the same difference of opinion; (2) All pieces have the same procedural starting points; (3) All pieces (except for those that are at issue) have the same material starting points; (4) The party whose proposal to use a certain proposition as a starting point was rejected in a certain piece of argumentative discourse has assumed the same position and the same discussion role in any of the preceding pieces of discourse under consideration.

The first condition excludes cases in which the issues that are discussed in the various pieces of argumentative discourse are not identical; the second condition excludes cases in which the same issue is discussed but different discussion rules are followed; the third condition excludes cases in which there are also other starting points that differ than the starting point that is at issue; the fourth condition excludes cases in which the protagonist of the starting point at issue made this proposal while being in a different dialectical position or having a different discussion role (e.g., as protagonist and defender of the opposite standpoint).[15] When taken together, these conditions guarantee that the proclaimed inconsistency between a starting point that a protagonist presently proposes and a starting point that this party proposed on a different occasion is an inconsistency in a sub-discussion at the opening stage of one and the same critical discussion.

At this juncture of our discussion of derailments in pointing out inconsistencies, it is worth reminding that for Johnstone all philosophical polemic is addressed *ex concessis* and is in this sense *ad hominem*. In Johnstone's view, this applies not only to philosophical argumentation that concerns self-referential refutation and the like but also to philosophical argumentation that makes use of the *tu quoque* argument. We pointed out that Johnstone's psychological criterion for distinguishing between sound and irrational cases of *tu quoque*—the arguer should display the appropriate attitude—does not fulfill the meta-theoretical requirement of externalization. After shedding some more light on the problems involved in invoking the notion of "(in)consistency," which is crucial to Johnstone's thinking and plays a central part in his work, we have now tackled the problem of distinguishing fallacious uses of *tu quoque* from sound uses by showing how in a sub-discussion in the opening stage of a critical discussion the soundness conditions can be identified of strategic maneuvering in which an inconsistency is identified in the other party's verbal and non-verbal behavior. We think that in this way we have shown that externalizable criteria can be established for identifying derailed—and therefore fallacious—occurrences of the *tu quoque* argument.

6. Conclusion

In this essay we hope to have shown that a comparison between the ideas on philosophical argument propounded by Henry W. Johnstone Jr. in the second half of the twentieth century and the ideas that are at the heart of the pragma-dialectical approach to argumentation developed over the last thirty years demonstrates, in spite of obvious differences, a relationship of real kinship. In both cases, only *ex concessis* arguments, whether they are philosophical or not, are considered potentially sound. And in both cases there is an articulated concern for combining a critical approach to arguments with a realistic view of their persuasive function. The critical interest leads in both cases to adopting a regulative ideal of validity that is broader than formal validity and the interest in persuasion leads in both cases to formulating well-considered constraints on the use of rhetoric. We are convinced that the commonality is no coincidence, for one thing because the core ideas of the two approaches are to a considerable extent inspired by common sources, most notably the methodological thoughts of Rupert Crawshay-Williams (1957) concerning the combination of problem-validity and conventional validity that is vital to achieving the desired integration of the critical and the persuasive in the study of argumentation.

Department of Speech Communication,
Argumentation Theory and Rhetoric
University of Amsterdam

Notes

1. The model of a critical discussion is a design of what argumentative discourse would be like if it were optimally and solely aimed at methodically testing the tenability of a standpoint by resolving a difference of opinion concerning the acceptability of that standpoint.

2. The notions of "problem-validity" and "conventional validity," which are based on insight developed by Crawshay-Williams (1957), are introduced by Barth and Krabbe (1982). Problem-validity refers to an assessment of the suitability of certain theoretical tools to fulfill the purpose for which they are designed, conventional validity to their acceptance by the company of people that is supposed to apply them. In van Eemeren and Grootendorst (1988) an account is given of the problem-validity of the pragma-dialectical norms; the conventional validity of these norms has been investigated empirically in a series of experimental tests, e.g., van Eemeren, Meuffels, and Verburg (2000).

3. Van Eemeren, Grootendorst, Jackson, and Jacobs (1993) demonstrate that some pieces of real-life argumentative discourse that, at first sight, seem strikingly unreasonable should not be

condemned as such out of hand, because a certain second-order condition concerning the required attitude of the participants or a certain third-order condition concerning the power relationship between the participants was not satisfied during the exchange.

4. Using the label "rhetorical" in this way does not necessarily imply a conception of rhetoric that equates rhetoric without any ado with "winning," let alone with "winning at all cost" (or a similar goal). It does mean, however, that rhetoric, whatever safeguards are added, is in the end always, and undeniably, associated with getting your point across to the audience.

5. A pragma-dialectical analysis benefits in at least three ways from using this conception of strategic maneuvering. By getting a clearer view of the rhetorical aspects of the discourse, a better and more comprehensive grasp is gained of argumentative reality. By achieving a more thorough and subtler understanding of the rationale behind the various discussion moves, the analysis becomes more profound and also more clearly justified. By gaining more insight in the strategic design of the discourse, a more mature sense is developed of the whys and wherefores of the various fallacious moves.

6. In the way we use the term, there are *aggregates of topical potential* or "topical systems" for all discussion stages, not just for the argumentation stage.

7. For the notion of "disagreement space," see van Eemeren, Grootendorst, Jackson, and Jacobs (1993, 95).

8. It is often wrongly assumed that audience adaptation is the overriding, if not the only, characteristic of rhetoric. There is also a tradition in which the use of presentational devices is taken to be the main characteristic of rhetoric. Rhetoric is then primarily viewed as stylistics. In fact, topical selection could just as well be seen as the general umbrella of rhetoric, in which case rhetoric is the art of finding the appropriate loci of persuasion. In our view, none of these one-sided conceptions of rhetoric does justice to the intricate relationship inherent in every form of adequate strategic maneuvering.

9. For the sake of clarity, we distinguish terminologically too between a certain type of strategic maneuvering (e.g., "argument from authority") and a derailment of this type of strategic maneuvering (e.g., "*argumentum ad vercundiam*"), reserving the traditional labels of the fallacies for the derailments.

10. This predicament does not necessarily mean that that there must always be a grey—or even dark—zone.

11. From a different perspective, Crosswhite (1993) makes a similar distinction between argumentative moves that are in the one case sound and in the other case fallacious when he shows for the *argumentum ad baculum,* equivocation and composition and division that none of these ways of arguing is necessarily always a fallacy. His solution, however, is different from ours: "[To make the distinction,] we have to know to what audience it is addressed, and how this audience understands the argument" (1993, 380).

12. For a discussion of some more or less institutionalized and conventionalized argumentative activity types, see van Eemeren and Houtlosser (2005), and for a discussion of the "dialectical profiles" that describe the various turns in the argumentative development, see van Eemeren, Houtlosser and Snoeck Henkemans (2005).

13. A distinctive characteristic of our approach is that it takes as its starting point the various *types of strategic maneuvering* instead of the traditional (or some other) list of fallacies. This approach makes it possible to clarify the *relationship* between the fallacies and their "sound counterparts" and to explain from a new perspective the potentially *persuasive character* of the fallacies and the fact that they often go unnoticed. As Hamblin (1970, 138–40, 158) points out, scholars such as Ramus and, in his wake, Fraunce already saw fallacies as the "captious" counterparts of sound argument forms known as—dialectical and rhetorical—topics.

14. Maxims such as "Practice what you preach" may, when turned around to mean that one should not say things that are at odds with what one practices, even be regarded to point at the existence of a general agreement that carrying out actions precludes having commitments that are inconsistent with these actions.

15. In the classification of types of outcome of an argumentative dialogue proposed by Barth and Martens (1977), our conditions apply to a thesis T being *tenable ex concessis against opponent O* because it can be successfully defended against this opponent on the basis of a set of concessions C.

Works Cited

Anscombre, Jean-Claude. 1994. "La nature des topoï." In *La Théorie des Topoï*, ed. Jean-Claude Anscombre, 49–84. Paris: Editions Kimé.

Barth, Else M., and Erik C. W. Krabbe. 1982. *From Axiom to Dialogue: A Philosophical Study of Logics and Argumentation*. Berlin: Walter de Gruyter.

Barth, Else M., and Jo L. Martens. 1977. "*Argumentum ad Hominem*: From Chaos to Formal Dialectic. The Method of Dialogue Tableaus as a Tool in the Theory of Fallacy." *Logique et Analyse* 20:76–96.

Crawshay-Williams, Rupert. 1957. *Methods and Criteria of Reasoning: An Inquiry into the Structure of Controversy*. New York: Humanities Press.

Crosswhite, James. 1993. "Being Unreasonable: Perelman and the Problem of Fallacies." *Argumentation* 7:385–402.

Eemeren, Frans H. van, and Rob Grootendorst. 1984. *Speech Acts in Argumentative Discussions: A Theoretical Model for the Analysis of Discussions Directed towards Solving Conflicts of Opinion*. Berlin/Dordrecht: De Gruyter/Foris.

———. 1988. "Rationale for a Pragma-dialectical Perspective." *Argumentation* 2:271–91.

———. 1992. *Argumentation, Communication, and Fallacies*. Hillsdale: Lawrence Erlbaum.

———. 2004. *A Systematic Theory of Argumentation: The Pragma-Dialectical Approach*. Cambridge: Cambridge UP.

Eemeren, Frans H. van, Rob Grootendorst, Sally Jackson, and Scott Jacobs. 1993. *Reconstructing Argumentative Discourse*. Tuscaloosa: U of Alabama P.

Eemeren, Frans H. van, and Peter Houtlosser. 2002a. "Strategic Maneuvering in Argumentative Discourse: A Delicate Balance." In *Dialectic and Rhetoric: The Warp and Woof of Argumentation Analysis*, ed. Frans H. van Eemeren and Peter Houtlosser, 131–59. Dordrecht: Kluwer Academic.

———. 2002b. "Strategic Maneuvering with the Burden of Proof." In *Advances in Pragma-Dialectics*, ed. Frans H. van Eemeren, 13–28. Amsterdam/Newport News: Sic Sat/Vale Press.

———. 2005. "Theoretical Construction and Argumentative Reality: An Analytic Model of Critical Discussion and Conventionalised Types of Argumentative Activity." In *The Uses of Argument: Proceedings of a Conference at McMaster University*, ed. David Hitchcock and Daniel Farr, 75–84. 18-21 May 2005.

Eemeren, Frans H. van, Peter Houtlosser, and A. Francisca Snoeck Henkemans. 2005. "Dialectische Profielen en Indicatoren van Argumentatieve Zetten." *Tijdschrift voor Taalbeheersing* 27:6–138.

Eemeren, Frans H. van, Bert Meuffels, and Mariël Verburg. 2000. "The (Un)reasonableness of the *Argumentum ad Hominem*." *Language and Social Psychology* 19:416–35.

Hamblin, Charles L. 1970. *Fallacies*. London: Methuen.

Johnstone, Henry W., Jr. 1965."Persusasion and Validity in Philosophy." In *Philosophy, Rhetoric, and Argumentation*, ed. Henry W. Johnstone Jr. and Maurice Natanson, chap. 9. University Park: Pennsylvania State UP.

———. 1978. *Validity and Rhetoric in Philosophical Argument: An Outlook on Transition*. University Park, Pa.: The Dialogue Press.

———. 1993. "Editor's Introduction." *Argumentation* 7:379–84.

Walton, Douglas N. 1998. *The New Dialectic: Conversational Contexts of Argument*. Toronto: U of Toronto P.

———. 2001. "Ad Hominem Argument." In *Encyclopedia of Rhetoric*, ed. Thomas A. Sloane, 1–7. Oxford: Oxford UP.

Walton, Douglas N., and Erik C. W. Krabbe. 1995. *Commitment in Dialogue: Basic Concepts of Interpersonal Reasoning*. New York: SUNY Press.

Rhetoric Achieves Nature: A View from Old Europe

Philippe-Joseph Salazar

I would like to quote a well-known example used by Frege to illustrate the difference between *Sinn* and *Bedeutung,* as a point of departure for this essay: Venus is the morning star and the evening star—it depends on the beholder[1]—but Venus, the celestial body, it objectively is. In the eyes of the beholder lies "sense" (*Sinn*); in an objective view, resides "reference" (*Bedeutung*). Or, to put it rhetorically: Venus is this or that, according to a given set of commonplaces, it is address-bound; whereas, in an objective and cohesive language, it is what science explains it to be.

Henry Johnstone, in his 1973 article "Rationality and Rhetoric in Philosophy," gives his own version of this aphrodisiac exemplum. In his essay, "rationality" behaves not unlike Venus, as for the philosopher rationality awakes at dusk, in the flight of the Hegelian owl, while, for the rhetor, it shines at sunrise, when arguments begin to be exchanged on the market place. Hauser neatly encapsulates this when he writes, "the addressed character of philosophical argument . . . [does] not permit a clear dividing line between what [is] philosophical and rhetorical in an argument" (2001, 5). Rationality is bound by the "addressed" nature of arguments that, prudentially, make our civil life bearable or, at the very least, less beastly, and help believers in the morning star to live side by side with those of the evening star. The recent success of the French referendum (in May 2005) when, following deliberative mobilization by a large number of non-governmental organizations, voters declined to accept a choice presented them by media and politicians united, as the only rational option, and voted "no," has highlighted the *Sinn*/*Bedeutung* political tension. I would go as far as to say that the *Sinn*/*Bedeutung* game is democratic or republican civility's aphrodisiac. Without its incentive, argument in politics may be reduced to a handbook of quotations held as "truths," with no escape from "rectification," in the words of Chairman Mao Tse-Tung (no date, 9).

This aphrodisiac tension between *Sinn* and *Bedeutung* enters civil life every time political choices offered the sovereign, either directly (through popular vote) or by simulation (through elected representatives), are pre-cast by rational choice practitioners as no-alternative decisions. When the latter face defeat, as in May 2005, for failing to understand the energy coiled within the tension, they often resort to admonishments that "more pedagogy is needed." The sovereign is treated as unreceptive to reason, stuck in the ("rhetorical") illiteracy of "senses." The professional political class, by contrast, heroically defends "reference." Politicians, indeed, trained in rational choice theory and whose skills are honed in business or public administration schools, those two great mirages of scientific-like politics, of objectified politics, must be staunch believers in *Bedeutung* although they play, of course, on *Sinn* whenever it suits them. The despairing side of this game is that republics that wish to embody the lessons of the eighteenth century, and to a different degree non-republican Western democracies, live a life whereby the political class keeps telling the sovereign that *Sinn* is good so long as national security is not at stake. The people are conceded, for instance, the right to have different "senses" of community rights or religious beliefs—"diversity" is the ruling commonplace, activating the topics of quality and posteritas, should we say if we were Quintilianists—but national policies must rest on "reference," this *Bedeutung* being the precinct of those who practice a scientific-like language, that of modern governance, made of interrelated "truths." International relations are of course a prime locale for the fabrication of *Bedeutung*.[2] Never has the game between sense and reference been so widely played in our Enlightenment-inspired democracies than today. Never has Venus known so many unprofessed idolaters.[3]

I should like now to leave Venus to her own devices and—without making any claim, however, to be a better interpreter of the French situation on matters of rhetoric, argument and rationality than some—to present how in France the vexed situation of "argument" in relation to rhetoric and philosophy, and politics, presents itself.[4] It is also a way of paying homage to Johnstone's interest in French philosophy of rhetoric.

I will seize upon three illustrations, the first borrowed from an actual debate, the second from an actual practice, and the third from the most recent scholarship. The first concerns the historical positioning of philosophy vis-à-vis rhetoric in France. The second gives direct insight into the teaching of argumentation at school by philosophy teachers. The third illustrates the treatment given rhetoric in the massive *Vocabulaire européen des philosophies* (Cassin 2004). All three hinge, of course, on what it is to argue in a republic.

1

Once upon a time, twenty-four years ago, there was a debate in France concerning the teaching of philosophy in secondary education. Must it be maintained, why, how, by whom? This very interrogation led, in 1983, to the chartering of the *Collège international de philosophie,* an initiative initially driven by Derrida, Deleuze, and Lyotard. The *Collège* was, in part, a response to the necessity of redefining education at large, "philosophy as a life science,"[6] at a time when the French had voted in a Socialist government and backed a social agenda—which is still today, in spite of the derision heaped upon the "French social model," the fountainhead of resistance to a market-based European Union with its disdain for social, republican justice. In essence, in France and since the Enlightenment, any sound debate on the teaching of philosophy is linked to a two-fold meditation on "what is a citizen" and "what is good government." This redoubling of philosophy in politics is a fundamental tension, which can be traced back to Descartes's allegory, in the *Discourse on Method,* on well-constructed cities and properly aligned buildings—metaphors for an ordered metaphysics, but also for an ordered, reasonable, reasoned, humane civil life.

Closer to us, it is worth recalling how the updating of Kantian ethics in the mid-nineteenth century was, singlehandedly, the work of Charles Renouvier (1815–1903). If his epoch-making *Philosophie analytique de l'histoire: les idées, les religions, les systèmes* (1896–1897) was the result of his new understanding of practical reason, it also was the outcome of his long-standing Socialist engagement: Renouvier had been a Republican activist under the ill-fated Second Republic, when he authored a *Manuel républicain de l'homme et du citoyen* (1848) and helped conceive a non-presidential and non-parliamentary constitutional dispensation, the *Organisation communale et centrale de la République* (1851). Silenced under the Second Empire (which saw, to its credit, the fast development of primary and secondary popular education under the supervision of historian Victor Duruy), Renouvier dedicated himself to reforming Kant and fashioning a "critical" and rationalist philosophy, profoundly republican and unashamedly centered on moral responsibility, soon to be called "personnalism" (*Le Personnalisme,* 1903). As the leading rationalist philosopher of his time, as a republican, as an anti-dogmatic, Renouvier envisaged the teaching of philosophy as a "resistance" against political oppression and moral illusions. Not surprisingly, its influence on *Esprit*, a leading progressive force in the 1930s, was more than perceptible and gave some of its steadier, intellectual roots to wartime *Résistance* itself. The constitution of a new social democracy, a republic that cares, after World War II, was the direct result of *Résistance* that, apart from being a fighting organization, represented an unusual and unique alliance of intellectual forces. During the debate that led to the French rejection of the European constitutional treaty in 2005, the moral imperative of a "return to 1945" was often heard in different quarters, a return to a foundational moment of reflection concerning the nature of the Republic. For Renouvier and its descendants philosophy and civic education are closely related. There cannot be a true "republic," and a responsible citizenry, without a philosophical education.

However, such education implies the eradication of rhetoric. In simple terms, the consolidation of the republic at the turn of the twentieth century, namely when church and state were separated (1905), was perceived as the achievement of the spirit of 1789, that of a polity based solely on the exercise of reason, itself structured by universal, rational truths. Education was the heart of the matter (already, in 1882, primary education had been made free, compulsory, and secular) and rhetoric was branded as a tool for religious indoctrination, obscurantism. Simultaneously, the republic affirmed the expulsion of religion from public and political life, and confirmed philosophy upon the ruins of rhetoric.[7] The anti-rhetorical move initiated by Condorcet in 1792, when the last of the great *Philosophes* presented a Report on Education to the revolutionary assembly, that eliminated rhetoric—"the seed of destructive corruption"—and replaced it with logic (Salazar 2003, 246–51), had found its completion. In fact, during the Revolution, the denial of rhetoric extended beyond the religious sphere and its previous absolute control over education. Indeed, the anti-rhetorical republic saw no benefit in forensic rhetoric, and disestablished the Bar. The law was applied, logically one hopes, outside the contest of evidence and effects of prestige and the activity of emotions, by "expert-judges."[8] In addition, the promotion of Thomistic philosophy by pope Leo XIII (encyclical *Æterni Patris,* 1879), while it restored Aristotelian logic and dialectic above rhetoric, confirmed in rationalists' eyes the Church inability to meet the challenges posed by modern, scientific argumentation.

One would have thought the debate about rhetoric and the best way for citizens, in a republic, to gain practice in duties and servitudes, joys perhaps, of the "mild voice of reason," long buried.[9] However, in 2000, the French Education minister raised, in a circular, the question of rhetoric at school. A public debate ensued, in the columns of left-wing daily newspaper *Libération,* over a good two months (Dubet and Merlin, 2000).

The most striking point of the exchanges was the open coupling of philosophy and rhetoric. The protagonists were not philosophers looking down onto the plebs from academic ivory towers. French teachers of philosophy enjoy great prestige, they form a sort of republican nobility in the sense Bourdieu speaks of "a nobility of State"—himself a reluctant exemplar of it—even though they may pursue careers in the secondary school system they often are published writers of influence, public intellectuals. In the popular eye, they remain a respected, intellectual bridge between secondary and tertiary educations. Every year, at examination time, philosophy exam questions make national news headlines. Philosophy is, in many ways, the acme of a citizen's education. Philosophy is supposed to prepare future citizens to reflect, to argue, to decide, to vote in reason and in conscience, in short: to vote "freely," that is free of obscurantist preconceptions. Renouvier would approve.

In this instance, the couple rhetoric–philosophy found itself, again, at the core of a debate about the formation of good citizens. The minister articulated his viewpoint with distinct clarity as he urged teachers to "construct situations of oral exchanges conducive to constituting the subject [meaning, pupils] as an efficient speaker." It assigned a clear objective: "A progressive command of expression is an essential element in accessing citizenship" (quoted in Merlin 2000, my translation). It seemed apparent that rhetoric was to find a new status, on the spoils of what used to be "civic instruction," which had itself replaced "religious instruction" in France's secular republican education. Philosophy was under no threat of being deposed.

Yet a professor of literary theory, who entered the fray against rhetoric, made explicit the social dangers implicit, in her opinion, in rhetorical rationality. She asked, "Is this, at last, by means of a proposed curricular change, the Republic's long-awaited definition of what a citizen is?" The new curriculum, she adds, "cuts short debates about the nature of language (is language intentional, is it a substitute for violence, does it make room for renouncing the will to command?), and settles the issue. It says: a citizen is an efficient speaker able to adapt to any verbal situation and to make an argument. This raises a more fundamental question. The new curriculum affirms that culture, if used with rhetorical dexterity, will be perceived as yet another capital acquired through dubious means" (Merlin 2000, my translation). In her argument, the re-introduction of rhetoric at school, far from building up citizenship, would for instance and in practice reinforces the republic's inability to reduce social violence, and in particular violence at school, where education shapes the republic.[10] Rhetoric at school, far from inducing a *cedant arma togæ,* the substitution of the contest of words to physical violence, would increase actual violence as well as "symbolic violence." Rhetoric would create new communicative inequalities and reinforce the idea that mastery, command, power, already perceived as the attributes of the culturally and economically dominant bourgeoisie, are the norm and must be acquired. Rhetoric would provide an added, institutionalized, advantage to those pupils who are already better equipped than others in material wealth and access to culture, and help them secure, later in life, increased power. In this argument, largely based on Bourdieu's reading of social reproduction, the teaching of rhetoric buttresses the bourgeoisie's ethos by having working-class, immigrant, subaltern children adopt its ways, internalize its "signs of distinction," and reproduce oppression.

This critique is polemical and severe. The analysis is rigid and mechanical. Yet, their common purpose is to reserve for philosophy the deliberative shaping of future citizens—with the help of history, especially social history as developed by the *Annales* school as, in the course of the debate, a republican alliance of sorts was indeed perceptible between philosophers, that is anti-rhetorical ones, and historians.[11]

Apart from their merits and demerits, such neo-Marxist strictures underscore how support for rhetoric is assimilated, in France, to the disparagement of democracy and the continuation of class violence by persuasion. Ironically, the remarkable body of scholarship on the Sophists—philosophical, philological, historical—consolidated in the past thirty years, far from dissipating doubts on the positive value of rhetoric for civility, has worsened rhetoric's position, as battle lines between advocates and detractors of rhetoric do not follow political ones, left and right, which is a case rare enough in France to be noted. In fact, apologists of the Sophists often belong to the same political spectrum as their detractors, and their advocacy of a deliberative, popular, "communal" democracy is firmly set in the Socialist lineage initiated by Renouvier. To unravel this idiosyncratic intellectual and political history would require another essay altogether.[12]

As a result, rhetoric did not re-enter the school curriculum.

2

However, this defeat of rhetoric at school brought the question of "argumentation" into the limelight, among concerned teachers of philosophy who are pursuing the earlier interrogation raised at the creation of *Collège international de philosophie.* How does one teach argumentation with citizens in mind?

In 2004, an association of philosophy teachers (ACIREPH) engaged in developing their discipline held a workshop on the subject (ACIREPH 2004). Their manifesto and colloquium program are documents of a practice.

In the manifesto, we read the following: "Making the teaching [of argumentation] an object for reflection reduces [the secondary school curriculum in] philosophy to 'argumentative rhetoric' or to 'public debate.' This objection shows the traditional reluctance of philosophers toward rhetoric, which it is not without grounds. None of us wishes to turn our pupils[13] into apprentice sophists trained to put in practice the artifices of language mechanically. Far from it. The great majority of pupils are safe from the risk of exposure to an excess of rhetoric. The problem rather lies in their lack of the most basic tools in most elementary rhetoric, most necessary and most legitimate ones to elaborate and develop their thoughts. For instance, they do not know how to go about constructing an argument (*raisonnement*) and its refutation, formulating an objection and rebutting it, developing a notion or a problem analytically. They do not know how to write it down, or how to read it in a text, or how to express it verbally or listen to it in live situations (*discussion orale*).[14] It is up to teachers to teach them all of this, to make them discover rules, to help them acquire competence" (my translation). The manifesto, having gone through this neat exordium (with a fair combination of appeals to pathos and ethos, even a preliminary refutation of sorts) goes on to identify two main arguments.

The document begins by stating that, if "the ability to reason well is an essential finality of the teaching of philosophy," this "ability" (*aptitude*) is the "minimum condition for any intellectual activity" and teaching it is an "eminently democratic task." The manifesto then deplores that "no collective" reflection on this "training" has so far been undertaken, deploring even further that if logic is indeed part of the curriculum in epistemology (called "*demonstration*") logic itself is not taught at all, in contraposition to the epistemology of, say, history, that accompanies the teaching of history. Pupils have to reflect on a discipline they are not practicing. The derisively over-ambitious curriculum ("a grandiose task") works on the assumption that learners possess an innate knowledge of logic's basic operations. Yet, "for instance, to understand the following examination questions, 'Is the end of the State to maintain order or promote justice?' and 'Is power founded on force or consent?' they must have learned to distinguish between the inclusive 'or' which gives its full meaning to the former statement, and the exclusive 'or' to the latter." The manifesto laments—union-style—the lack of clarity of instructions given teachers by the minister (himself a scholar of some repute).

Having, negatively, established logic as the sole conveyor for fulfilling the dual task of teaching good reasoning and equipping citizens with the voice of reason, the manifesto moves to defining "reasoning" (*raisonnement*) and argumentation in philosophy.

A first statement dismisses formal logic as somewhat "useful" but "insufficient," on the dual ground that, on one hand, philosophical concepts can rarely be rigorously formalized and, on the other, that inferential soundness does not concern itself with "material truth." Oddly, but not for rhetoricians, the manifesto adds that "premises must be acceptable" to the audience, the classroom, and that, in any event, an argument proved correct by a formally sound deduction hardly ever "reduces to nothing" arguments invoked against it. The manifesto then proposes, as an evident implication, that "for all these reasons, the notion of argumentation expresses best what is the philosophical way of proceeding (*démarche*), in keeping with the legal, political and esthetic fields." Having established why "the logic of argumentation" fits better the teaching of philosophy, as defined earlier, than formal reasoning and, in one clean move, having co-opted forensics, politics, and art, the manifesto disposes of an objection arising from within its midst: "many colleagues are allergic to this very word, 'argumentation,' an hostility stemming from binary thinking and perfectly expressed by the pair 'to convince/to persuade' which leaves us with no other choice than the search (*souci,* "care") for truth or the seduction of sophistry." The manifesto then moves to dissolve the contradiction by playing Perelman against Descartes. It derides Cartesian dogma that "if two persons are in disagreement, one must be wrong or, rather, none is right for the mere exposition of reasons, if valid, should have sufficed to convince the wrong party"—a taken-for-granted view that shows "no pedagogical care" (*souci,* again). It adds: "We owe Chaïm Perelman, an author practically unknown under our latitudes,[15] a critique of this Manichean model and a defense of a logic of argumentation which recognizes the value of opinions (*vraisemblable*) and the relative weight of arguments." The manifesto concludes with a recommendation—to determine what procedures need to be taught—and on a plan of action—to hold a working colloquium.[16] Ironically, it is structured like a French essay, a dissertation with an introduction, a thesis, an anti-thesis, and a synthetic, *Aufhebung* style, substantial third part and conclusion. (Non) rhetorical habits die hard.

The Manifesto would elicit smiles from rhetoricians both outside and inside France, if what is at stake was not the education of a polity, placed at the heart of Europe and not unimportant for the idea of the republic. This document gives a direct insight into prejudices and difficulties, as well as the "care" (*souci*—as in Foucault's *Le Souci de soi,* "The Care of the Self") French philosophy teachers do take of their charges. Without laboring the point, it is self-evident that rhetorical argumentation, although attractive in social terms, leaves many of them with a sense of discomfort, if not of betrayal of philosophy. By insisting on the tag word "logic," however informal, they wish to retain philosophy's eminence over other forms of reasoned discourses (history, for instance), in full knowledge that the standard written test remains, across the humanities, their philosophical dissertation, although its procedures are still unexplicated.

Rhetoric, once again, is left in abeyance as its rapport with philosophy and logic remains dependant upon ideological concerns—here, the tension between the *Bedeutung* philosophy teachers wish to assign to their profession and the "senses" that, as concerned citizens, they need to attach to their pedagogical activity.

What of, then, philosophers who, besides being teachers, are fashioning enquiry itself? How do they reflect on the essential relationship between rhetoric and rationality?

3

Philosophical encyclopedias are good indicators of how knowledge is perceived at a given time. As it happens, in 2004, a team of European philosophers completed an imposing decade long task, the modestly named *Vocabulaire européen des philosophies* (Cassin 2004). The *Vocabulaire* is an analytical dictionary of philosophical "words" (French, English, German, etc) that present cases of "unstranslatability" across European languages. For our purpose, the interest presented by the *Vocabulaire* is threefold. On the one hand, many of the contributors are well versed in rhetoric and have for *logos* the respect post-Heideggerians would and should feel. The editor in chief is herself a leading exponent and translator of the Sophists and the Pre-Socratics.[17] In addition, many of them are closely associated to the renovation of philosophy initiated at *Collège international de philosophie.* Finally, their multi-lingual approach, which allows concepts to be approximated, compared, and even left suspended in between possible translations, is proof enough they are not bent on forcing problems into whatever "French" mold. These are favorable conditions for re-opening the issue of (rhetorical) reasoning and the *Vocabulaire* cannot fall under any suspicion of anti-rhetoricism. Simply, we cannot expect rhetoric, *rhétorique, retorica,* etc. to be given an entry, for—unlike belief, *pravda, praxis, quiddité, stato*— the word, in any of these languages, does not present a case for "untranslatability."

Nonetheless, rhetoric is present in the *Vocabulaire*. Voice, style, sublime appear in dedicated entries, notions that have some incidence on rhetorical matters.[18] *Actio* receives a brief mention under "*Acteur*" (an unusual entry in a philosophical encyclopedia); so does *Kairos* under "Moment." More pointed notions, "Performance" and "*Dialectique*" and "*Sophisme*," have brief, handy notices. The *Vocabulaire* seems to maneuver around rhetoric. However, the index of Greek words cited (not dedicated entries) lists *rhêtorikê,* with two references to articles on "*Lieu commun*" (commonplace) and "*Mimêsis.*" The words *rhétorique,* rhetoric, *Rhetorik,* etc. are not indexed at all. Even-handedly, the *Vocabulaire* has no entry for "argument" or "logic." In order to piece together a philosophical narrative concerning rhetorical reasoning, we have to turn to three extensive articles: "*Lieu commun,*" "*Logos,*" "*Acte de langage.*"

The article "*Lieu commun*" (721–26), written by the best French specialist,[19] in a style not devoid of humor ("*Doxa* was akin to Wisdom, it now is akin to Stupidity") (727), differs from the "Commonplace" entry in the *Encyclopedia of Rhetoric* (Sloane 2001, 119–24). It is a detailed emphasis on the shift of meaning, and rhetorical practice, from Aristotle (meaning #1, *topos*), to Cicero (meaning #2, *locus communis*), and to the Renaissance (meaning #3, commonplace book, digest). The author carefully unravels the Aristotelian meaning, indispensable to understand, and to put into practice, rhetorical, enthymematic reasoning. Just as skillfully, he explains how Ciceronian commonplace is an event of discourse (in a forensic speech, it is this moment in a peroration when the argument on a particular case proceeds to stirring generalizations and eloquent vehemence). The analysis of the pedagogical value of Renaissance digests does not differ in substance from the *Encyclopedia*'s entry.[20] The article deals therefore with three aspects of rhetorical rationality: (1) the production of enthymemes relevant to a category of discourse (a judicial speech is not "located" in the same stock as a celebratory one); (2) the moment of persuasive speech when an orator leaves behind reasoned arguments, appeals to an audience's moods or ethics, and has it adhere to a thesis that, henceforth, will be "common" knowledge; and (3) the lists of topics readily usable in rhetorical exercises, the stock in trade of speechmaking.[22] Furthermore, it contains a large insert, entitled "Rhetorics of '*topos,*' rhetorics of '*kairos*'" (722).[23] There, we find an unexpected and short history of rhetoric. The author recalls the critique leveled by Plato, in philosophy's name, against rhetoric. The word *rhêtorikê* appears only to disappear as referring to a *tekhnê*: Plato dismisses indeed the "art of rhetoric" as *alogon pragma,* a "practice without reason" (*Gorgias*, 465a)—setting on its course the duality between rhetoric and philosophy, the duel of rhetoric argumentation and dialectical demonstration, the doubling up of persuading and convincing. This is standard history. However, the author displaces it. She posits a distinction between a Protagorean interpretation of rhetoric as opportunistic, enunciation driven, stupefying argumentation, and an Aristotelian interpretation of rhetoric where reasoning needs space to unfold, may it be in syntactic arrangement or in speech composition. By implication, there are two sorts of rhetorical rationality or reasoning—the Sophistic, with its reliance on *kairos* and paradoxes of enunciation; and the Aristotelian, with its reliance on *topos* and systematic layout or "placing" of arguments. There are rhetorics of time, and there are rhetorics of space. In sum, the near "untranslatability" of *topos* by *locus communis,* and of both by commonplace, allows to recognize both Sophistic and Aristotelian logics of argumentation as "practices that reason," in rebuttal of Plato's own dismissal,[24] and to further propose that these two forms of reasoning are articulated to either time or place, two "logics." However, what does *logos* mean?

The substantial article on "*Logos*" relays the analysis given in "*Lieu commun*" (727–40).[25] Warn the authors: "It is important to bear in mind that Greek *logos* stems from a polysemous etymon in which the seme 'to gather' is welded to the seme 'to speak.' This is the point of departure for any philosophical enquiry on *logos*" (729). This peremptory claim is somewhat idiosyncratic[26] but is borne out by an erudite and cogent analysis. How does it figure in the debate between rhetoric's reasoning and philosophy's rationality?

The article presents a history of (mis)translations, from *logos* (729–33), to *ratio* (733–38), and "vernacular word games" (738–41). Seven inserts focus on specific topics.[27] The treatment of *logos* begins with the devaluation of Sophistical *logos* at the hands of Plato, proceeds to the latter's appropriation of *logos* as "correct reasoning," *orthos logos* (*Phaedo*, 73a8). This "right"[27] *logos* offers itself to grammatical analysis, an essential tool for dialectical reasoning. The authors tersely remind us the word "*logos* can simply denote a combination of a noun and a verb, either true or false" (by reference to *Sophist* 262c–263b). Rhetoric is hardly a concern in the developments on Aristotelian "networks of sense," and Stoician "systematicity," regarding *logos* or *ratio*. For the second time, rhetorical reasoning is essentially harnessed to the Sophists. Further, and final, evidence of the surreptitious, or "encyclopedic," defense of (sophistical) rhetoric lodged in the *Vocabulaire* network of cross-references is found in a referral, at the beginning of "*Logos*": "See *epideixis* under '*Acte de langage*'" (729).

"*Acte de langage*" (11–21)[28] opens with translations for French *acte de langage:* Greek *epideixis*, (Medieval) Latin *actus exercitus,* English speech act and performance, and German *Vollziehung* (11). Perfunctory homage is paid to Austin, whereupon the authors declare interest in "those moments in Greek and Roman traditions when language was considered for what it does and not what it expresses." They go on: "Unlike the Anglo-Saxon approach, concerned with the ethics of speech, the question they [Greeks and Romans] raise is that of the difference between culture and nature, and of the invention of politics, which revolves around the problem of Sophistical *epideixis,* rhetorical efficiency" (11, my translation). The opening analysis, entitled "*Epideixis,* performance and performativity of *logos*," is an apology for rhetoric (11–14), and its beginning sentence surveys the entire Ancient tradition of rhetoric and sums it up: "*Epideixis* is the word which traditionally denotes sophistical discursivity, from Plato to the *Lives of the Sophists*" (11). Epidictic rhetoric is, technically, a genre, but, philosophically, it is about the invention of culture and politics, the power of speech (*dunamis*). *Epideixis* goes further than generic celebratory rhetoric, it is the art of "showing," the "monstration" of what theoretical knowledge can "demonstrate" (in Thales' case, astronomy applied to economy, and making money, and "showing it off") (*Politics* 1259a 9–19). Similarly, Gorgias can "demonstrate" that Helen of Troy, although reviled by the Greeks, is innocent.[29] Rhetorical performance performs reality. The authors show their colors: "*Epideixis* disturbs philosophy [by creating] an opposition between two discursive modalities, two world models even: a physical one where demonstrations adhere to and explain Nature's principles, in relation to which truth is an unveiling and a correspondence (see Truth); a cultural and political one where performing common values takes place at every opportunity and continuously produces consensus and political self-recognition [*identité*]" (my translation). In short, the world of reasoning is divided between *apodeixis* and *epideixis,* a frontier blurred by the univocal prefix "de-" in "de-monstration"—both epi- and apo-. Think of "public demonstration" and "mathematic demonstration" to feel how confusing, and close, they can be. We could stop here, agree to this philosophical and Heideggerian history of epi-/apo-deixis,[30] and retreat to the comfort of the hackneyed opposition between rhetoric and philosophy, flawed logic and true logic. The authors of the article would have none of it.

In an insert on "*Apodeixis* in Aristotle" (14),[31] the authors show how Aristotelian apodictic reasoning has two faces, one in the *Analytics,* the other in the *Rhetoric* (14). Apodictic syllogism is one degree up from probability-based dialectical syllogism and two up from short-cut rhetorical enthymeme because its premises are demonstrated or evident truths (one step up), and is fully articulated (two steps up). However, if its scientific function is to establish universal causality and finality in phenomena, it is a procedure that, in inductive argumentation (*Posterior Analytics,* 18, 81a 40–b2), makes us understand what is universal in a singular phenomenon, or that part of universality lodged in an individual (Socrates is mortal because he is a human being). Now, in *Rhetoric* III, 13 Aristotle declares "there are two parts to a speech; for it is necessary [first] to state the subject and [then] to demonstrate (*apodeixai*) it."[32] Simply put, rhetorical demonstration mirrors dialectical demonstration, *prothesis* mirrors *problema*—in both cases, the prefix tellingly denotes what is "placed in front of," literally "pro-posed" (hence the technical meaning of "proposition," statement of argument "thrown at" the audience, a "proposal" really). *Apodeixis* mirrors itself in rhetorical proofs. Even better, argue the authors: in the bi-partition between atechnic proofs and entechnic, "artistic," ones, the latter bring rhetorical reasoning to its plenitude not through arguments of *ethos* and *pathos*, but thanks to arguments of *logos*. The superiority of this category of "artistic" proofs, to those issuing from orator's granted prestige or conceded prudence, and to those activating listeners' emotional receptivity, resides in the "monstration" of *logos*. For the authors, the achieved form of rhetorical reasoning is apodictic reasoning inasmuch as it is an *epideixis* of *logos* "as constitutively rhetorical."[33]

The *Vocabulaire*'s argument rests on a phenomenological view, for which they provide us with an Aristotelian key. Citing *Physics* II, 8, the authors return afresh to their rebuttal of the anti-rhetorical indictment of rhetoric as non-art, a non *tekhnê:* "Art imitates nature [194a 21] . . . and generally art completes what nature cannot bring to a finish [199a 15]."[34] In short, the ontological difference between rhetorical and non-rhetorical reasoning is minimal: as signaled by their shared adherence to apodictic proofs, they both help us perceive, through the singularity of events and cases and persons, underlying universals, and make "phenomena manifest." Rhetoric completes Nature; in particular, as far as human beings as political animals are concerned, rhetorical "art" achieves our political nature, by making it "manifest." The question is, what sort of phenomenon does rhetoric manifest? We are referred to the (beautifully written) article on "*Erscheinung*" (372–77).[35] If the rhetor's art simply consists in slotting phenomena into persuasive arguments, to make things already there evident for the sake of a cause to win (a policy to implement, a case to adjudicate, a value to promote), then this "art" does not "bring nature to a finish"—nature as a policy-making, nature as justice, nature as values. The answer lies in the difference between "phenomenon" and *Erscheinung*. The article retraces the philosophical history of this dual nomination from Kant to Husserl, and finds its resolution with Heidegger: "Phenomena never are *Erscheinungen*." Put differently: *Erscheinung* refers to what does not appear by itself. Then, by folding this definition onto that of rhetoric as a "practice that reason," via the mediation of the argument about *epideixis,* we realize what the authors of this interconnected series of entries intend to mean: that rhetorical reasoning makes manifest what never appears by itself. This is why Rhetoric brings Nature to a finish.

*

We may or may not like or accept—or unhappily disagree with, or concede with distaste—the argument developed by the *Vocabulaire* concerning rhetorical reasoning. This is an unmitigated defense of rhetoric from the standpoint of philosophers who have sided with the Sophists, and Aristotle. It upsets roles. Rhetoric reasoning stands, here, on the "right side," achieving what neither dialectic nor logical rationality can possibly deliver. This rhetoric restores to daily, human, civil life a measure of discovery, and invention and "apparition" (*Erscheinung*), which no other "art" can provide. It performs for humanity in its human milieu, politics or life-together, what scientific reasoning does for humanity in relation to its physical milieu. Moreover, it does so by making appear what cannot otherwise appear, just as astronomers make manifest, in equations, stars before senses or instruments can experience them. Venus the star, as I mentioned at the beginning of this essay, has this or that sense for beholders, while as an object for science it is duly referenced. In sum, the questions raised by a number of French philosophers concerning rhetoric—first, in strictures against its power of social subjugation, second, in the inadequacy of a philosophical education deemed a requisite for political education, third, in a complex elaboration on the nature of philosophical language across European cultures—are not analogous to what beholders think of Venus, regardless of what it is. This is not about relativism, this travesty of free thinking. The general problem is quite different, and so is the answer. The problem is not that of the civil diversity of commonplace, "digested," viewpoints, and of their eloquent or communicational marketeering, but of the possibility afforded by rhetoric to provide a recourse against such pre-cast "senses," which, in addition, are dismissed as irrational or unwise by those who say they possess "knowledge" (*Bedeutung*), unless, of course, they find them expedient. The answer is that rhetoric can manifest un-apparent viewpoints, go beyond topics, and achieve—true—politics, by bringing our human nature, our political nature, to a finish. This may well be the real *kratos* of democracy.[36]

Centre for Rhetoric Studies
University of Cape Town

Notes

1. St. John of Damascus indeed notes that Arabs worshiped Aphrodite, the Morning Star, until Muhammad rose among them; by contrast, the Prophet hails the Evening Star (Qur'an, LIII) (Saint John of Damascus, *Writings,* ed. and trans. F. H. Chase, in *The Fathers of the Church,* vol. 38. New York: 1958).

2. I refer to Beer and Hariman (1996) and draw attention to the issue "The Rhetorical Shape of International Conflicts," *Javnost—The Public* 12(4), 2005.

3. This contribution forms part of a suite of essays on Republican idealism: "Censorship: A Philological (and Rhetorical) Viewpoint," *Javnost—The Public* 11(2): 5–18, 2004; two forthcoming

papers in *Revista de la Antropologia Social,* ed. J. Fernandez, 2006; and a volume co-edited by I. Strecker and S. Tyler, *Rhetoric Culture Theory.*

4. Let me mention my two colleagues at *Collège international de Philosophie*, Barbara Cassin, author of the seminal *L'effet sophistique* (1995), and Dominique de Courcelles (for instance, her work for the Report on Corruption, "On Separation," presented to the French Prime Minister in 2004: http://www.justice.gouv.fr-publicat-scpc2004.pdf.url). Otherwise, an international colloquium is to be held in Paris, in May 2006, on "Rhetoric and Its Others."

5. Beside his publications in French journals, his sustained interest in Chaïm Perelman.

6. Significantly the first seminar report published in the *Cahier* (*Collège*'s annals), in 1985, was by Miguel Abensour, "Philosophie politique et socialisme," *Le Cahier du Collège international de philosophie* 1:8–24. Quote: 21.

7. Rhetoric was the crowning part of secondary education from 1809 to 1902. Until 1904 (for *Concours général,* a national competition between the best final-year secondary pupils), yet only until 1890 for the literary part of *baccalauréat* (examinations at the end of secondary education, giving access to university education), the final examination in French consisted in three exercises, straight from rhetoric: a narrative, an epistle, a speech. In 1890, the speech component was replaced by an essay (dissertation), a new form invented for the purpose of the philosophy examination in 1864, and fixed in 1866 by Charles Bénard (*Petit traité de la dissertation philosophique*). In 1902 the replacement of rhetoric by philosophy is complete, and the dissertation form spread across the humanities, the main if not sole standard for rational argument. On all this, see Douay-Soublin (1999), Compagnon (1999), Salazar (2003).

8. The Bar was only reconstituted in 1810. The French revolutionary system is—I believe, without being at liberty to present my arguments here—the rhetorical model for Stalinian trials.

9. The history of its abrogation is complex. I recommend reading Douay-Soublin (1999) and Compagnon (1999); in addition, documents provided in my *Art de parler* (2003).

10. Violence, from racket to rape, between pupils and against teachers has reached, in France, staggering heights—schools are places for enacting social violence, otherwise controlled and corralled in definite areas (statistics on the Ministry of Interior website). Laws prohibiting private ownership of weapons have merely prevented violence to spawn many a Columbine massacre at French schools.

11. Note that Communication is absent from this debate. French intellectuals generally hold "la com" in the lowest regard. However, ironically, Dominique Wolton, a popular sociologist of the mass medias, in a recent "apology for communication" attempts to restore the civil validity of mass communication in general, and to dispel the belief it is intellectually vacuous and politically un-prudential, by celebrating its persuasive and argumentative value for a responsible citizenry—of course, he stops short of making reference to rhetoric. As a dual defender of communication and rhetoric he would deal himself a double coup de grâce (Wolton 2005).

12. A footnote is not the place to sketch out such a description. Nonetheless, here are a few pointers, in chronological order: Marcel Detienne and Jean-Pierre Vernant, *Les Ruses de l'intelligence* (1974)/*Cunning Intelligence in Greek Culture and Society* (1978); Nicole Loraux, *L'Invention d'Athènes (Histoire de l'oraison funèbre dans la cité classique)* (1981)/*The Invention of Athens* (1986) ; Jacqueline de Romilly, *Les grands Sophistes dans l'Athènes de Périclès* (1988)/*The Great Sophists in Periclean Athens* (1992); and Barbara Cassin, *L'effet sophistique* (1995). See also Cassin's brilliant analysis of Perelman's reworking of the Sophistic question (Cassin 1995, 428–35). As a reviewer of Loraux's posthumous work *La Tragédie d'Athènes* points out, Loraux's argued belief in *stasis* as central to Athens cannot be detached, today, from a reflection on the "power" of masses and elites'recoiling at *demokratia* (Mossé 2005). By contrast, the belletristic revival of rhetoric, in the wake of Marc Fumaroli's work on French Classicism, is by and large marked to the Right.

13. I translate élève as "pupil," not "student," because it reflects the French notion that secondary education is just that, a preparation to tertiary education, in a free access system. Hence, no need to glorify secondary learners with a premature title all, by right, can have, in due course.

14. Underlining, here and below, indicates emphasis in the original text.

15. This aside sheds light on an ungenerous situation. In recent years there has been a growing cottage industry of primers in argumentation, mainly directed at elite students (distant inheritors of the "rhetoric" class and direct beneficiaries of secondary-level teaching of philosophy). The most recent one, by Plantin (2005), opens with a statement about Perelman's re-foundation of rhetoric/

argumentation, yet it avoids referring altogether, even in its otherwise up-to-date bibliography, to the work of Michel Meyer, whose own, latest, guide is largely self-referential (2005).

16. The Program lists seven working groups on set themes (argumentative structure of texts, with a presentation of Toulmin's work; reasoning and enunciation; reasoning outside philosophy; "patient" reasoning and oral debate; argumentation and the standard dissertation essay; rewriting of philosophical texts; fallacies and deficient reasoning). Further plenary presentations were made by Frédéric Cossuta (for an insight, see Cossuta 2003) and philosophers from Spain, Portugal, and Italy—bearing witness to a largely southern European shared concern.

17. Cassin has produced an unrivalled commentary and translation of Parmenides (1998).

18. The *Vocabulaire* offers word indexes in several languages; entries are either brief, in point form, or extensive with, sometimes, inserts. An elaborate system of references allows navigating across entries.

19. Francis Goyet.

20. Ann Moss. Goyet and Moss cross-reference one another.

21. Trent and Friedenberg caution against the expression "stock speech" in political communication as it seems to imply that campaign speeches are "set" (2000, 182). Aware of the commonplace tradition, they underscore and, in fact, explain how commonplaces, "modules," enter the assembly line of speechwriting (182–98).

22. By Barbara Cassin.

23. I leave aside the Platonician melting away of rhetoric into philosophy, whereby rhetoric is no longer an art of persuasion but a psychagogical dialectic (*Phaedrus* 266b and 261b).

24. By Clara Auvray-Assayas, Barbara Cassin, Frédérique Ildefonse, Jean Lallot, Sandra Laugier, and Sophie Roesch.

25. French philosophy has a strong sense of philology or the history of concepts—think of Derrida's art of reading into and from etymologies—in part a legacy of its illustrious Heideggerian tradition and in part a long familiarity with historical linguistics, in this case Emile Benveniste's (see Benveniste 1969, tr. 1973).

26. In this order: (1) A review of Greek etymology; (2) A review of how *logos* is handled in dictionaries—Bailly and Liddell-Scott-Jones; (3) Plato's treatment of *logos* in *Theaetetus* 206d–208c, and problems of translation in French, German, Italian posed by 201e–202c; (4) Definitions collated in the Byzantine *Scholia in Dionysii Thracis artem grammaticam*; (5) A short note on the ambiguity of Hebrew *dâvâr,* "speech" and "fact, thing"—as in Faustian *Tat*; (6) Three translations of Heraclitus's Fragment 50; (7) The three meanings of German *Wort*, with a recall of Heidegger's citation of Hamann, *Vernunft ist Sprache, λόγος."*

27. It could be useful here to look at Benveniste's take on *rectus,* and to draw a parallel between the rectitude of dialectical reasoning and that of the moral and political "direction" (Benveniste 1969, 2:14).

28. The authors are Barbara Cassin, Sandra Laugier, and Irène Rosier-Catach (author of *La Parole comme acte,* 1994).

29. Insert # 1 is about Gorgias' *Praise of Helen* and "From orthodoxy to creation of values."

30. One reference is to Heidegger's *Sein und Zeit,* 7.

31. Insert # 2.

32. This quote, Greek excepted, is taken from Kennedy's translation (1991).

33. Kennedy's translation of *Rhetoric* 1356a4 says that persuasion happens "through arguments when we show the truth or the apparent truth" (Kennedy 1991, 39). In the *Vocabulaire*: "by the fact that it [*logos*] shows or seems to show." Notably, Garver's reading, and promotion of *ethos,* is antithetical to the *Vocabulaire*'s argument (Garver 2004).

34. I quote from the Hardie-Gaye translation.

35. By Françoise Dastur.

36. My gratitude goes to Michael Leff, who, by way of an invitation to deliver a keynote paper at the 2004 Institute of the Rhetoric Society of America (Kent, Ohio), gave me the opportunity to develop some of the thoughts sketched in this essay—and to Gerard Hauser for the opportunity to have them in print.

Works Cited

Abensour, Miguel. 1985. "Philosophie politique et socialisme." *Le Cahier du Collège international de philosophie* [Paris: Editions Osiris] 1:8–24.

ACIREPH. 2004. Manifesto for the Teaching of Philosophy and Program of the 6th Colloquium, "Apprendre à raisonner." October 23–24, Lycée Paul Valéry, Paris. <www.acireph.net>.

Aristotle. 1991. *On Rhetoric: A Theory of Civic Discourse.* Translated with an introduction by George A. Kennedy. New York: Oxford UP.

Beer, Francis A., and Robert Hariman, eds. 1996. *Post-Realism: The Rhetorical Turn in International Relations.* East Lansing: Michigan State UP.

Benveniste, Émile. 1969. *Le Vocabulaire des institutions indo-européennes*, 2 vols. Paris: Minuit, 1973. Indo-European Language and Society. Coral Gables/London: U of Miami P/ Faber and Faber.

Cassin, Barbara. 1995. *L'effet sophistique*. Paris: Gallimard.

———. ed. 2004. *Vocabulaire européen des Philosophies.* Paris: Le Robert/Le Seuil.

Compagnon, Antoine. "La rhétorique en France à la fin du XIXe siècle (1875–1900)." In *Histoire de la rhétorique dans l'Europe moderne. 1450–1950,* ed. Marc Fumaroli et al., 1215–50. Paris: PUF.

Cossuta, Frédéric. 2003. "Dialogic Characteristics of Philosophical Discourse." *Philosophy & Rhetoric* 36:48–76.

De Romilly, Jacqueline. 1988. *Les grands Sophistes dans l'Athènes de Périclès*. Paris: De Fallois, 1992. *The Great Sophists in Periclean Athens*. Translated by Janet Lloyd. Oxford: Clarendon.

Detienne, Marcel, and Jean-Pierre Vernant. 1974. *Les Ruses de l'intelligence. La mêtis des Grecs.* Paris: Flammarion, 1991. *Cunning Intelligence in Greek Culture and Society.* Translated by Janet Lloyd. Chicago: U of Chicago P.

Douay-Soublin, Françoise. 1999. " La rhétorique en France au XIXe siècle à travers ses pratiques et ses institutions." In *Histoire de la rhétorique dans l'Europe moderne, 1450–1950,* 1071–214. Paris: PUF.

Dubet, François. 2000. "La fin de l'école sanctuaire." Libération, February 16. <www.libération.com/quotidiens/debats>.

Foucault, Michel. 1986. *The Care of the Self.* New York: Random House.

Frege, Gottlob. 1980 (1892). "On Sense and Meaning." In *Translations from the Philosophical Writings,* ed. P. T. Geach and Max Black. Oxford: Oxford UP.

Garver, Eugene. 2004. *For the Sake of Argument: Practical Reasoning, Character and the Ethics of Belief.* Chicago: U of Chicago P.

Hauser, Gerard A. 2001. "Henry Johnstone, Jr.: 'Reviving the Dialogue of Philosophy and Rhetoric.'" *Review of Communication* 1:1–25 [electronic version].

Javnost—The Public. 2005. "The Rhetorical Shape of International Conflicts." 12(4).

Johnstone, Henry W., Jr. 1973. "Rationality and Rhetoric in Philosophy." *Quarterly Journal of Speech* 59:381–89.

Kennedy, George A. 1991. "Introduction." In *Aristotle. On Rhetoric: A Theory of Civic Discourse,* translated with an introduction by George A. Kennedy. New York: Oxford UP.

Loraux, Nicole. 1981. *L'Invention d'Athènes* (Histoire de l'oraison funèbre dans la "cité classique"). Paris: Mouton/1986. *The Invention of Athens*. Cambridge, MA: Harvard UP.

———. 2005. *La Tragédie d'Athènes*. Paris: Le Seuil.

Mao Tse-Tung. No date. *Quotations from Chairman Mao-Tse-Tung*. Peking: Foreign Language Press.

Merlin, Hélène.2000. "Le temps d'apprendre." *Libération,* March 20. <www.libération.com/quotidiens/debats>.

Meyer, Michel. 2005. *Qu'est-ce que l'argumentation?* Paris: Vrin.

Mossé, Claude. 2005. Review of Loraux's *La Tragédie d'Athènes. Le Monde,* September 9.

Parménide. 1998. *Sur la nature ou sur l'étant*. Translated and Greek-French ed. by Barbara. Cassin. Paris: Le Seuil.

Plantin, Christian. 2005. *L'argumentation.* Paris: PUF-Que Sais-je?

Rosier[-Catach], Irène. 1994. *La Parole comme acte*. Paris: Vrin.

Salazar, Philippe-Joseph. 2003. *L'Art de parler: Anthologie de manuels d'éloquence*. Paris: Klincksieck.

———. 2004. "Censorship: A Philological (and Rhetorical) Viewpoint." *Javnost—The Public* 11(2): 5–18.

Sloane, Thomas O., ed. 2001. *Encyclopedia of Rhetoric*. New York: Oxford UP.

Trent, Judith S., and Friedenberg, Robert V. 2000. *Political Campaign Communication*. Westport, CT: Praeger.

Wolton, Dominique. 2005. *Il faut sauver la communication*. Paris: Flammarion.

On Rhetoric as Gift/Giving

Marilee Mifsud

In this essay, I explore the possibilities of rhetoric as gift. I begin with the Homeric gift economy and the rhetorical resources of this economy.[1] My use of "economy" here is not reducible to a monetary exchange system, but rather a more general system of practices orchestrating cultural identity and relations. As Georges Bataille suggests, studying a general economy may hold the key to all the problems posed by every discipline (1991, 10). For Bataille everything from geophysics to political economy, by way of sociology, history, and biology, to psychology, philosophy, art, literature, and poetry has an essential connection with economy. So, too, rhetoric. Henry Johnstone once defined rhetoric as the art of getting attention (1990, 334). We cannot attend to everything at once, so something must call our attention, invite our focus, and this something is rhetoric. Rhetoric's desire to dispose its audience to invest in the object of attention connects rhetoric to economy. Rhetoric can be said to enact a disposition to invest, or a *cathexis,* a certain kind of savings. As such it is subject to economic movements and displacements, a dimension seen as well through Lyotard's figure of the *dispositif* (1993, x).

My use of "gift" here draws broadly from work in anthropology and philosophy on "the gift" starting with Marcel Mauss's groundbreaking anthropological work on archaic gift cultures. Mauss argues that as far back as we can go in the history of human civilizations, the major transfer of goods has been by cycles of gift-exchange. Each gift is part of a system of reciprocity in which the honor of the giver and recipient are engaged. That every gift must be met with a return gift, even if delayed, sets up a perpetual cycle of exchanges within and between cultures. In some cycles the return is equal to the gift, producing stable systems. However, in some cycles the return exceeds the gift. Such excess creates a competitive generosity, an escalating contest for honor. Mauss's work shows there are no free gifts: a gift economy creates for members permanent commitments that articulate the dominant institutions of law, politics, culture, and interpersonal relations. The theory of the gift is a theory of human solidarity.

From Mauss, the gift has taken off as a subject not only of sociological and anthropological interest, but of philosophical. Alan Schrift makes the case that the theme of the gift is located at the center of current discussions of post-modernity, discussions ranging from deconstruction, to gender, to ethics. The gift is, as Schrift argues, "one of the primary focal points at which contemporary disciplinary and interdisciplinary discourses intersect" (1997, 3). As a sampling, and an insight into theories of the gift underwriting this essay, consider the encounters Bataille, Derrida, and Cixous have with the gift. Bataille encounters the distinction between restrictive and general economies, and theorizes general economy through an economic logic based on the unproductive expenditure of excess associated with gift cultures. Derrida encounters the impossibility of the gift, that is, once a gift is recognized as gift, it is no longer a gift but an obligation demanding reciprocity. Hélène Cixous encounters the difference between masculine and feminine economies in terms of the latter creating relations with others through gift-giving where the gift does not calculate its influence.

My exploration of the archaic Homeric gift economy takes me eventually to explore what such postmodern theories of the gift offer rhetoric, but not before moving through the classical Athenian polis economy. In the Western tradition, the polis is a familiar economy. For the most part, this familiarity arises because of the marketplace and state structure of the polis, so familiar still in modern capitalism. However, in particular regard to the study of rhetoric, this familiarity arises from the historical claim that the polis invented rhetoric as an idea and practice of serving its needs (e.g., arguing in the public assembly about the administration of the state, in the courtrooms to administer justice, and in the agora to proclaim and persuade the values of the culture). The polis has become so familiar as the economy of the Western tradition, and the situation of exchange in which rhetoric takes place, that it has become normalized. This normalization makes the polis economy visible only as *the economy,* rather than as a particular form of economy. This normalization masks a more archaic past where gifts not markets, and people not entities, regulate cultural economy, including rhetoric.

When the Homeric gift economy is taken as the starting point for theorizing rhetoric, the Athenian polis and its rhetoric seem alien and strange, not at all "normal." Just as the Homeric Greeks are aliens to the Athenian Greeks and vice versa, so too the gift economy is alien to the polis economy and vice versa. The two economies are not only alien, but incommensurable. Drawing from Paul Feyerabend, I posit incommensurability as a means by which to articulate cultural alterity. This creates an orientation of distinction between these economies, where the alien is both between and within each economy. Such an orientation works to resist trading a relation of difference for a regime of domination.[2] Moreover, such an orientation allows the relation of difference to be generative of directions beyond these incommensurable economies.

My approach in this essay is not so much, if at all, about history, and getting it right, or rescuing its lost virtues. My approach is, in Deleuzian terms, a becoming, that belongs to geography, not history. Becomings are "orientations, directions, entries and exits" (1987, 2). Deleuze writes of a woman-becoming that is not the same as women, their past, and their future, but that is essential for women to enter to get out of their past and their future, their history (2). Likewise, there is a philosophy-becoming that has nothing to do with the history of philosophy and that happens through those whom the history of philosophy does not manage to classify (2). And, I add, there is, too, a rhetoric-becoming that has nothing to do with the history of rhetoric, and that happens through those whom the history of rhetoric does not manage to classify. Such is Homer to me in rhetoric. Yet, as we shall see, Homer is not a savior. Rather, exploring Homeric gift economy and rhetoric offers an experience of alterity. What Cixous calls a *sortie* and Deleuze a *becoming* opens in the rub between the archaic gift and the classical polis. This opening allows for rhetoric becoming, not so much *gift,* but *giving.*

Homeric Gift Economy

The Homeric gift economy is situated in the home: the *oikos*.[3] The same could be said of all economy, for *oikos* is the root of "economy." In the Homeric gift economy, we see how the home serves as the space of cultural orchestration. The aorist passive, middle sense of the verb *oikew* (to live) means, of a people, to settle, organize or dispose themselves. This disposition gives rise to the Homeric economy, the systems of exchange, both material and symbolic, by which a people dispose themselves.

The dynamism between the home and the disposition of a people shows the significance of hospitality in Homeric economy. Archaic hospitality, the virtue of being a host to a guest in the home, or vice versa, generates the obligation of friendship and solidarity, as well as the acquisition and amplification of honor within and between peoples. Hospitality involves the *xenos,* meaning both guest and host. That the term *xenos* is one of Zeus's epithets marks the particularly sacred association of guest-host relations, and signals the significance of hospitality rituals.

Homeric depictions of hospitality rituals are lavish. In the *Odyssey,* Odysseus's arrival at the palace of Alkinoös, King of the Phaiakians, presents such an occasion for Homer to tell the details of greeting a guest, welcoming him as a stranger with guest gifts, offering to him a feast, and the occasion for story telling, as well as preparing a splendid departure for the guest, with more guest gifts, another feast, and still more occasions for the exchange of speeches. Whereas action generally passes quickly in Homer, the story of Alkinoös' hospitality and guest-friendship offered to Odysseus spreads from Book 8–13, a remarkable dedication to the details and dynamics of gift-exchange.

Details of the luxurious items exchanged during hospitality rituals abound as well: silver, gold, tunics, fine fabrics, wines, cauldrons, baskets, mixing bowls, tripods, decorated armor, and swords. Homer tells of the gifts given to Helen and Menelaus from the King and Queen of Egypt: the silver work-basket with wheels underneath, edged in gold, to hold yarn for spinning, a golden distaff with dark-colored wool, two silver bathtubs, a pair of tripods, and ten talents of gold (*Od.* 4.125–35). We are told as well of the gifts of the Phaiakians to Odysseus: the surpassingly beautiful tripods and caldrons, the intricately wrought gold, and all the fine woven clothing (13.217–18) that the Phaiakian men of counsel gave to Odysseus, man by man, to create a most generous collection of treasure (13.7–15). Menelaus gives to Telemachus, not utilitarian gifts, but the single most precious gift in his storehouse of treasure, a silver fashioned mixing bowl, edged in gold, made by the god Hephaestus (4.615–17).

The luxury of the gifts and the liberality of hospitality rituals portray in the orchestration of relations in and between peoples a competitive generosity. Competitive generosity directs the Homeric gift economy. Menelaus must bestow precious treasure on Telemachus not only to establish his honor, but to communicate to Telemachus the deep bond, the solidarity, he feels for Odysseus (4.612–19). The elaborate hospitality of the Phaiakians not only ensures their honor in the moment with their guest, but that their honor transcends the moment into the future as Odysseus will tell great stories of them upon his return to his homeland. Generosity is the primary means by which characters acquire and sustain honor, as well as create a network of obligations to each other that can carry this honor into the future, and to many different peoples. This network of obligations creates solidarity both within and between cultures, and this solidarity engenders trust. One who expends his surplus so liberally by giving feasts and treasure is not only honorable, but trustworthy.

The Homeric gift economy is situated in the home, structured through norms of hospitality, the highest of these being generosity, and directed toward creating the obligations of friendship and solidarity, as wells as acquiring honor.

This does not mean, however, that the gift is always a friendly economy. Examples abound of the gift being a source of trickery and enmity, as is the case with the infamous Trojan horse, given in the guise of a luxurious hospitality gift to the Trojans. That such examples exist does not, however, undermine the structure of the gift economy through hospitality rituals. The Trojans were obligated to receive the lavish horse as a gift because of the norms of gift cultures. How else could they have been so duped?

Of note in this sketch of the Homeric gift economy are the inextricable relations between public and private, and between persons and things. First, no radical separation between the public and the private makes sense in the Homeric world. Even in what might be considered the public world of Homeric men (assembling in the *Iliad* to orchestrate war, or in the *Odyssey* to orchestrate the return of a hero and the security of the hero's kingdom), private rituals of guest-host relating, friendship, and gift-giving structure the public assembly. Moreover, the site of the assembly is often the home, the palace of the King. This private space in which the public disposes itself connects the public to the intimate, as do the private rituals of hospitality.

The intimacy of the gift economy inextricably links the person and the private to the public. Moreover, this intimacy links the person to the thing, and vice versa, creating an animistic quality to the gift. The power of the gift is, in Maussian terms, a laying hold of both persons and things. In gift cultures, no absolute boundary between persons and things can be drawn. No radical separation exists between the two. Things are an extension of persons, and people identify with the things possessed and exchanged. Mauss describes worlds where the relation between persons and things is one between souls, because the thing itself possesses a soul (2000, 12). To make a gift of something to someone is to make a present of some part of oneself (12), hence the thing given is not inactive. The thing is intimately connected to the person, hence it is invested with life (13).

A gift economy is an intimate economy, where things have not yet become distant, abstract, objectified commodities, and acts of exchange between people have not yet become less about the people and more about the things. In the gift economy, things and people imitate each other, as do the private and public. Things represent and portray the people who give them, and vice versa. The private represents and portrays the public, and vice versa. Hence things and people, and the private and public, in a gift economy are mimetic: they represent or portray one another. Their mimesis allows for the gift "to be less an entity or object than a matrix of relations" (Naas 1995, 150). "Entities" or "objects" can be treated as independent analytic units. A kind of abstraction and distance figures their being. The gift as "a matrix of relations" resists treatment via analysis of isolated parts as independent of the whole, or of inanimate objects to be exchanged, or of public assembly divorced of private rituals of hospitality. Not only does the gift as thing represent or portray the person as giver, and vice versa, but it represents and portrays the past as present and the present as past, thus constituting the future out of both simultaneously. Gifts always bear the traces of others, and of the past. Gifts link generations to each other, representing or portraying not so much a present value as the figure of past and future relations. Hence, the significance of gifts lies not so much in their material worth as in their creation of cultural intimacy and cultural memory.

The consciousness required for such intimacy and memory is a consciousness of aggregation, not division. Aggregation guides relations in the gift economy. Archaic aggregation is a product of archaic paratactic consciousness and speech. Parataxis is a style of thought and speech that holds multiple related and divergent things in mind simultaneously, not "as one unified entity" but "as ones in the aggregate" (Feyerabend 1975, 179–180n.51).

We can see how parataxis stylizes ideas in and through aggregation in the following passage from the *Odyssey:*

> We came next to the Aiolian island, where Aiolos
> lived, Hippotas' son, beloved by the immortal
> gods, on a floating island, the whole enclosed by a rampart
> of bronze, not to be broken, and the sheer of the cliff runs upward
> to it; and twelve children were born to him in his palace,
> six of them daughters, and six sons in the pride of their youth, so
> he bestowed his daughters on his sons, to be their consorts.
> And evermore, beside their dear father and gracious mother,
> they feast, and good things beyond number are set before them;
> and all their days the house fragrant with food echoes
> in the courtyard, and their nights they sleep each one by his modest wife,
> under coverlets, and on bedsteads corded for bedding. (10.1–13)

In this passage, we encounter paratactic style: the presence of grammatically co-ordinate propositions fashioned through "and," and in place of "and," the comma. We can see as well the absence of logically subordinating connectors such as "then" and "because." The aggregate quality of parataxis parallels the absence of elaborate systems of subordinate clauses in the early Greek language. This absence of subordination in Homeric language as well as style displays a simultaneity operating in archaic rhetoric, where many and multiple ideas can be strung together, to proliferate meaning and connection. In the passage cited above, a rhetorical intimacy can be experienced where the detail of the corded bedsteads is as significant to the passage's offerings as the details of sleeping under coverlets, being given over to one's siblings in marriage, and feasting all one's days in the courtyard of one's family home. In the multiplicity in unity, minority ideas are equalized with majority, allowing for a liberality to meaning not offered by majority rule.

A paratactic consciousness allows for aggregation, and in turn allows, as archaic mimetic consciousness allows, cultural intimacy and memory. Multiple and divergent things can be seen as touching. The possibilities of connection proliferate. One thing cannot be thought without simultaneously thinking of some digressively incidental thought (Feyerabend 1975, 179–80n.51). An intimacy emerges in parataxis. In the process of simultaneously entertaining a digression with the thought that sparked it, we experience a connection and connectedness and both particular and general awareness of our situation. This intimacy forges a cultural memory of general relations, a memory that is ever-present yet always becoming.

Cultural intimacy and memory work within a general economy. In Batail-lean terms, with an orientation toward a general economy, exchange cannot be studied in isolation as an independent act, or as collection of independent acts all coordinated to perform a specific end. Bataille writes that when it is necessary to change a car tire, it is easy to manage a quite limited operation. It is possible to act as if the elements on which the action is brought to bear are completely isolated from the rest of the world. One can complete the operation without once needing to consider the whole, of which the tire is an integral part (1991, 19). Bataille considers the whole, general economy at play—not just the particular operations of the changing of a tire but the more general economy that expands even to the production of cars. The changes brought about do not perceptibly alter the other things, nor does the ceaseless action from without have an appreciable effect on the conduct of the operation. However, something changes when the question becomes that of economic activity in general. A certain kind of intimacy and memory are at work in general economy—an intimacy where elements on which action is brought to bear are not completely isolated from the rest of the world, but are brought into contact with it—and a memory is forged of general relations, not merely of operations, at play in any cultural activity. The gift is not a series of technical operations, nor an exchange of entities and objects as inanimate things. Nor is the gift a private ritual separate from the public. The gift is an economy of intimacy and memory, where exchange wrought from hospitality structures cultural identity and relations.

Polis Economy

The polis transfigures exchange to meet the needs of the nation-state, an idea wholly alien to the Homeric Greeks. A striking portrayal of the transfiguration of exchange in the polis economy can be found on the Temple of Hephaestus, looming directly above the bouleterion, on the crowning hill of the agora.[4] Decorating the face of the temple is a configuration of the labors of Heracles. This configuration is quite different from the mythic tales of the labors. On the temple, the labors are organized differently, some are excluded, one is included twice, and one offers a different portrayal altogether of a labor from the mythic portrayal. This different portrayal is of Heracles giving the golden apples of the Hesperides to Athene. Moved to the climactic metope on the frieze of the temple's face (in the myth this is Heracles's eleventh labor; in the temple frieze it is his twelfth and final labor), this portrayal signals the transfiguration of exchange from the gift economy to the polis economy. In this climactic metope, we see Heracles wearing the impenetrable pelt of the Nemean Lion, whom he killed for its magical protective skin. He has other objects around him, perhaps the other commodities he secured in various labors. He has in his hands the golden apples of the Hesperides, which he cunningly stole from Atlas. He is giving these apples to Athene, who in turn gives him an olive branch.

That Heracles's gift of the apples is not an extension of himself, but rather a yield from his labor, is significant. The apples are actually things intimately connected not to Heracles but to the Hesperides. That Heracles was not given them as a gift, that rather he secured them through trickery as a commodity that would fashion a favorable future for Athens (not the Hesperides), is significant. That the impenetrable skin that Heracles flays and uses for his own protection is intimately of the Nemean Lion not of Heracles, yet the Nemean Lion is not the giver of its own skin, is significant. The significance of all this lies in the distance between the gift and the giver, the abstraction of the thing from the person, which in turn creates a commodity out of the apples, and of the Lion's skin, and a trader (traitor?) out of Heracles for putting these commodities in circulation for the benefit of the Athenian polis, a benefit wrought from the robbing and murder of the proper givers.

That the metope tells a different story than the myth, too, is significant. In the myth, Heracles tries to give the apples first to Eurystheus, who hands them back to him; then to Athene, who returns them to the Hesperides, the nymphs who tended and protected Hera's orchard, making them the proper givers. Some tellings of the myth hold that Athena was angry with Heracles's offer as it was an affront to gift exchange. In the metope, we see none of this. Gift exchange is transfigured from the myth to the metope. In the metope, the apples are not a gift, but a commodity, exchanged for the good of the state. Moreover, Athena's participation in this exchange, as depicted in the metope, sanctions the exchange. In the myth, Athena's rejection of the apples as a gift marks the wrongfulness of the exchange of "gifts" figured as such. In the metope, this kind of exchange is not only depicted as right, but as requisite for Athenian peace and prosperity.

The practice of exchange as depicted in this final metope of the labors of Heracles on the Temple of Hephaestus spirits exchange in the agora and bouleterian in particular kinds of ways, in and through relational distance, abstraction, commodification, technical operation/procedure, and utility. This spirit of exchange expresses itself in actual practices of the polis, such as ostracization, liturgy, and antidosis. These practices of the polis present figures of exchange in a polis economy.

First let's consider the practice of ostracization. When the last tyrant, Peisistratus, was driven from Athens, Athenian citizens were left to create a system of rule appropriate to freedom, not only in political situations but economic too. The tyrant, after all, was likely as hated for his accumulation of wealth and resources as his despotism, not that these two are necessarily separate phenomena. We see evidence of the suspicion of over-accumulation of resources in the ancient practice of ostracization. This practice came into favor in the early years of the polis and continued through the fall of Athens. Whenever a citizen began to amass too much—too much wealth, too much loyalty, too much social status—anyone perceiving this excess as a threat to the polis could call for a vote of ostraka. The council would gather. Speeches would be made about the threat of the man who had accumulated such great wealth and resources, and on pottery shards, or ostraka, councilmen would scratch the name of the person feared to have accumulated too much. If five hundred ostraka were cast, the citizen in excess would be ostracized for a period of seven years. Seven years was thought to be sufficient for the destruction and redistribution of one's excess so upon re-entry to the polis the once overly accumulated citizen would be appropriately reduced to the norm, or even below. Over-accumulation happens because the over-accumulator never gives anything away; he has no competitive generosity. Rather, he hoards, in a spirit of generous competitiveness. Ostracization worked as a state mechanism to force the exchange process when members of the polis economy felt no obligation to keep wealth in circulation.

Another such practice illuminating the transfiguration of exchange in the polis economy is the practice of antidosis. Literally "a giving in exchange," antidosis was a practice of the newly developing Athenian democracy. The practice came about when a man wished to avoid his duty of performing a liturgy.

Liturgies were related either to the army or to the state. The trierarchy (ship keeping) was an "extraordinary liturgy" directly related to wartime. "Ordinary liturgies" comprised such acts as theatre sponsorship, running the gymnasia, providing civic meals, and horse-breeding. A liturgy is a practice of taxation that transfigures the gift through the mechanism of a state apparatus. The liturgy, in theory, was to inspire pride in the Athenian taxpayer, for it placed his estate at the service of his city. The practice called for the wealthiest Athenian men to come forward to carry out various services for the good of their polis in the best possible fashion. They were to get out of it notability and self-respect. Yet, the liturgy, because of expense and responsibility, could be received as a compulsory act that some might want to avoid performing. A man who was nominated to perform a liturgy could avoid this duty if he could name another citizen who was richer and better qualified to perform the task, in effect, shifting the burden of hospitality to another. If the man challenged agreed that he was richer, he had to take over the liturgy; if he claimed to be poorer, then the challenger could insist on an exchange of all their property to test the claim in which case the challenger would himself perform the liturgy as the new owner of the supposed greater estate. This process of exchange was called *antidosis*.

The advantage of antidosis and ostracization as formal systems from the viewpoint of the democracy was that they encouraged the rich to be suspicious of each other, instead of being hostile toward the state. In both the practice of ostracization and antidosis, we can see how suspicion structures citizen relations. This is not to say that members of the gift economy did not also get suspicious of each other. They certainly did. We know well, for example, that the *Iliad* is as much a story of Achilles' suspicion of Agamemnon as it is a story of the Trojan War. Yet, the gift economy did not have a state mechanism constructing operations that formalize suspicion as an orientation toward others. The distinctness of the gift economy, as it structures relations through rituals of hospitality, is not that of technical operations formalizing suspicion. The state cultivation of suspicion works as a safeguard against tyranny, but it works against cultural intimacy and memory.

The polis economy transfigures exchange to meet the needs of the nation-state. The transfiguration works through positioning people and things differently. Relative to the gift culture, things and people in a polis culture are related through distant, abstract mechanisms of power, rather than personal relations, and through technical proceduralism and utility, more so than through relational obligations, luxury, and honor.

In terms of cultural memory, exchange in a polis economy spirits the future, using the present and the past as means to a desired end. The confluence of past and present brought forward in memory creates points of closure from which the future can be built. These points of closure prevent memory of peoples and cultures as givers prior to the point at which the gift is transfigured into the commodity. Polis exchange operates in and through distance and commodification. Things are distant—by this I mean non-intimate—from people, and people distant from things. Things become means or tools to be used by people—a use governed by techne. Technics overwhelms mimetics. And in the technic culture, intimacy and memory suffer. How intimate is a techne? In what way memorable? In technics, intimacy is transfigured into fetishism—as when Heracles wraps himself in the skin of the Nemean lion, and memory becomes particular and operational rather than general and relational. Rather than remembering relational experiences in their general economy, brought forward to shape present and future relations, we now remember the particular reward for particular labors well executed. We remember the particular operations of our labors that secure a desired outcome, and our cultural memory develops from this restricted economy. We don't remember the Nemean Lion as he wore his own skin, and as he came into relation with Heracles. We only remember Heracles in the operation of his kill, and the yield of his labor, which secured a desired future—impenetrability in the quest to civilize Athens by ridding her of beasts, monsters, and the uncivilized Other.

Not only is the mimetic power in a gift economy transfigured by a polis economy, but so too its paratactic power, and again cultural intimacy and memory suffers. The polis economy figures exchange through a hypotactic consciousness, not paratactic.[5] Hypotaxis figures relations in and through logical subordination. This logic of subordination is essential to making judgments in the public sphere on matters of politics, law, and culture, and it exists as well in archaic culture. The difference is that classical hypotaxis overwhelms exchange with its demand for subordination. Hypotaxis as the sanctioned style of speech constrains a general consciousness where subordination can be one of the many in an aggregate, and cultivates a restricted consciousness where subordination figures thinking and relating.

Rhetoric-Becoming

The rub between the gift and the polis economies can be generative of rhetoric's possibilities. The possibilities, in the positive, of the rhetoric of the polis are well known, since so much of the history and theory of rhetoric is situated and understood only in the context of the polis economy. Yet the polis economy and its rhetoric can be encountered otherwise when juxtaposed with the gift economy and its rhetoric. When rhetoric is put in the situation of the polis economy, in light of the gift, we can suppose a rhetoric operating in an ethic of abstraction, approaching its situation with a fundamental distance between self and other. In this distance, the other's assent becomes regarded as a commodity to secure, and rhetorical techne the tools for the task. We can suppose technical attention to operations in the successful design of persuasion transfiguring persons into things or objects, and in so doing undermining cultural intimacy and cultural memory, turning the former into fetishism and the later into proceduralism.

We can suppose, too, rhetoric's utility in structuring citizen relations through suspicion. Note that ostracization and antidosis are rhetorical situations, the latter so much so that Isocrates' *Antidosis,* an imaginary antidosis fashioned to protect his wealth of rhetorical teachings from being given over to the suspicion of the polis, has become a mainstay of education in rhetoric.

Perhaps more than these suppositions, we can suppose a rhetoric wrought from the polis economy to be a rhetoric of generous competitiveness, and not competitive generosity. The agonistic impulse of rhetoric in the polis aspires to win, to conquer, and, in so doing, to establish one's honor. This kind of honor is wrought from a spirit of domination, not friendship. We can suppose, then, the worst case scenario of rhetoric's effects in a polis economy: Fetishism. Proceduralism. Suspicion. Domination.

Henry Johnstone did more than suppose such a rhetoric when he wrote about technology and ethics (1982). He showed such a rhetoric as a logical consequence of technological process. A process, e.g., rhetoric, is technological in the sense when it is a series of steps in which either a given step or the project as a whole determines the sequel to the given step; or else the question whether the successor is fitting to its predecessors does not arise. In such a process, the means are determined by the end. A technological procedure is distinct from a creative process. A creative process consists of a series of steps none of which is strictly determined by its predecessors but each of which, once taken, is seen to have been a fitting sequel to its predecessors. One salient feature of a creative process is that two or more people are cooperating, taking turns to make the step that is retrospectively seen to be appropriate. A technological process fixes in advance the relationships among the steps, and requires no cooperation between those involved in the process to accomplish its task.

Johnstone writes that creative communication occurs only among persons, and persons require creative communication. The only alternatives to creative communication are technological communication and no communication at all. And technological communication is in fact only an unstable phase of a transition that leads to no communication at all. If I am so exclusively occupying myself with the procedures for winning a rhetorical position that I end up simply manipulating my listener in order to win, clearly I am no longer communicating with my listener. My listener stops being a person to me, and becomes instead a commodity, a thing abstracted, better yet robbed, from the listener for the benefit to me. The commodified listener then becomes my fetish, rhetoric the procedure for feeding it, and brutalization the outcome. If I am surrounded by things and disconnected from persons, not only do I get no cooperation, but nothing calls for my own cooperation. There will be no occasion for me to exhibit my own humanity. Johnstone writes of the probability that under such circumstances a person could not survive as a person: "His environment would sooner or later brutalize him. From the role of sole technological manipulator of things around him, he would pass to the final phase of his degradation; he would become a thing himself, a thing interacting with other things in a minuet of meaningless transfers of energy" (48).

When rhetoric is put in touch with the legacies of the gift economy, we can imagine it not so much as a tool but a gift. We can suppose rhetoric as a gift to be creative, intimate, memorable, luxurious, and liberal. Creativity is the antinomy of technical procedure. Intimacy is the absence of commodification and fetishism. Memory is of general relations or persons, not particular operations on things. Luxury is surplus of meaning produced. And liberality is a feast-like expenditure of surplus. However, that the gift is well known to be both remedy and poison complicates too romantic a view of the gift.[6] Gift recipients in a gift economy can become burdened by the debt of compulsory reciprocity and obligatory exchange. Moreover, strict lines of exchange tend to be culturally coded in gift cultures, hence defining and reifying class stratifications. Not just anyone can give to or receive from just anyone. And that women are wares of exchange in gift culture offers plenty of caution about romanticizing the gift.

The archaic Homeric gift economy is not our savoir. However, exploring this archaic economy in contradistinction to the classical polis economy creates an experience of alterity. This experience becomes generative of new theoretical directions for rhetoric, so as to get out of the historical trappings of both the gift and polis economies. In recognizing the radical otherness that the polis is to the gift, and vice versa, we can resist trading a generative relation of difference for a deadly regime of domination. If we resist such a trade, we will be given two incommensurable economies in the study of rhetoric, neither of which should be the only economy, nor even should both be considered the only two. Instead, we can work with the generative relation of difference between (and within) the two to create something new.

Whereas the gift economy is incommensurable to the polis economy, they are both economies. This becomes a problem for the gift. We see in the gift economy a certain kind of savings. The savings of the gift comes in the form of cultural memory, and while this cultural memory saves obligations to create solidarity and honor into the future, it also creates permanent cycles of obligatory reciprocity. Derrida points out that the gift that is recognized as a gift ceases thereby to be a gift, but an economic exchange. The gift, as Derrida notes, is figured through antinomy, so that the conditions of its possibility are precisely its conditions of impossibility (1997, 128). The gift, once recognized, collapses into a system of exchange. The return to the giver nullifies the act of giving. As Cixous writes of the ever-presence of economy in history, even the gift brings in a return (1986, 87).

Mauss never denies the gift's return; rather, he attempts to calculate the circulation of the gift under a law of return somewhere between the economic and the aneconomic. The question becomes whether this return can be denied. Can the gift be aneconomic? Can we imagine giving, not figured through cycles of obligatory return, i.e., not savings, but squander; not return, but release?

Both Derrida and Cixous suggest that we can, and both bring this suggestion to bear upon writing, the privileged term for rhetoric in the vocabulary of these philosophers. Derrida writes of the demand in writing for excess, with respect to what the writer can understand of what she says. The demand is "that a sort of opening, play, indetermination be left, signifying hospitality for what is to come" (2001, 84). Yet "whoever gives hospitality ought to know that she is not even the proprietor of what she would appear to give" (84). There is no "I" that ethically makes room for the other in the act of giving, but rather an "I" structured by the alterity within it. Derrida writes, "The other is in me before me" (84). The hospitable "I" is itself in a state of self-deconstruction and of dislocation, and from this state writing acts as aneconomic gift of excess meaning.[7]

Cixous is not so much interested in aneconomic space, but in transfiguring economy from its masculine to its feminine body. She takes Mauss's construction of the return of the gift and Derrida's deconstruction of this return and inscribes it within the gendered unconscious. The masculine economy of giving is always associated with debt. The desire to save and to invest so as to receive a return on one's investment in the form of increased savings directs a masculine economy. Cixous suggests we call this economy "masculine" in part because it is erected from a fear that is typically masculine, namely of expropriation, of loss. In contrast, feminine economies transfigure return. They are not restricted economies where giving is a means of deferred exchange in order to obligate a counter-gift in return. Rather, giving becomes in a feminine economy an affirmation of generosity that cannot be understood in terms of exchange economies. Yet, women's giving does not escape the law of return:

> You never give something for nothing. But all the difference lies in the why and how of the gift, in the values that the gesture of giving affirms, cause to circulate, in the type of profit the giver draws from the gift and the use to which he or she puts it. (Cixous 1986, 87)

We can see this feminine economy as an alien within the Homeric gift economy. In Cixous's terms, the dominant norms of giving in Homeric gift economy are masculine. Givers give in expectation of a particular, calculated return, as when the Phaiakians give such liberal and luxurious departure gifts to Odysseus, among all the pomp and circumstance of a public hospitality ritual, in return for his spreading their honor to his home. This scene of gift-giving stands in stark contrast to the scene of Circe sending off Odysseus. Circe, with no pomp and circumstance, stocks the ship with the departure gifts of a ram and black ewe, and she does so without being detected by Odysseus and his men: "for easily had she passed us by. Who with his eyes could behold a god against his will, whether going to or fro?" (*Od.* 573–74).[8]

This example of Circe's giving shows that the masculine gender of the Homeric gift economy is not essential, but yet another accident of history. Something other is already within the gift. The other is a feminine giving able to resist the gift that calculates influence.

This escape from calculation of return makes possible Cixous' feminine writing. This writing puts the abstracted, autonomous self at risk, bringing the self into intimate contact with alterity, so intimate that the alterity is already within. The self recognizes its own radical alterity, and writes from this recognition. This writing is not about saving, or holding in reserve, but sending, not about return but release. We women, Cixous notes (without excluding men in her sexual qualifier "women"), do not find our pleasure in "employing the suitable rhetoric" (92):

> indeed, one pays a certain price for the use of a discourse. The logic of communication requires an economy both of signs—of signifiers—and of subjectivity. The orator is asked to unwind a thin thread, dry and taut. We [women] like uneasiness, questioning. There is waste in what we say. We need that waste. To write is always to make allowances for super-abundance and uselessness while slashing the exchange value that keeps the spoken word on its track. (92–93)

For Cixous, a feminine economy of the gift is a launching forth and effusion without return. Woman giving doesn't try to "recover expenses" (87). She does not have to return to herself: "she is not the being-of-the end (the goal), but she is how-far-being-reaches" (87). This giving makes possible a feminine writing that like woman's cosmic libido can only go on and on, in a paratactic flow, without ever inscribing or distinguishing contours:

> *Voice*! That, too, is launching forth and effusion without return. Exclamation, cry, breathlessness, yell, cough, vomit, music. Voice leaves. Voice loses. She leaves. She loses. And that is how she writes, as one throws a voice—forward into the void. She goes away, she goes forward, doesn't turn back to look at her tracks. Pays no attention to herself. Running break-neck. Contrary to the self-absorbed, masculine narcissism, making sure of its image, of being seen, of seeing itself, of assembling its glories, of pocketing itself again. (94)

Such a rhetoric that Derrida and Cixous theorize as writing through giving requires not investment and savings, but a spending of excess, waste, and surplus. If rhetoric is not a disposition to invest, then it is an expression of excess.

Henry Johnstone seemed as well aware of this dimension of rhetoric, as he was of rhetoric's *cathexis*. His work on pankoinon attends to the way in which rhetoric offers surplus meaning. In formal logic, a tautology is an instantiation of a logical truth such as the Law of Self-Identity ("X=X") (2000, 7). In rhetoric, a pankoinon is, as Johnstone writes, a paradox: "it consists in the assertion or assumption that although a tautology, and thus logically true, it can nevertheless, have implicatures—one or more of them—the truth or falsity of which does not depend on logic alone" (2000, 10).

Take, for example, the following definition of rhetoric: rhetoric is rhetoric. This pankoinon came from a conversation I had with Johnstone about the trouble with definition, and in particular how this trouble wrecks havoc on rhetorical scholars asked to define their subject. Johnstone asked why we could not be content to say, "Rhetoric is rhetoric." Read as a pankoinon, this definition is quite evocative. A pankoinon becomes a figure of speech, in part, when it is assumed that its implicatures need not take the form of an explicitly stateable proposition (8). What the pankoinon conveys may amount to no more than the sense that something is being adumbrated that is indefinable, elusive, and mysterious (8). In pankoinon, we have an open, playful, indeterminate speech, offering surplus meaning, a giving rhetoric, or a rhetoric giving.

Rhetoric as giving goes beyond meaning that is known or that can be understood, readily translated, commodified, and exchanged. Such a rhetoric holds in mind many meanings not for the sake of meaning, not for the sake of savings and return, but for the sake of liberal expenditure. A hospitable rhetor becomes, then, a producer of possibilities rather than a judge of meaning. In Deleuzian terms, a hospitable rhetor is like Bob Dylan organizing a song: "as astonishing producer rather than author" (8). To be "no longer an author" but a "production studio" takes a very lengthy preparation, says Deleuze, yet no method, nor rules, nor recipes apply (9). The enterprise is a wholly creative one. The creativity of production has an absolute speed, its does not slow down for reason's plan, nor is its line of flight predetermined as a technical process.

Rhetoric as giving enacts a rhetorical hospitality, a sumptuous expenditure of surplus meaning, whether produced by host or guest, speaker or listener. Such hospitality requires an aggregative consciousness of multiplicity. This consciousness harkens to Homeric culture, where a paratactic style and the absence of a "self" have led characters to be called schizophrenic for the many voices in their heads constituting multiple orientations to their experiences and the world around them. This schizophrenia allows for meaning to be decentralized, or, in Deleuzian terms, *deterritorialized.* It gives rise to an encounter, a becoming, and it operates, as we see in Homeric rhetoric and as Deleuze notes, in and through "and."

The power of rhetoric as giving is its power to generate surplus meaning, a power encountered only in its liberal expenditure. This expenditure, though, is beyond "exchangist" economic terms, beyond calculated return, beyond commodification and appropriation. A rhetoric as giving is a rhetoric becoming, betwixt and between the gift and the polis.

Department of Rhetoric and Communication Studies
University of Richmond

Notes

1. I am indebted to Henry Johnstone for introducing me to Homer. With Dr. Johnstone, I enjoyed a seven-year reading of the *Odyssey* in Greek. We began this work as friends, and it lead not only to my dissertation (*The Rhetoric of Deliberation in Homer,* Penn State University, 1997), which Johnstone directed, but to a body of continuing writing, from which the present essay is born.

2. The benefit of experiencing alterity "to resist trading a relation of difference for a regime of domination" was articulated by Michelle Ballif citing Lynn Worsham in "Rhetorical Gifting of the Other." Ballif presented this as a lecture in a course titled "The Gift: Theory, Culture, Language," which I taught in spring of 2004 with my colleague Gary Shapiro, Professor of Philosophy, University of Richmond. Diane Davis also presented a lecture to this course, which foreshadowed her recent publication, "Addressing Alterity: Rhetoric, Hermeneutics, and the Nonappropriate Relation" (*Philosophy and Rhetoric* 2005). Davis's distinction between the said and saying resonates with the distinction between the gift and giving that I will address in this essay.

3. For excellent commentary on Homeric gift culture, see Donlan (1982a, 1982b, 1989, 1993), Finley (1991), Grant (1988), Murray (1993), Naas (1995), Snodgrass (1990), and Tandy (1997).

4. For extended critique of the Temple of Hephaestus, and its significance to the polis economy and rhetoric, see Mifsud, Sutton, and Fox (2005). I am indebted to Jane Sutton for suggesting, in 1997, the significance of this temple. I am indebted to Lindsey Fox for her research on this temple culminating in her undergraduate honors thesis, "Illuminating a Space for Woman," Department of Rhetoric and Communication Studies, University of Richmond, 2004.

5. For Aristotle's comments on the hypotactic privilege of civic discourse, see *Art of Rhetoric* 1409a.29–1409b.4.

6. See Benveniste (1997) for extended linguistic critique of *gift*.

7. I am indebted to Ballif, "Rhetorical Gifting of the Other," for directing me to this passage in Derrida.

8. I am grateful to Henry Johnstone for pointing out during our reading the particularly feminine character of Circe's giving. Johnstone later gave to me an essay he wrote on this passage during his graduate work in classics at Bryn Mawr, "Potnia Kirkê" (1977).

Works Cited

Aristotle. 1991. *The "Art" of Rhetoric*. Trans. J. H. Freese. Loeb Classical Library. Cambridge, MA: Harvard UP.

Ballif, Michelle. "Rhetorical Gifting of the Other." Seminar Lecture in "The Gift: Theory, Culture, Language." MariLee Mifsud and Gary Shapiro, Instructors. Department of Rhetoric and Communication Studies and Department of Philosophy, University of Richmond. Spring 2004.

Bataille, Georges. 1991. *The Accursed Share*. Vol. 1. Trans. Robert Hurley. New York: Zone Books.

Benveniste, Emile. 1997. "Gift and Exchange in the Indo-European Vocabulary." In *The Logic of the Gift*, ed. Alan Schrift. New York: Routledge.

Cixous, Hélène. 1986. "Sorties: Out and Out: Attacks/Ways Out/Forays." In *The Newly Born Woman*, ed. Hélène Cixous and Catherine Clement, trans. Betsy Wing. Minneapolis: U of Minnesota P.

Davis, Diane. 2005. "Addressing Alterity: Rhetoric, Hermeneutics, and the Nonappropriate Relation." *Philosophy and Rhetoric* 38(3):191–212.

Deleuze, Gilles, and Claire Parnet. 1987. *Dialogues*. Trans. Hugh Tomlinson and Barbara Habberjam. New York: Columbia UP.

Derrida, Jacques. 1997. "The Time of the King." In *The Logic of the Gift*, ed. Alan Schrift. 121–47. New York: Routledge.

Derrida, Jacques, and Maurzio Ferraris. 2001. *A Taste for the Secret*. Ed. Giacomo Donis and David Webb, trans. Giacomo Donis. Oxford: Blackwell.

Donlan, Walter. 1982a. "The Politics of Generosity in Homer." *Helios* 9(2):1–15.

———. 1982b. "Reciprocities in Homer." *Classical World* 75(3):137–75.

———. 1989. "The Pre-State Community in Greece." *Symbolae Osloenses* 64:5–29.

———. 1993. "Dueling with Gifts in the *Iliad*." *Colby Quarterly* 29:155–72.

Feyerabend, Paul. 1975. *Against Method*. Atlantic Highlands: Humanities Press.

Finley, M. I. 1991. *The World of Odysseus*, 2nd ed. London: Penguin Books.

Grant, Michael. 1988. *The Rise of the Greeks*. New York: Charles Scribner's Sons.

Graves, Robert. 1977. *The Greek Myths*. Vol. 2. Middlesex: Pelican Books.

Homer. 1963. *Iliad*. Vol. 1–2. Loeb Classical Library. Cambridge, MA: Harvard UP.

Homer. 1965. *Odyssey*. Loeb Classical Library. Cambridge, MA: Harvard University Press.

Johnstone, Henry. 1977. "Potnia Kirkê." Seminar Paper, Department of Classics, Bryn Mawr.

———. 1980. "Pankoinon as a Rhetorical Figure in Greek Tragedy." *Glotta* 58(1-2):49–62.

———. 1982. "Communication: Technology and Ethics." In *Communication, Philosophy, and the Technological Age*, ed. Michael J. Hyde, 38–53. Tuscaloosa: U of Alabama P.

———. 1990. "Rhetoric as a Wedge: A Reformulation." *Rhetoric Society Quarterly* 20(4):333–38.

———. 2000. "Pankoinon as Paradox." *Rhetoric Review* 19(1–2):7–11.

Lyotard, Jean-Francois. 1963. *Libidinal Economy*. Trans. Ian Hamilton Grant. Bloomington: Indiana UP.

Mauss, Marcel. 2000. [1950]. *The Gift: The Form and Reason of Exchange in Archaic Societies.* Trans. W. D. Hall. New York: W. W. Norton.

Mifsud, MariLee, Jane Sutton, and Lindsey Fox. 2005. "Configurations: Encountering Ancient Athenian Spaces of Rhetoric, Democracy, and Woman." *Journal for International Women's Studies* 7(2):36–52.

Murray, Oswyn. 1993. *Early Greece*. Cambridge, MA: Harvard UP.

Naas, Michael. 1995. *Turning from Persuasion to Philosophy.* Atlantic Highlands: Humanities Press.

Schrift, Alan D. 1997. *The Logic of the Gift: Toward an Ethic of Generosity*. New York: Routledge.

Snodgrass, Anthony. 1990. *Archaic Greece: The Age of Experiment.* Berkeley and Los Angeles: U of California P.

Tandy, David W. 1997. *Warriors into Traders: The Power of the Market in Early Greece*. Berkeley and Los Angeles: U of California P.

Rhetorical Criticism and the Challenges of Bilateral Argument

Stephen H. Browne

To assume editorial responsibilities for *Philosophy & Rhetoric* after Henry W. Johnstone was to have assumed rather a lot. He was, for starters, a philospher, and I am not. This much appeared to bother Henry not a bit, and in fact it proved the occasion of many productive discussions and facilitated my apprenticeship in ways for which I am still grateful. By trade a rhetorical critic, I was particularly interested in what might be called philosophical style, and in what sense that style might differentiate itself from modes of expression that characterize my disciplinary conventions. Pressed on the subject, Henry observed that one such distinction turned on our respective ways of initiating an argument. Philosophers, he said, start their arguments in mid-sentence.

Now that is a curious thing to say, even by Henry's standards, and I have dwelt on it frequently in the years since his passing. At first I thought he must be referring to the various stratagems with which scholars inaugurate a line of thinking—the appeals to established literature, the staking of terrain within a crowded field of commentary, the documentary requirements that can burden the opening of a case nearly unto death. And indeed there is something to this, as any quick comparison will attest: let us recall first the manner in which most essays in the humanities begin, and turn then to Johnstone's own:

> In philosophy there is nothing in principle more authoritative than argument. (1959, 21)
> All valid philosophical arguments are addressed ad hominem. (1959, 121)
> It is only fair to say that while I am the editor of a quarterly journal, I am not an expert. (1971, 78)

On reflection, it is clear to me now that what is involved here is something more than style, or at least more than the ordinary sense of style. To begin an argument "in mid-sentence" is to forego the trappings of erudition familiar to most of us; it is, further, to acknowledge without saying so the capacity of one's interlocutor to understand what one is saying; there is presumption of a type at work. But above all it is to lay bare and grant immediate access to the structure of one's principles, claims, and arguments. Such an opening is strategic, to be sure, in that it represents a willed effort to establish a certain relationship as obtaining between disputants; it in effect extends an offer of contract, in which I agree to expose my reasoning at the outset under the expectation that you will do the same by way of response.

Johnstone's singular contribution was to establish a general theory of argumentation, of which philosophical argument was one subset. I wish here to suggest that another such subset is rhetorical criticism, and to explore how the practice of rhetorical criticism may benefit from this general theory of argument. What kinds of presumptions and obligations, like those noted in the above paragraph, might be said to apply to critics, seen now as practitioners of argument? The aim here is not to offer up an ethics of criticism, if by that we mean appealing to an independent set of norms as a way exposing the moral grounds of a given argument; it is rather to identify the obligations indigenous to rhetorical criticism conceived as a form of argument. The stakes here would seem to suggest more than an exercise if we are to take seriously Johnstone's oft-repeated insistence that argument is a medium for the disclosure of our selfhood and humanity. Taking that claim as a premise, it follows that as a subset of argument generally, rhetorical criticism is similarly one means through which we expose our structure of reasoning, acknowledge the agency of our interlocutors, and sustain our commitment to the ongoing practice of argument itself.

The following argument is exploratory, and claims neither a comprehensive nor a conclusive treatment of the subject. By way of focus, I invoke a composite version of Johnstone's "bilateral argument," identify practices in rhetorical criticism that in my judgment violate such argument, and suggest ways in which criticism might better meet its obligations as an argumentative practice. My characterizations, while highly general, are based on twenty years of editorial service in one capacity or another. My overall aim is to help us imagine how Johnstone's legacy might create a better version of ourselves as critics, as arguers, and as human beings.

Johnstone sought to formulate a theory of argument that was both constitutive and expressive of our shared humanity. To do this, he had to think through the possibility of conflict without coercion. The result is a substantial body of thought, a key component of which is his conception of bilateral argument. It proved a remarkably persistent feature of his thinking from the early 1960s until his death in 2000. Not surprisingly, his thinking on bilaterality changed and deepened through the years—notably as he extended its tenets from philosophical dispute to virtually of forms of communication—but for our purposes it is enough to sketch the rudiments of his theory. In the main, his point is captured in the maxim that "the arguer must use no device of argument he could not in principle permit his interlocutor to use" (1982, 95). Such a conception clearly stands in contradistinction to unilateral communication, characterized as that exercise of language which seeks its ends regardless of assent; communication, that is, that works coercively through disguised means, threat, authority, or other compulsions. It is important to note here that bilateral argument is thus not reducible to a sheer instrumental calculus; it possesses a disclosive function that is fundamental to the argumentative enterprise. If "there is an imperative to become or be human," Johnstone wrote, "and communication is an aspect of being human, then we communicate not merely to achieve the satisfaction of our needs but to participate in humanity" (96). Bilateral argument is that kind of communication through which the imperative is met.

Three correlates to this principle may be identified as necessary conditions for the fulfillment of genuinely bilateral argument. In principle and in practice, the interlocutor is obliged to (1) respect the capacity of the other to render free judgment of one's argument. "In bilateral communication," Johnstone explained, "each interlocutor speaks as if the others were capable of propagating a message fully as credible as his own. He treats his hearers with respect rather than as merely means to the end of their own credulity" (99). Here is the principle of free will.

The interlocutor additionally assumed the obligation to (2) risk failure. Precisely because we seek not to control but to induce, to secure assent to one's argument rather than command it, we must always accept the possibility that we will fail to do so: "To argue is inherently to risk failure, just as to play a game is inherently to risk defeat" (1965, 1). Unilateral communication, by contrast, may be defined as risk-less, at least to the extent that a given message is delivered in ways to best protect against the possibility of failing one's objectives. Again, the risk inherent in bilateral argument serves a humanizing function. For Johnstone, "the person willing to run the risks involved in listening to the arguments of others is open-minded and, to that extent, human. . . . It is an entirely new possibility. In making himself available to arguments, man transcends the horizons of his own perceptions, emotions, and instincts" (1965, 3). Here is the principle of risk.

Finally, the interlocutor is obliged to (3) assume responsibility for the outcome of the argument. Bilateral argument is thus marked by a mutual investment in the process and consequences of the activity itself, where such investment is understood to mean that one 's self is at risk of being transformed by the arguments of another. To relinquish this responsibility, Johnstone notes, "is to suggest that he has resigned from the control of his own action and belief—that he has transferred this control to the hands of the arguer, saying, in effect, 'You must decide for me'" (1965, 4). Here is the principle of mutuality.

These are, of course, very brief renditions of a complicated body of thought. They are nonetheless useful as a means of interrogating contemporary practices of rhetorical criticism and, more positively, to generate ways of thinking that can make such criticism more responsible, more bilateral, than has heretofore been the case. To that end, I organize the following observations with reference to the standards of free will, risk, and mutuality as they apply to the academic work known as rhetorical criticism.

The Principle of Free Will

What are some of the ways in which rhetorical critics fail to meet the standard of free will? To answer that question, let us recall Johnstone once again: "To argue with another is to regard him as beyond the scope of effective control, and hence precisely to *place* him beyond the scope of effective control. Provided he is a person capable of listening to an argument and knows how it is that we are regarding him" (1965, 1). The italics are in the original, and it provides a key to our answer. Wittingly or not, to argue is to locate oneself in relationship to another, and how we locate our interlocutor will be decisive—not necessarily to "winning" the argument but to ensuring its integrity *as* an argument. When we bring to bear premises, claims, or appeals that seek to control the ways in which an interlocutor might render judgment of our argument, then we have essentially located that person within a coercive relationship. We have sought, in effect, to ensure the defeat of any counterargument.

If we are to view rhetorical criticism as a subset of argument, then we have cause to ask whether critics place their readers (themselves critics) within a similar relationship. I would suggest that we do in several ways. Among the most persistent examples of such criticism is that which presupposes an unassailable norm and proceeds to argue as if that norm was in fact unassailable. The result is a type of criticism that in effect renders disagreement illegitimate because it violates a putatively consensual premise. To dissent from the argument, in short, is to deny the moral claim imposed at the level of frequently unstated assumptions. For better or worse, the politically charged environment of the last several decades has played an enabling role in this practice.

The current interest in the relationship between rhetoric and democratic theory and praxis offers a useful example of how this type of argument works. Democracy is taken as a premise to be a universal good. A given category of discursive or material practices is examined, and judgment is rendered as to whether such practices may be said to confirm or violate that good. To the extent that the premise is not itself made available for criticism (democracy: always? everywhere?), then we have withheld a means of counterargument from our interlocutor and have thus sought to place him or her within a coerced relationship. And to the extent that disagreement with the argument is interpreted as disagreement with the premise (by criticizing my criticism you are announcing yourself an opponent of democracy), then we have delimited the range of responses available to our interlocutor. Either way, we have protected ourselves as critics by refusing to allow for the possibility of legitimate opposition.

A second and often closely related practice involves the nature of the prose with which one advances an argument. I have in mind here language which obfuscates, relies on hermetic codes, or otherwise renders opaque the meaning of one's argument. At first glance this concern may well seem a relatively trivial matter of "style," a frustration for editors but remediable with a sturdy red pencil. It is more than that. In practice if not in principle, the use of such language operates to severely circumscribe the range of possible responses, withholding as it does the very basis upon which one's argument can be made intelligible. Aside from the fact that such willful obscurity dismisses readers not already in on "the game," it too serves to protect the critic from counterargument. How can we assess, much less attack, an argument that we cannot understand?

This is not an altogether easy matter to resolve. As a rhetorician, I am fully aware that certain disciplines generate vocabularies suited to their needs, and that frequently such vocabularies must make assumptions about what requires saying and how it is to be said. And, in truth, there are those aplenty who would attack a given discipline's language as "mere jargon" as an easy, indeed lazy way of dismissing arguments otherwise threatening to their own positions. Attacks on Foucault's prose by those unwilling to take his ideas seriously are a ready case in point. But if it is unacceptable to oppose the writing of others for this reason, it is equally unacceptable to refuse a good-faith obligation to make one's argument clear and therefore available for critique. To do so, in Johnstone's words, is to acknowledge that our interlocutor "is a person capable of listening to an argument and knows how it is that we are regarding him." That is to say, willful obfuscation is one other means through we deny the capacity of our audiences to make free and enlightened judgments of our views.

A third but certainly not final threat to the bilateral norm of free will consists in the effort to overwhelm one's interlocutor with the trappings of erudition. This is, again, a more complex matter than may first appear. It is a truism in most critical work in the humanities that we are obliged both to situate our argument within the relevant scholarship and to warrant our claims based on empirical evidence when appropriate. Indeed, it is scarcely possible to conceive of reputable rhetorical criticism as doing otherwise—it is, in a sense what makes our work *scholarship*. At the same time, it is not rare to find those who would seek to control the response to one's argument by so embedding it in the authority of others as to make it effectively unavailable to exposure and critique. Here is a variation on Johnstone's "game" that turns out to be a game not at all, at least to the extent that it secures itself against the possibility of failure.

I am of course not contesting the appeal to authority when such appeals are germane to the requirements of a given argument. I am seeking to draw attention to a critical practice—unhappily prevalent—in which the critic so loads the dice of authority that readers are discouraged from undertaking a serious examination of the argument at hand. We may note, for instance, the manuscript that comes across the editor's desk. The author wishes to make a case for the priority of "difference" over and above "identity" as a heuristic for our time. The argument, we discover, is so deeply embedded and so contingent on interpretations of Plato, Aristotle, Augustine, Aquinas, Leibniz, Locke, Descartes, Vico, Bacon, Hume, Rousseau, Kant, Hegel, Nietzsche, Heidegger, Derrida, Foucault, and Deleuze that it becomes readily unclear in just what a counterargument would consist. We have here a kind of bullying effect, playground strong-arming that camouflages whatever weaknesses the actual argument may possess.

The Principle of Risk

At the heart of Johnstone's conception of bilateral argument is the assumption of risk both by the arguer and to that person to whom the argument of addressed. It is fair, I think, to observe that his view of risk undergirds each and any constitutive component of his theory; without it, the others would lack grounding as non-arbitrary norms. Put briefly, Johnstone takes risk to be a feature of one's humanity, and the refusal to assume risk, at least in some cases, as destructive of that humanity. This is so because the willingness to risk one's beliefs through the process of argument is to accept the possibility of having one's self literally changed; and this requires an open mind: "The risk that the open-minded person takes," he stressed, "is that of having his belief or conduct altered. This risk, of course, is strictly correlative to the risk the arguer takes that his argument might fail." While it is true, Johnstone wrote, that we cannot always thus put ourselves at risk, "we cannot always have closed minds either, for the person with the totally closed mind cuts himself off from the human race. Such a person is inhuman, although he is not beastly, for we do not accuse animals of having closed minds, any more than we say that their minds are open" (1965, 3).

In this sense, the discussion above regarding the standard of free will is another way of talking about risk and those practices that seek to protect the critic from the dangers of failure. Here I wish to address a particularly knotty but important issue in the conduct of rhetorical criticism, and to examine it in light of Johnstone's conception of risk. The issue has to do with the function and effect of *method,* and to the role it may be said to play in minimizing risk within the critical enterprise.

Questions of method are as old as modern criticism itself. By this I refer not to preferences for one type of method over another, but of method as such. What, for example, is a critical method, how does it work, and why "use" one in the first place? Again, what is the relationship between method and object? Between method and critic? The answers have not always been self-evident, and indeed the history of rhetorical criticism may well be written as an account of how we have struggled to arrive at mutually satisfying resolutions to problems posed by them. Edwin Black's frontal assault on conventional methods of criticism is now forty years old, but the debate continues apace. Here I would like to state in very broad terms the case against method, when, in practice, it confounds the aim of bilateral argument. To be clear: I am not contesting the utility of method in principle. Of course criticism requires systematic, non-arbitrary, and warranted claim-making. I mean rather to identify ways in which method can serve to reduce or eliminate the possibility of risk and therefore of failure. Several such practices suggest themselves.

Rhetorical criticism is an interpretive practice in which a class of phenomena is identified as rhetorical and judgment is rendered as to the properties and moral implications of those phenomena. The key term here is judgment, inasmuch as the critic seeks to make sense of the object not simply by describing its several features, but ultimately with reference to the critics own set of beliefs, values, and commitments. To issue a critical judgment is therefore to give expression to oneself; it is, to use a Johnstonianism, to expose the self to counterargument and thus to the possibility of having one's judgment fundamentally altered.

We might now consider how this process is preempted by certain strategies of deploying method. When, for example, a given method is so mobilized as to deflect judgment away from the critic and toward the method itself, we would seem to have a case of risk-minimization. In this instance, the method in effect stands in for the critic, provides an apparently objective structure of inference, and issues claims and conclusions that are themselves a product of that method.

To wit: I seek to explain the rhetorical force of a certain film; I invoke a typology familiar to students of myth; I identify plot developments and characters with reference to that typology; and conclude by offering claims about how the filmic text operates according to mythical archetypes. What have I done? I have rendered a "judgment," if it may be called that, intelligible only within terms presupposed by the method. To what extent have I exposed myself to the risk of criticism, counterargument, or failure? None. The only available response is either to accede to the argument or to attack the method. I have deputized my obligations to a model, and relieved myself of the risk of actually having to alter my beliefs or, more to the point, beliefs about myself.

A second and closely related danger raises question about the relationship between method and the very possibility of judgment. At the very real risk of oversimplification, we might view judgment, or at least hermeneutic judgment, as an exercise in practical intelligence. By this I mean rendering decisions without access to universals or superintending rules. By their very nature, such judgments are indeterminate, contingent, and fallible. This is so because the person from whom such judgments are issued are themselves indeterminate, contingent, and fallible. And this is why interpretive judgment is always open to risk if it is to claim the status of a judgment at all. Now, when method is so used as to virtually eliminate the possibility of chance, variance, mistakes, or any other contingency, then we have grounds for suspecting such usage to be in violation of the bilateral norm. We see this most frequently in cases where the critic relies upon a method as a novice actor relies upon a script: both seek merely to operate according to the directions provided and conclude, so to speak, without blowing the lines. Conversely, the accomplished critic—like the accomplished actor—knows that real insight comes from operating in the improvisational spaces outside the script proper, in the undetermined zone of surprise, nuance, and, of course, risk.

All of this, again, is not to claim that critics ought to abandon method, if by method we mean an intelligible structure of inquiry guided by certain assumptions and standards of reason. This much is to be expected. It is rather to remind us that method is a way of proceeding in view of specific questions or problems. Method is in this sense posterior to the need which gives rise to it. Any interpretive practice that in effect deflects judgment away from the critic, or predetermines its own outcome, may be said to reduce not only the risk essential to such criticism but the humanity of the critic as well.

The Principle of Mutual Investment

What is the point of argument? Not the point of a given argument, but of the process itself? What is at stake when we argue? In one way or another these questions wove themselves into the fabric of Johnstone's work for much of his scholarly career. And while we cannot hope to summarize his thinking on the matter here, we can at least attempt a characteristic view. We argue, Johnstone believed, because in the process we learn who we are and where we stand. We learn this by exposing ourselves to risk, by countenancing scrutiny of our positions and adapting ourselves, when necessary, to the claims of our interlocutors. And so to the question "What is at stake when we argue?" the answer is "the Self is at stake." That is why, he writes, "argument is in fact essential to those engage in it—a person who chooses argument does in fact choose himself" (1965, 6). If I understand Johnstone's point, this means that to argue is to put ourselves at risk, and that putting oneself at risk is a positive condition of our humanity. Such a view runs counter to what he takes to be a standard conception of argument as " transaction that has no essential bearing on the characters of those who engage in it. The arguer attempts to persuade the listener. If he succeeds, well and good; if he fails, he may either resort to nonargumentative techniques or else give up the effort. But the argument is in no way definitive of either the arguer or the listener" (5). Johnstone was by contrast preoccupied with the ways in which argument was in fact constitutive of both. In this view, it is unthinkable that such an undertaking could command anything except a resolute and mutual investment in its outcome.

The politics of academic labor being what they are, it is tempting to acknowledge Johnstone's point without taking it seriously. We may say, for example, that we are invested in the outcome of our criticism to the extent that it gets published, cited, or otherwise adds to our scholarly credentials. These are not trivial concerns, as any untenured faculty member is well aware. But this is clearly not Johnstone's point. He is rather attempting to identify the nature of our commitments when we enter into an argument, and to underscore the obligations we assume thereby. Otherwise, as he noted, "arguments would have no more than a strategic function, and the milieu would collapse into a game in which open-mindedness and tolerance would no longer be possibilities" (7).

The principle of mutual investment strikes me as applying with disturbing force to the practice of rhetorical criticism in our time. We operate within the peculiar economy of academic print, where traffic in scarce resources is required for professional success. The economy is peculiar in several senses. We may, by virtue of having an essay deemed publishable by editors, contribute to the production of arguments, yet without any guarantee that our efforts will be read, much less engaged as an argument. Indeed, it is not inconceivable that one may enjoy considerable academic success without ever having one's work read save by members of an editorial board. If, on the other hand, our work is read, what then? What does it mean to enter into an argument—bilateral argument—with a printed essay of rhetorical criticism? We may, to be sure, be prompted into organizing a conference panel, or compose a counterargument that aims for publication. But we still seem a distance from the ready exchange of arguments that define the dialogic moment.

Without attempting to resolve these dilemmas here, we can nevertheless identify those modes of criticism that reduce risk by reducing commitment to the consequences of our arguments. The more obvious examples of such work would include the featuring of pseudo-problems; manifestic statements in which argument is neither evident nor invited; and writing simply for the sake of getting published. More interesting, I think, are two motivations we have touched upon already.

For reasons that should now be apparent, a preoccupation with questions of method is almost certain to discourage the kind of investment essential to bilateral argument. The fine tuning, correction, and elaboration of critical method can serve in this case only to reproduce to problems noted above. Why? Because such tinkering further deflects critical attention away from the basis of all interpretation—the judgment of the critic. Put another way, it is one thing to dispute the efficacy of a given method, quite another to dispute the assumptions, reasoning, and conclusions of one's interlocutor. We do not say of a method that it is morally untenable; instruments are not susceptible to that kind of claim. But a critic is not an instrument, and a person who renders a judgment must be assessed in terms of moral tenability.

A second guarantee against securing against the investment of both arguer and audience is the appeal to incorrigible political convictions. By this I refer to a critical practice that is, so to speak, overly invested in its own commitments. In this sense, the argument proffered is understood to be a means simply of giving otherwise unshakable tenets their most forceful articulation. Such a position means that even if the argument is exposed as faulty, the overriding set of convictions remains unchanged. Here the entrenched beliefs of the arguer serve as a kind of breaker switch, overriding objections and ensuring the continued operation of the value system at work. "You can defeat my argument," the reasoning goes, "but that is all you have done; my convictions remain in place." Needless to say, the appeal of investing in such a process as an audience is negligible, as is the integrity of the process itself.

Conclusion

When Henry Johnstone was skeptical about the ways of rhetoric, it was frequently because of what he perceived to be its didacticism. To the extent that this essay is rhetorical, it must admit to a certain tendency in that direction. I make no apologies for this, if only because a similar quality underwrites a good deal of Johnstone's own work. I hope, in any case, that my comments will not be read as if written by a scold; I have sought, rather, to take an honest look at some dimensions of rhetorical criticism that invite scrutiny, and to suggest that Johnstone offers us an expert guide to what is essentially a healthy process. He spent much of his career holding a mirror before the face of philosophy, and was able thereby to discern the sinews that give to philosophical argument its character, appeal, and, sometimes, its warts. Rhetorical critics can and should do the same.

Department of Communication Arts and Sciences
The Pennsylvania State University

Works Cited

Johnstone, Henry W., Jr. 1959. *Philosophy and Argument.* University Park: Penn State UP.

———. 1971. "Some Trends in Rhetorical Theory." In *The Prospect of Rhetoric,* ed. Lloyd F. Bitzer and Edwin Black. Englewood Cliffs, N.J.: Prentice-Hall.

———. 1982. "Bilaterality in Argument and Communication." In *Advances in Argumentation Theory and Research,* ed. Robert J. Cox and Charles Willard. Carbondale: Southern Illinois UP.

Johnstone, Henry W., Jr., and Maurice Natanson, eds. 1965. *Philosophy, Rhetoric, and Argumentation.* University Park: Penn State UP.

The Faith and Struggle of Beginning (with) Words: On the Turn Between Reconciliation and Recognition

Erik Doxtader

> No justificatory discourse could or should insure the role of metalanguage in relation to the performativity of institutive language or to its dominant interpretation.
>
> —Jacques Derrida

> The words that are a "riddle" from the outset contain a symbolic core, beyond the meaning communicated in it, a core that is the symbol of noncommunicability. For this reason many riddles can be solved simply through an image, but they can be redeemed only through the word.
>
> —Walter Benjamin

In a beginning that strives to constitute the grounds for understanding from the terms of fate's violence, the promise of the word is not (self) fulfilling. Caught within those conflicts that ban the self from its own voice and which use the codicils of law's precedent to deter expression and collective (inter)action, the power of language is simultaneously rendered absolute and suspect. As such "signs of the times" strive less to negate resistance than to ensure that it replicates and thus confirms the legitimacy of their logic, the "gift" of the word that claims to interrupt this cycle and make human relationships anew can be "taken" only as its potential is turned against itself. A hinge in which we are called to create a beginning in the light of its own cost, the experience of this contingency is a moment in which we are confronted with the question of whether the word('s) power to invent (or discover) unity in the midst but not at the expense of difference inaugurates the productive opposition of reconciliation's promise or marks the onset of recognition's struggle.

In the name of beginning that which cannot be dirempted from a beginning named, we have come to speak a great deal about reconciliation and recognition. In the violence from which we seek exception, we have come to place significant faith in the power of their words. (Re)presenting the hope of a new beginning, reconciliation and recognition promise something basic if not fundamental, a (trans)formative event that beckons the subject from the bindings of mastery and slavery and which crosses the isolating corners of enmity in order to fashion the subjectivating bonds of friendship. This work appears in a variety of places and contexts. It may, for instance, be held in the very name of this journal, at least insofar as Henry Johnstone's tremendous initiative in 1968 provokes the question of whether its (transgressive) conjunction between philosophy *and* rhetoric expresses a conciliatory interest or opens a space for the mutual acknowledgement of (inter)dependence. Very close by, at least if we are receptive to Adorno's claim that the divorce of philosophy from rhetoric is a division "leagued with barbarism," reconciliation and recognition are concepts that both ground and focus contemporary debates over how to best promote democratic pluralism, foster democratization, and repair the wounds wrought by gross violations of human rights.

Does it matter if we speak of reconciliation or recognition? Whether in the halls of the academy, the public square, or the killing fields, the appearance of deep historical division beckons this question. It is a question not just of value but of relation. In the midst of certain conflicts, we are sometimes called to the language of reconciliation. At other times, we turn to words of recognition. In still other moments, we compose and rely on a vocabulary that sets these ideas into an unsteady play, a connectivity that can be seen to variously blur and codify their difference. In all cases, it is frequently difficult to discern the rhyme of our reasoning. Consider that on the first page of its first issue, this journal's editorial vision appeared just above the listing of an editorial board that was strictly divided between those in "philosophy" and those hailing from "Speech and English." Does the tension between these "announcements" hint that recognition more than reconciliation was the order of the day? The matter can be debated. It is debated by those concerned with dynamics of democratic politics and transitional justice. In the name of making a timely future from the wreckage of authoritarian rule, the pragmatic need to build peace and displace standing justifications for violence has been set out as a reason why the process of reconciliation trumps recognition's strict if not juridical attention to equality and the obligations of justice. In a reversal of the equation, the problem of how to sustain such transitions has been taken as an indication that the lofty goal of reconciliation is a dangerous abstraction if it is not prefaced by recognition, a process given to acknowledging historical experience, taking stock of individual interest, and recuperating the identity and dignity of those that have been subjected to and divided by violence.

Appeals for reconciliation and recognition often come in the same breath. And yet, there is something deeply puzzling about such calls, an ambiguity that serves to both provoke and simultaneously defer the question of how these concepts are (best) related. In many contexts and discourses, arguments about the meaning of recognition and reconciliation are rife with the imprecision of ordinary language and shot through with assumptions that appear to warrant both their differentiation and alignment. Even as they are alleged to do different things and wield different powers, each is given to the creation of "unity in difference" and oriented to (re)constituting the basis and form of human (inter)action, a process that involves turning alienation and conflict toward mutual understanding and productive (dis)agreement. How then do we distinguish between reconciliation and recognition? Do the terms of our distinction figure a relationship? What difference does this relation make?

In light of controversy over whether reconciliation is necessarily cheap and if recognition promises only more of the same, these questions have grown more urgent.[1] Without singular or formulaic reply, they are problems that appear in both critical-theoretical accounts of reconciliation and recognition and political discourses dedicated to their practice. In this essay, I pursue the relationships between these relation-making goods across both "fields."[2] Initially, I reflect briefly on the difficult meaning of these concepts and make a case for how critical accounts have tended to construct and rely on an "ambivalent distinction" between reconciliation and recognition. A reflection of the Hegelian legacy to which many of these positions owe a substantial debt, this dynamic suggests that the conceptual relationship between reconciliation and recognition may be held in their rhetorical potential, a form of power that was constituted, deployed, and troubled by the South African Truth and Reconciliation Commission (TRC). Thus, from an early moment of testimony that was presented to the Commission and which posited a normative relationship between recognition and reconciliation, I move to the TRC's larger attempt to explain and enact the (inter)play between these two concepts, an argument and performance that sets them into a complex constellation, a relationship in which struggles for recognition and the promotion of reconciliation are seen to betray one another's risk, a danger that abides in their respective beginnings.

* * *

Reconciliation and recognition are "difficult terms." Both familiar and controversial, these concepts, if they are concepts at all, have each provoked and sustained theological, political, and philosophical debate over the nature and value of their power. This instability cannot go unnoticed. In part, it means that the question of how these notions are related requires us to ask after the intersection of ideas that upset and sometimes refuse their own grounds. Thus, if their connection is to be grasped in an immanent way, the task at hand is far less to resolve this contingency than to work within it, an exercise that involves moving from our (pre)understanding of recognition and reconciliation to a reflection on the ways in which the characteristic ambiguity of each has served to call for(th) the other. A clear echo of Hegel, this dynamic is not the prelude to an equation but a way of grasping how the often unspoken movement between recognition and reconciliation holds a rhetorical question, a (double) problematic in which their relation appears in the potential of their words, the capacity of speech to constitute bonds whose meaning cannot be dirempted from the provisionality of their own power.[3]

In an attempt to recover an important and often overlooked gift, Paul Ricoeur begins his "course" of recognition by considering the "breadth of the lexical field in question," a field of ordinary language in which *reconnaissance* shows some fifteen different meanings (2005, 247).[4] Within the *Dictionnaire de la langue française,* however, he finds that recognition's somewhat vertiginous "polysemy" rests in three "major senses": (1) "to grasp (an object) with the mind, through thought, in joining together images" and "to distinguish or identify the judgment or action, know it by memory"; (2) "to accept, take to be true (or take as such); and (3) "To bear witness through gratitude that one is indebted to someone for (something, an act)" (12). While Ricoeur claims that the idea of gratitude is largely absent from its German counterpart, this tripartite definition echoes the connotations of *Annerkennung,* a term that extends beyond the cognitive process of perceiving something at hand to a sense of acknowledgement that includes the provision of equality and an expression of respect or esteem.[5]

Both an action and judgment, recognition (versus re-cognition) is an event that may grant a kind of status, attribute worth to historical experience or interest, commend a form of life, engender dignity, confess transgression, or honor an individual's (intrinsic) value.[6] It is, in Robert Pippen's view, a "certain form of social relation" in which the freedom of the "sovereign" agent is disclosed and enabled within an (intersubjective) exchange, a process in which who I *am* is grasped and affirmed by an other (2000, 156). If, as Allen Wood puts it, "I am 'recognized' by another when the other self-conscious being has an image of me as a being self-conscious like itself and I am aware of this other having this image" (1990, 86), the work of recognition expresses a desire for self-certainty that finds satisfaction only within a mutual relation, a social (and socially constitutive) bond in which a "binding form of dependence," the self's willingness to risk it-self in the name of embracing and being with an other, marks the potential for an individual and collective "form of independence" (Pippen 2000, 162).

It is this problem that opens and centers the struggle over the "struggle for recognition," a philosophical and political debate dedicated to both tracing the paradoxical yet productive negativity of recognition, the "one-sidedness and the reciprocity that mark the act of recognizing," and grappling with the ambiguity that attends its practice and outcome, that is, whether "what is to be confirmed [vis-à-vis the self] is at the same time what the act of recognizing must yet establish" (Düttmann 2000, 181, 47).[7] Today, much of this inquiry proceeds from and troubles Charles Taylor's familiar work on multicultural politics, an argument that locates the need for recognition in those histories of subordination, exclusion, and marginalization that constitute a "form of oppression, imprisoning someone in a false, distorted, and reduced mode of living" (1994, 25). Beneath its overt concern for dignity and democratic equality, Taylor's position rests on a (largely undeveloped) claim that the desire for recognition is rooted in a "basic human need," an interest that has been set variously onto ontological, epistemic, political, and ethical registers and that has provoked the question of whether recognition is an ongoing event that cannot (or refuses to) "transform the insecurity and uncertainty that it effects into a secure ground or foundation" or if it is a formal (pragmatic) process given to creating and stabilizing the "structural elements of ethical life."[8] At the heart of this debate is the question of what recognition *does* with identity. Following Taylor, many commentators contend that recognition is an individual or collective struggle that proceeds from, constitutes, and secures an authentic identity.[9] Increasingly, however, this promise of self-certainty has been criticized as hollow and self-confounding, a naive hope that risks replicating precisely the violence that occasions recognition struggles and that thus suggests why recognition may be better pursued through an attitude of vulnerability, a willingness on the part of individuals to oppose and perhaps even sacrifice their identity in the name of embracing a sense of finitude and self-contingency that opens the door to mutuality.[10]

If recognition marks a "change which effects otherness" (Düttmann 2000, 48), there are several reasons why it makes sense to approach the idea of reconciliation as an otherness that affects change. First, this interpretation reflects the longstanding notion that reconciliation begins with a certain experience of alterity, a form of division that the ancient Greeks cast as an occasion and need to change "enmity to friendship."[11] In the politics of antiquity, this turn frequently rested on the provision of indemnity or amnesty, a legal edict that suspended the law's demand for punishment in the wake of divisive transgression or domination. In moments of *stasis* that reduced the force of precedent to an instrument of violence, reconciliation's calling marked the (meta)normative need to (re)constitute the commons and (re)figure the common good.[12] Carried by letter, this exceptional turn from the law promised, according to the Apostle

Paul, a break in given time, a moment in which, "The old things [are] passed away; behold! All things have become new."[13]

Second, reconciliation's transformative power is often viewed as a gift from the Other, an unjustified offer of renewal (from God) made in the name of breaking (self) negating cycles of violence.[14] In both interpersonal and socio-political contexts, this gesture is a source of controversy, particularly as it appears to demand (yet another) sacrifice from victims of violence and seems to legitimize peace-building at the expense of accounting for history and its injustice.[15] In recent work, Pablo de Greiff (2005) shows how this problem leads many to conceptualize reconciliation as an "over-arching process," one that functions as a marker or placeholder for the simultaneous pursuit of reparation, truth, and mutual understanding. As it risks a "naive normativism," de Greiff counters this tendency by arguing that reconciliation may be better understood as a process that attempts to redress the "resentment" which follows from violations of "norm-based expectations" about individual and collective ways of life (16–17). Tied to a logic of apology in which the self shows and discloses itself to an other, reconciliation thus unfolds as an "exchange of power" given to constituting forms of trust that hold "community-building effects."

Third, as it seeks to fashion what *is* into what *is not,* reconciliation calls for individuals to be(come) otherwise. If it does not proceed by fate or fiat, such work holds a difficult problem of motivation, the question of whether reconciliation offers a chance for "learning to live together" that depends on the displacement of self-interest, an opposition to ontological, epistemic, and political interpretations of identity that provide unity at the potential cost of an engagement with difference.[16] Much like the debate over recognition, this turn from identity to identification leads some to shudder and then retreat to the idea that reconciliation is best conceived as a condition or state in which individuals, groups, or cultures have "become reconciled."[17] Along with its refusal of the possibility that reconciliation's constitutive promise is one which "bars its affirmation in the concept" (Adorno 1973, 160), this definition has been criticized for discounting the *processual* quality of reconciliation, an open-ended form of (ex)change that counts not as the achievement of peace but a moment in which aggrieved and alienated parties discern and fashion the ground for clash over what counts as peace, how it can be created, and the ways in which it might be sustained.

At first glance, reconciliation and recognition appear to have a good bit in common. They seem to share a concern for the "formation of a genuine and peaceful relationship" between human beings and the creation of a "shared present" characterized by an intersubjective "agreement to settle accounts"

(Borneman 2002, 281). So, too, each proceeds from and enacts a complex and constitutive negativity, an opposition to violence and an explicit interest in discerning how standing rationales for conflict contain the grounds for productive (dis)agreement that energizes individual and collective action. In many critical-theoretical accounts, this congruence is underscored by an evident and curious movement, a terminological code switching and analytic slippage in which dedicated accounts of one concept make a subtle shift to the ordinary language of the other. Working in both directions, from recognition to reconciliation and vice versa, these appeals rarely question the meaning of their "second(ary)" term even as it is used to redress (or cover) a lacunae in the "primary" position.[18] Thus, for instance, Michael Hardimon's single-minded effort to erect a social theory of reconciliation makes an unexplained turn to recognition at the point when it becomes necessary to account for the breaches and wounds that constitute reconciliation's object (1994, 90–91). Much more striking, Ricoeur's attempt to recover the "gift-logic" of recognition, a logic of "mutuality" that aims to offset the juridical violence embedded in appeals for "reciprocity," closes with an argument as to why the necessary dissymmetry between human beings is crucial to "the power of reconciliation attaching to the process of recognition" (2005, 262). More forthright but no less puzzling, Andrew Schaap finds cause to underwrite the *achievement* of reconciliation with a form of recognition that is itself supported and modified by an ongoing *process* of reconciliation (2003, 7).

As it (re)calls and (re)turns reconciliation and recognition to one another, theory comes to reflect if not mimic the work of the philosopher who struggled most fully with the operativity and significance of these two concepts. Indeed, the silences that appear in contemporary accounts can be cast as the problem of how to read between Hegel's early theology of reconciliation and the *Phenomenology of Spirit's* sustained concern for recognition.[19] Literally and figuratively, both positions may be addressed to the same *subject,* a subject that confronts the question of how to turn within and from a conflict that threatens to render it the (self) same.

In "The Spirit of Christianity and its Fate," Hegel considers the experience of violence that renders life hostile to itself, a transgression that finds redress only through the dissolution of law's form and a refusal of the "right" that promises universality at the cost of a "wealth of human relations" in which the hatred borne in the demand for equality gives way to the productive opposition of a love united with reflection (1948, 216, 253). A capacity to annul enmity with a disposition that invites the mutual constitution of life in relation, reconciliation is thus not salvation but a (messianic) time *given* to repairing the injuries of e(x)ternal law—slavery, political domination and subservience—through the (re)formation of a bond in which the self is (re)turned to what it is not.[20] Later, moving from the alienation of the master and slave to the call for forgiveness that haunts the beautiful soul's retreat from the hard heart's confession, the *Phenomenology* seems decidedly less concerned with reconciliation than pursuing a path of "reciprocal recognition" in which "self-consciousness is in and for itself in and through the fact that it exists in and for itself for another."[21] Marked nevertheless by a "reconciling yea," this struggle is described by Hegel as the move toward the "unity of the different independent self-consciousness which in their opposition, enjoy perfect freedom and independence" (Hegel 1977, 110). A process that begins with the self coming out of itself in its encounter with an other, this recognition is staked first by the risk of death and later as the negativity that underwrites the "formative activity" needed to realize the subject's intersubjective potential, an "'I' that is 'We' and 'We' that is 'I.'"[22]

What *is* a relationship of unity *in* difference? This question stakes Hegel's accounts of both recognition and reconciliation. Sitting between and within the two positions, it hints that the connection between the two concepts may turn on the problem of the relational, the issue of how to move between an ontological desire to confirm a sense of self through the other and the ethical need to render this work contingent on the idea that human relationships defy full control or submit to timeless definition. Indeed, much hangs on this "between." Marking a "middle course of beauty" and a "play of Forces," Hegel's interpretations of reconciliation and recognition hold an attitude of "indeterminacy" that plays between necessary acts of (self) assertion and the (self-confounding) transgressions that they necessarily enact. As the creation of a relation that is equally the experience of a negativity which marks creativity's limit, this suggests that reconciliation and recognition are best understood as a form of potential, a modality of power in which the chance to be(come) is equally the risk of not coming-to-be.[23] Distinguished from those "natural potencies" that constitute fate and haunt idealism, Hegel's renderings of recognition and reconciliation are shot through with this sense of potential, particularly as he claims that both move between a desire to renew the "spontaneity of life" and the loss attached to a "life known and felt as not being" (1977, 397; 1948, 231). Far from an accomplishment and standing in excess of (identitarian) law, reconciliation and recognition strive for the (be)coming of those relations that do not disavow the impossibility of their "end."

In a double sense, the "language of potential" is a mainstay of contemporary accounts of recognition and reconciliation. Charles Taylor, for instance, locates "a universal potential" at the heart of recognition's "fundamental principle" and contends that the politics of difference that it supports must both respect and help to enable "the potential for forming and defining one's own identity" (1994, 42). So, too, Axel Honneth's rereading of Hegel rests heavily on an argument as to how the struggle for recognition is best dedicated to "realizing potentials for subjectivity" (1997, 169), a claim that is challenged (somewhat) by Düttmann's contention that recognition is best considered a "medium of uncertainty" (2000, 7) and extended by Ricoeur's thinking about the productive negativity of recognition's (reconciling) gift (2005, 176–77). Without attempting to resolve the disagreement, what is crucial is the way in which Ricoeur discerns and characterizes this power: "By launching the idea of capacity by way of that of being able to say things, we confer on the notion of human action that extension that justifies the characterization of the self as the capable human being recognizing himself in his capabilities" (94). Close to Alex Boraine's claim that reconciliation requests our faith in words (2000, 79), Ricoeur's suggestion is both that language reflects the potential of recognition and that the action of speech puts its power into play.[24] Recalling Hegel's concern to cultivate a living connection between word and action, the potential of reconciliation and recognition manifests in language, an operativity of *logos* given to making and (re)turning to relations of unity and difference (1948, 218).[25] If so, the question of the relationship between reconciliation and recognition is a rhetorical question, a problem that demands a consideration of the ways in which each concept mounts and sustains a struggle for those words that trouble, fashion, and enable the potential for relation-making. Put differently, the connection between these concepts may appear through inquiry about what each presupposes about speech, how they compose presuppositions about what it means to speak in and for a relation, and the costs that attend putting these assumptions into practice. What are the features of discourses that "problematize" reconciliation and recognition, that lend it conceptuality, objectivity, and practicality? How is this talk (about talk) addressed and do the rhetorical operations of recognition and reconciliation (in)cite one another? Together, these questions hint that the relationship between reconciliation and recognition is not a matter of comparing normative "states" or a problem that that can be resolved by an identitarian comparison or unilateral attribution of their respective meanings. Indeed, the issue is not what the relationship *is* but what abides in the play between the words that hold the potential of their relational gestures.

* * *

Within the threat of an endless violence fed by righteousness, the difficult work of (be)coming into (self) relation appears in the difficult words of the subject accused of being an askari, the subject who is alleged to have betrayed the very historical causes that have left it alone to face the causality of fate that manifests as the experience of "hard living and not existing"(Henry 1996, 7). Heard in a country and within a "quasi-juridical" forum that has theorized, enacted, and troubled reconciliation and recognition in the name of constituting a (heterogenous) unity in a (manifold) diversity from within the midst of deep and violent division, this figure raises the question of their relation, the question of their relative potential to broker a coming to terms and (re)make human relationships at a moment when the action of speech confronts the need to hold and turn between its constitutive power and the cost of its invention.

Created not long after the 1994 election of Nelson Mandela, the Truth and Reconciliation Commission was charged to "promote national unity and reconciliation" by helping South Africans to "walk the historic bridge between the past of a deeply divided society characterised by strife, conflict, untold suffering and injustice, and a future founded on the recognition of human rights, democracy and peaceful co-existence and development opportunities for all South Africans, irrespective of colour, race, class, belief or sex."[26] Concluding only in 2003, the pursuit of this mandate saw the TRC devote substantial attention to the conceptual and practical relationships between recognition and reconciliation. Here, beginning with a telling moment of testimony that illustrates the stakes of this relation within the TRC's rhetorical architecture, I trace how the Commission offers four interpretations of their connection. Figured in the TRC's Final Report, a fragmented seven-volume text that is equally a description of the Commission's work and a normative defense of its efforts, procedures, and vision for how best to energize South Africa's transition, my suggestion is that these accounts are motivated and bound by an underlying negativity, a shared opposition that binds reconciliation and recognition through the question of their constitutive violence.

"*And to whoever may listen, ja, I don't know, I think maybe it's best to start so that we can get into it*" (Henry 1996, 1). Tentative and attuned to the fact that the moment was one that held no guarantee of audience, these words brought Yazir Henry to the precipice of his testimony to South Africa's Truth and Reconciliation Commission, a "statement about a story" that Henry choose to present to the Commission's Human Rights Violations Committee (HRVC) on 6 August 1996. One of several thousand individuals who took the chance to testify publicly about their experience of apartheid-era violence during the TRC's altogether brief tenure, Henry began his "statement that is about my story" by invoking his "former name" of Mark Henry, a name that he changed to Yazir owing partly to religious reasons and partly because "it brought me shame and it brought me great danger." Taking this turn as an indication that some in the audience could "know nothing about my history," the then twenty-six-year-old student of politics at the University of Cape Town defined the purpose of his "submission" to the TRC, a subjection designed to "recapture an experience at the hand of the state that has scarred me for life and has caused me immeasurable psychological trauma" and a hope for subjectivation, a moment in which "to wake up from this nightmare that I have lived ever since November 16th, 1989" through a "telling" of experience shot through with "gaps in my memory."

"*Wat praat julle nog met die fokken donner—why are you still speaking to this fucking man, it wasn't a man, they said die fokken donner, they said why are you speaking to this fucking man*"(Henry 1996, 4). Along with this account of how a security force officer interrupted one of the abusive interrogations that occurred during his legally indefinite (Section 29) detention, Henry's testimony has much to say about the experience of having words deemed not fit to hear. Beginning with his decision at age seventeen to enter exile for purposes of military training with the ANC's armed branch, Umkhonto we Sizwe (MK), Henry details the terms of his return to Cape Town two years later and his unhappiness with the domestic struggle's disorganization and mistrustfulness. Arrested shortly after he left the ANC's fold, Henry was bounced from police station to police station until the moment when several notorious security officials threatened to "kill my mother and nephew who at the time was only 4" if he did not disclose the whereabouts of a (former) comrade. Observing how he was left with "no choice basically," Henry testified to how he revealed Anton Franz's whereabouts and the fact that he was then forced—on "the floor of the car, with my head between my legs and my hands cuffed behind my back "—to accompany police on the raid that ended with Franz's assassination, a death that was surely preceded, according to Henry, with the question "who sold me to the police?"

Released only after several additional weeks of torture, Henry's return home brought questions from activists and a growing awareness that he "was being viewed as a sell-out and an askari." An object of distrust and cut off from the ANC's "membership and leadership alike," Henry held hope that the "law of the underground" would vindicate him even as his written accounts of his detention were rejected as inadequate and as he "began to disintegrate" and suffer an erosion of "self-confidence, self-esteem, and dignity." Adamant and at moments defensive, Henry closed his testimony by arguing that he could "not be held solely responsible" for Franz's death and then disclosing his specific "expectations of the TRC." Specifically, Henry asked:

> That I am publicly cleared of all rumors that I am an askari and I want to reiterate that I have remained faithful and committed to the struggle of oppressed South Africans for the human rights and the human dignity. That there is public acknowledgment—where am I—of my integrity and the restoration of my dignity. I wish to be recognized for who and what I am so that the falsification of my history be rectified. That the truth about the circumstances leading to my arrest and the names of those individuals or individual who informed on me be made known to me. Only then would I be able to reconcile myself with my own experiences and with the death of Anton.[27]

While I will return shortly to the precise terms of this position, the story does not end here. In the weeks and months that followed his appearance at the TRC, Henry's testimony was first picked up by the national media and then (re)presented as a "narrative of betrayal" in Antjie Krog's *Country of My Skull,* an influential account of the TRC's early work.[28] Thus, concerned that the Commission had "trivialised the lived experience of oppression and exploitation," and confronted with the way in which his testimony had been "taken out of my control and done without my permission," Henry was motivated to author a short essay in which he reflected on how his efforts to "face the past" and recover a basis to "interact with anybody other than the members of my immediate family" had led to a misunderstanding of his position and the imposition of a history, the public attribution of a "hurtful" identity that placed him "as the agonized confessor or the betrayer that should be pitied" (Henry 2000, 167). In Henry's terms, the "complexity of this maze" that was the TRC offered a space rife with contradiction, a forum in which the hope for human beings to "face each other as human beings" through the expression of experience and the breaking of silence sat in deep tension with the vulnerability that attended mediated publicity and the "hollow sound" of "never again" at the moment when it became apparent that the Commission was unable to "provide a precedent for deciding who is to be held accountable" for the crimes of the past (2000, 171).

As it concludes with the truisms that "everyone has a story to tell" and that the TRC was an important but flawed "beginning to the healing process," Henry's position echoes a number of statements presented to the TRC.[29] Along with his subsequent reflections on his experience at the TRC, the testimony can and has been taken as evidence that the Commission either fulfilled or fell short of its charge to "promote national unity and reconciliation in a spirit of understanding which transcends the conflicts and divisions of the past."[30] Still, appearing only four months into the TRC's human right violations hearings,

Henry's testimony is provocative for the way that it links the logics of recognition and reconciliation. In his terms, the "wish to be recognized for who and what I am" composes the basis if not the prerequisite for a capacity to reconcile, a potential that is then complicated and perhaps thwarted by the misrecognition that followed from his testimony, an alleged misappropriation of his narrative and the false attribution of an identity that set Henry in the midst of a historical conflict and left him without words that could stand for truth.[31]

Is Henry's position realistic or even consistent with how the TRC viewed its mandate and the way in which the Commission sought to fulfill its charge? If at all, how did the TRC envision and establish a relationship between reconciliation and recognition? In many ways, these questions were present at the beginning.[32] In February 1994, as most South Africans were looking ahead to the April election, a small but ultimately influential conference was convened in the name of looking back. Sponsored by a prominent NGO led by the future vice-chair of the TRC, the event was dedicated to reflecting on the nature of South Africa's transition and whether the negotiations that ended statutory apartheid needed to be supplemented with a formal process designed to "deal with the past" in a morally acceptable way.[33] At the end of several days of deliberation and in the immediate wake of a contentious debate over the (in)justice of the amnesty agreement that was brokered at the close of the constitutional talks, Andre du Toit reflected on the situation, noting that "one hardly knows where to begin," warning that the country's ability to move forward depended on its commitment to "use words such as reconciliation, amnesty, and amnesia in their serious sense or not at all," and then contending that "measures of amnesty can be used in a new society, but if we want to establish the rule of law and have a society in which the dignity of the victims is recognised, then we must take on the task of dealing with the past" (1994, 148). Less than a year later, in the midst of the public hearings on the draft TRC legislation held by the Portfolio Committee on Justice, du Toit deepened his argument, arguing that the transition's constitutive compromise rested on the pursuit of a reconciliation that offset the cost of amnesty with a moral logic of recognition (1995, 67).[34]

From its first hearings in mid-1996 to its controversial and overdue close in 2003, the TRC wrestled conspicuously with the question of how to define and link the ideas of reconciliation and recognition. Early in its Final Report, the Commission attributed a significant portion of the ambiguity to the terms of its complex mandate, a charge that it described this way:

> One of the main tasks of the Commission was to uncover as much as possible of the truth about past gross violations of human rights—a difficult and often very unpleasant task. The Commission was founded, however, in the belief that this task

> was necessary for the promotion of reconciliation and national unity. In other words, the telling of the truth about past gross human rights violations, as viewed from different perspectives, facilitates the process of understanding our divided pasts, whilst the public acknowledgement of 'untold suffering and injustice' (Preamble to the Act) helps to restore the dignity of victims and afford perpetrators the opportunity to come to terms with their own past. (TRC-I 1998, 49)[35]

Here, the concepts of acknowledgment and recognition appear to take center stage in the Commission's process while reconciliation is deemed an outcome, a condition to be produced through these or other means.

Yet, as the TRC conceded in its report, this logic "proved to be riddled with tensions," partly because of the fact that the Commission's was forced to "hit the ground running" and partly due to the ways in which the Commission's key terms shifted in response to the unfolding and frequently unexpected demands of the larger transition (I, 104). This fluidity is evident in the Final Report's discussion of its basic "concepts and principles." Initially, the TRC's conception of recognition develops from its mandate to "create as full as picture as possible" of apartheid-era violence, a revelation of truth dedicated to "helping citizens to become more visible and valuable citizens through the public recognition and official acknowledgement of their experiences" (I, 110). The creation of this picture (logic)—itself a goal of the Final Report—required, according to its chairperson, that the Commission "listen to everyone" and provide all South Africans with a "chance to say his or her truth as he or she sees it" in the name of *giving* meaning to "multi-layered experiences," restoring human dignity, and contributing "to the reparation of the damage inflicted in the past" (Desmond Tutu, quoted in TRC-I 1998, 112, 114). In these terms, the TRC's goal to discern and acknowledge the truth was defined not only as a forensic-institutional accounting or conferral of *status* but also as a dialogic event with "healing potential," a narrative and restorative process of truth-telling that aimed for a deeper sense of recognition: a "validation of the individual subjective experiences of people who had previously been silenced or voiceless" (I, 112). Linking the two forms, the Commission contended that:

> Acknowledgement refers to placing information that is (or becomes) known on public, national record. It is not merely the actual knowledge about past human rights violations that counts; often the basic facts about what happened are already known, at least by those who were affected. *What is critical* is that these facts be fully and publicly acknowledged. Acknowledgement is an *affirmation* that a person's pain is real and worthy of attention. It is thus central to the restoration of the dignity of victims. (I, 114)

With this implicit call for critique, the TRC claimed that the promise of recognition turned on a process that reflected "the essential norms of social relations *between* people" and took pains to ensure that the "truth of experience [that] is established through interaction, discussion, and debate" (I, 113). Thus, linked partly to a controversial claim about the "little perpetrator in each one of us," the Commission routed its definition and defense of recognition through the potential of public speech, an interchange and exchange dedicated to disclosing and narrating one's "*own account*" of history, accepting responsibility for past transgressions, (re)presenting self interest, and fostering the mutual understanding needed for the "restoration of our humanity" (I, 112).[36]

What then of reconciliation? In its Final Report, the TRC makes clear that this crucial and "highly contested term" did not admit to a "simple definition" and that while "it was obviously impossible for the Commission to reconcile the nation," its work did aim to "constitute signposts on the long road towards making individual, communal, and national reconciliation a living, lasting reality in South Africa" (V, 350). In the TRC's terms, reconciliation's promise of a "new way of life" marked both a distant goal and a dedicated process "where the building or rebuilding of relationships was initiated" (V, 350). Relevant across a variety of contexts and referring to different kinds of conflict, this practice of reconciliation was defined as an attempt to make peace with (historical) events, encourage the development of a culture of human rights and democracy, and lay a foundation for individual and collective healing (I, 107–8). A demand for neither love nor even friendship, the TRC maintained that much of reconciliation's potential lay in its capacity to cultivate a form of "peaceful co-existence" characterized by indemnity from the past's violence, the (re)constitution of memory, and the nation's embrace of ubuntu, an ontological and political concept that expresses the idea that "people are people through other people."[37] Relying significantly on testimony presented to its Human Rights Violation Committee, the Final Report argues that these goods depend on speech that occurs in "face to face meeting" and which seeks the grounds for productive dispute from within the historically given causes of violence (V, 392). Without a requirement of forgiveness but attuned to the question of its value and limit, the TRC argued that reconciliation was less a way of transcending disagreement than an occasion for undertaking meta-discourse, a process of deliberative norm creation dedicated to provoking and sustaining public debate over the demands of transitional justice, the appropriate reference for reparation, and the translation of deep division into a process of "healing broken human relationships" (I, 110, 117; V, 382). In short, the Commission's view of reconciliation rested heavily on the claim that it could open a shared space and build a common interpretive framework given to questioning how the violence of the past continued to distort and undermine the grounds for collective interaction (V, 424, 351, 426).

In accounts of its mandate and practices, the TRC suggests that reconciliation and recognition are both given to enacting a beginning. This (meta-transitive) turn is one that calls those subjected to historical violence to the work of subjectivation, a "coming to terms" through the (re)presentation of those words that are claimed to hold the potential for understanding. This does not mean, however, that the TRC rendered these concepts synonymous. In fact, the Final Report suggests that the Commission's interest in facilitating the transition from apartheid led it to advance four different but ultimately interlocking arguments about the relationship between reconciliation and recognition. First, the TRC made the case presented by Yazir Henry, a familiar argument as to how recognition is the basis for moving toward or achieving reconciliation. In its report, the Commission draws heavily and approvingly from testimony in which victims of gross violations of human rights contend that a "full acknowledgement" of the past and the public-social recognition of their existence and experience is a necessary condition for reconciliation (V, 364). On this view, recognition is first an event that composes an appearance, a word-picture (or relational form) that discloses and breaks the self's silence (for the self). Freed from history's foreclosure on expression, the subject's recognition is a moment for the announcement and ratification of identity commitments, a power of self-definition that enables and folds citizenship into a prior rule of law (V, 423). While this rehabilitation is deemed by the TRC to contain the potential for individual and collective action, a capacity to move forward with others toward a state of reconciliation, it is also an argument as to why recognition is a vital check on the constitutive power of reconciliation, a mode of invention—used at the constitutional bargaining table—that may bracket history at the cost of accounting for its own violence. In other words, recognition's claimed priority at the TRC is rooted partly in the expressed need to unravel the logic of indemnity that was used to both support the transition and justify the Commission's formation.

Second, the TRC's Final Report reverses field and contends that reconciliation is a precondition and foundation for recognition.[38] In large part, this formulation rests on the Commission's argument that reconciliation is less a state of affairs than a process that interrupts those cycles of totalizing violence that preclude a meaningful or productive struggle for recognition. Citing the efforts undertaken by former apartheid security officer Brian Mitchell in the community of Trust Feed, for instance, the Commission suggests that the opposition through which recognition develops may hinge on reconciliation's (constitutive) power to rhetorically break the historical precedent that sustains endless clash, compose a common space for talk, and invent a provisional vocabulary with which combatants can begin to address one another (V, 375, 394, 397). In those forms of violence so extreme that they leave one side or another to experience (the risk of) death as a "joke," and within a persisting system of sociopolitical division that renders basic forms of publicity not only incoherent but sanctionable, reconciliation's "reading of the signs of the times" creates space for recognition's work.[39] Closely related, the TRC claims that reconciliation's capacity to engender "talk about talk" is a starting point and referent for recognition. In a moment when language itself is deeply suspect, an instrument of the "undecidable" identitarian logic that was used to rationalize apartheid and the shifty vocabulary of so-called terrorists who are thought to harbor the desire to "throw whites into the sea," reconciliation holds out the gift of words.[40] Put differently, the claimed priority of reconciliation is rooted in a need to refuse the power of self-definition promised in its defense of recognition, a commitment to identity that the TRC held to be both a crucial cause of apartheid-era violence and an ongoing threat to the development of human rights culture.[41] Evident both in the fierce parliamentary debate over whether the TRC would leave crucial elements of the old regime intact or lead the country on a witch-hunt, the depth of this mutual distrust in the identity-forming potential of language ought not to be underestimated. At the TRC, in hearing after hearing in which the testimony of victims failed to produce *any* reaction from or interaction with perpetrators, the problem of the word's capacity to sever and isolate in the name of setting like only and always with like is the question of how reconciliation might indemnify the unraveling of recognition's narrative promise into a string of claims that is neither coherent nor heard.[42] Indeed, amnesty figures centrally in the TRC's contention that reconciliation sets the stage for recognition. A deeply controversial way of setting the perpetrators of a crime against humanity into (conceptual) relation with those who fought a just but sometimes excessive war for liberation, the reconciling quality of amnesty is deemed a form of disclosure that opposes historical justifications for identity-based violence with a form of publicity that aims to promote identification through debate over how a society can displace and reconstitute memory outside the confines of law.[43]

Tied closely to the second, the TRC's third argument is that recognition has the capacity to thwart reconciliation. Routed partly through the exception to law constituted by amnesty, the claim here is that reconciliation stands before the law, an event that both defies precedent in the name of its reconstitution and opposes the privilege ceded to the law's liberal subject. Thus, a reflection of the larger constitutional negotiations and enabled by appeals to ubuntu, the TRC sets the promotion of reconciliation over recognition to the degree that the former is a way to oppose and refigure the "given moral order," an ideological regime that severed the connection between law and justice to such a degree that the meaning of both, along with their relation, must be reconstituted by those that they are intended to serve.[44] While the recognition of experience is a vital referent for this effort, the TRC's hedge appears with the question of whether recognition presupposes precisely those norms of justice that must be reforged in the crucible of transition, a process in which citizens are given the chance to question, author, and consent to the rule of law. Put more bluntly, the risk of recognition is its legitimation of a form of collective memory that presupposes the timeless right of the liberal subject, a figure that neither represents a crucial dimension of South African history nor cedes to the interim constitution's claim that the law's promise will be realized only as it gives itself away to the good faith of reconciliation's beginning in relation, a mode of sufficient consensus that does not contain the risk of turning unity *in* difference to unity *as* difference.[45]

The TRC's fourth position turns this coin. Specifically, the Commission offers a case for why reconciliation may confound recognition. Recalling the early debates over whether South Africa needed a formal means of dealing with the past, the argument is partly that the TRC was created in direct response to the shortcomings of the constitutional negotiations, a set of talks that relied on reconciliation to both exclude "lesser" political parties from the design of the transition and set aside the question of justice in the name of avoiding breakdowns at the bargaining table. Thus, as the invention of the "new" nation engendered the risk of exclusion and impunity, the TRC presents itself as a counterweight, a quasi-juridical body dedicated to checking the heady promise of reconciliation in the name of first accounting for history's barbarism and the ways in which it carries into the present, an inheritance cut short by interpretations of reconciliation that presuppose the need to "draw a line in the sand" and move forward in the name of a future yet (or never) to come. Perhaps ironically, this work stands in some tension with the TRC's own claims about the value of forgiveness. Indeed, the Commission's Final Report contains a history of how it advocated, vacillated, and then backed away from the reconciling quality of forgiveness, in part because witnesses at its hearing began to contend that the call to forgive amounted not only to an inappropriate appeal to Christian tradition but as a call to forge a homogenizing national unity at the cost of expressing constitutive difference. In this way, the forgiving *ethos* of reconciliation was seen as an abstract harmony that cut against if not deterred the struggle for recognition.

* * *

Reconciliation and recognition betray one another. From testimony given to rendering the subject named as an askari otherwise to the discourse of a forum dedicated to the gift of coming to terms, recognition and reconciliation stand in opposition, a negativity through which they enter constellation and come to disclose the risk of the other, a potential to engender words (for and about words) that may not come to be. In reconciliation, the difference made by recognition appears to replicate unity's pathology, a coherence and assumption of identity that refuses if not distorts the creativity held in the experience of mutual vulnerability. In recognition, the promise of reconciliation's unity is the hope to make a difference that is always but yet somehow never at hand, a promise of renewal that may leave those most in need to wait for a time to (be)come.

At the TRC, the relationship between recognition and reconciliation appears in an interplay between forms of rhetorical power, a movement in which the creative speech action that (re)constitutes human relationships is confronted with the violence that attends and follows from its creation. As the Commission suggests, this dynamic connection neither allows nor warrants the construction of a matrix dedicated to showing how each concept balances the shortfall of the other. The anxiety that spurs the desire for such a (dialectical) system of mutual compensation, an anxiety with which the TRC itself struggled, may bring order only at the cost of making an exception for the very contingency on which the potential of recognition and reconciliation depend. Indeed, I want to close by suggesting that this exception contains the basis for a critique of violence, a critique that challenges several of the presumptions about the presence, coherence, and power of speech that tend to (silently) underwrite contemporary theories of recognition and reconciliation and which may undermine the transitional quality of transitional justice.

The hope for recognition and reconciliation holds a certain double-bind. In theory and practice, these concepts ask for and invite words in situations that mark the limit of language. Expressed more fully, the problem is that reconciliation and recognition call for speech in the name of fashioning relationships that have been foreclosed or rendered violent by a deprivation or lack of voice, the deterrence of expression, and the distortion of speech. Beneath his claim that human life has a "fundamentally dialogic character" and his demonstration that human beings define their identity through forms of dialogue which may perform or yield degradation, exclusion and homogenization, Charles Taylor's account of recognition, for instance, pays almost no attention to the difference between that speech which functions as a balm and that which wounds (1994,

32–33). In fact, the position's widely accepted assumption is that dialogic activity is a given, stable, and undistorted faculty. Whether inside or outside of Taylor's struggle for recognition, we can speak.[46] Echoed in accounts of reconciliation that pin its power on the production and expression of narrative, the "semantic bridge" that recognition calls us to cross is a structure that has already been built (Honneth 1997, 163).

Recalling Hilda Bernstein's claim that "opponents of apartheid are forced into a semantic trap: once you begin to use the language of apartheid, you have already accepted something of the premise" and echoing Vaclav Havel's contention that citizens in (post)totalitarian societies may lack a certain language of truth, the TRC's case for reconciliation appears to question and in many cases refuse the assumption that language stands intact and ready to serve. Perhaps more than Frantz Fanon (1967), it is the voice of Steve Biko that supports this gesture, particularly as the latter's philosophy of Black consciousness is addressed directly to the ways in which the "Black man feels a bit like a foreigner in the linguistic field" and how the apartheid system grew from and relied on one language to divest citizens of their voice, denigrate the power of other tongues, and violently name the terms and bounds of identity (1978, 108–11).

In this light, as it was tasked to undertake an effort that would "acknowledge *untold* suffering" and hear from those left "voiceless and silent" by the violent logic of apartheid's ban, the TRC's (re)presentation of reconciliation as more than a state of affairs is important to the degree that it marks a process for (re)building the conditions for speech, opening a space for talk, and creating moments in which individuals can speak with the hope of an audience. In situations of conflict that mark the limit of the word, reconciliation discerns and opposes this distortion in a manner that figures a basis for recognition. Or, more accurately, the gift of reconciliation's word is a vocabulary with which to begin the struggle for recognition, a struggle that the TRC then defines as one that turns back on its enabling to gift in order to ask after its cost and whether its semantic field is broad and deep enough to support the expression of historical desire, interest and need.

The TRC's play between reconciliation and recognition marks the problematization of speech, a dedicated concern for if and when there are words that will suffice and how the invention of expression is neither a miracle nor a historical inevitability. This interest in the condition of speech and the conditions for speaking leads directly to the question of what words do and the risks that are borne in the act(ion) of speaking. Reflecting the widespread perception that struggles for recognition are given to an exchange that recovers, composes, and validates identity, Yazir Henry's testimony speaks to the priority of securing a sense of self and disclosing "a repressed past," a history left from the official-public annals and displaced from the terms of individual and collective memory. The TRC, however, appears to complicate this position when it suggests that recognition's reconstitution of identity may involve not a productive (mutual) struggle but the incitement and repetition of the identitarian logic that underwrote apartheid's violent law and that runs counter to a cross-cultural historical suspicion of liberalism's self certain-subject. Confronted with this potential fault-line, the TRC contends that reconciliation is a form of speaking in relation that can indemnify struggles for recognition from the risk of their own collapse or devolution. Concerned less with identity-formation than with the cultivation of identification, reconciliation's productive opposition is a turn from violence to talk about how to usefully disagree that is carried partly by the idea of ubuntu, a communal ideal that allows the Commission to claim that the relation-making power of speech depends on the willingness of individuals to refuse something of their own status and interest (TRC-V, 387). With this claim as to how reconciliation sets the stage for recognition, the Commission also illustrates why the ensuing struggle may be dedicated partly to the question of whether reconciliation's unifying script(ure) offers the opportunity for understanding at the expense of experience and if its challenge to identity amounts to an undue subjection, a demand to enter into relation at the expense of the justice that it purports to serve.

The point is neither that the TRC discerned the proper formula nor that it simply shifted between recognition and reconciliation in order to conserve its own legitimacy. As a "scene of address" that did not take the capacity and operativity of speech for granted, the TRC's (concern for) language offers, in Daniel Herwitz's terms, a way to question the "abstraction of (certain kinds of) philosophy" (2003, 17). Specifically, its attempt to constellate and speak to the relationship between reconciliation and recognition suggests several ways that the theoretical discourse dedicated to these concepts might deepen its account of speech's operativity and the ways in which words hold the potential to make human relations anew. While still the order of the day in many accounts of recognition, originary and teleological accounts of language betray what Adorno called an "allergy to expression" and serve to smuggle fate into the work of beginning, a usually covert operation that affords little insight into how to generate the grounds for understanding in those moments of conflict when pleas for mutuality are dismissed as duplicitous or the short road to an unjust capitulation. The potential for coming to terms is not given. If it is, there may be violence close at hand, an invitation that must be turned against itself in the name of discerning the costs that attend the naming of the new. What's more, the availability of those words that sustain reconciliation and recognition does not assure their expression. The motive to speak at a distance from self-interest is frequently a recipe for resistance just as attempts to recognize historical experience and identity may be complicated by deep-seated arguments that throw the difference between the master and slave into question.[47]

For all of its ambiguity, the TRC's work suggests ultimately that a closer appreciation for the relation between reconciliation and recognition may be a way to open and underwrite an important critique of violence. In part, this is to say that the potential of the words that sets reconciliation and recognition into play is directed to the work of constitution, the transitional beginning-in-relation that endeavors to unravel (law's) precedent in a manner that does not negate the promise of (its) justice. Recalling Walter Benjamin's claim that such work is confounded by the false promise of formless freedom and the abstraction of revolutionary redemption, the relative power of reconciliation and recognition may demonstrate that the formation of human agreements which exceed the logic of the contract, may occur only with an unstable mixture of divine and mythic violence (1996). In practical terms, this means that the promise of *transitional* justice may recede quickly if it continues to demand either the priority of recognition or a reconciliation bereft of opposition.

What is held between these goods may yet make a difference. In the constellation formed by reconciliation and recognition, the form(ation) of human relationships is the problem of how to move between the word that constitutes by calling for the sovereign's (self) sacrifice and the (self) constitutive word that discovers sovereignty only in the acceptance of (its own) sacrifice. It is around this puzzle that reconciliation and recognition turn. Between them, they hold the singular question of the (non)violence of the word's potential to define and sustain a human relationship that would not otherwise come to be.

Department of Communication Arts, University of Wisconsin, Madison, and The Institute for Justice and Reconciliation, Cape Town

Notes

The positions advanced in this essay do not necessarily represent the views of the Institute for Justice and Reconciliation. This essay developed out of long and much appreciated conversations with Philippe Salazar, Charles Villa-Vicencio, and Sarah Burgess.

1. Today, in an age where the recognition of truth and the promotion of reconciliation have become nearly compulsory elements of democracy building, the connection between these ideas is increasingly contested and frequently staked to the question of how to simultaneously achieve political stability and justice. Moreover, there is an evident trend to fix the relation between reconciliation and recognition by equation. In her account of transitional justice, Eva Hoffman, for instance, argues—on side of the debate—that there is a "broad notion of recognition" which leads

to reconciliation (2002, 280). The benefit of this math is conceptual and practical comfort. By defining reconciliation as a condition, achievement, or state of affairs, we gain a bit of distance from a notion that is frequently burdened with religious baggage and that often seems to undermine the obligations of justice, a commitment that can be fulfilled through a (prior) struggle for recognition dedicated to the acknowledgement of identity and the recover of dignity. Its cost, however, may be an account of reconciliation's processual quality, an appreciation of how both reconciliation and recognition call the identitarian premise of liberal subjectivity into question, and an understanding of why their (trans)formative promise may depend on and unfold within their interplay.

2. In fact, one of the implicit suggestions of this essay is that the lack of attention to the interplay between reconciliation and recognition is a reflection of how conceptual and practical accounts tend to refuse one another on the respective grounds of avoiding either an "unphilosophical" particularism or abstract theory-building that paralyzes public policy-making.

3. Of course, this is already to take sides to the degree that the position that I pursue here does not presuppose a prior or given capacity for intersubjective dialogue.

4. This terministic breadth runs back to antiquity and includes a concern for the idea of recognition that appears in Aristotle's treatment of tragedy. See Markell (2003) and MacFarlane (2000).

5. For a systematic treatment, see Inwood (1993).

6. In Ricoeur's survey there is an interesting but yet undeveloped connection between the act of recognizing and the praise that abides in the epidictic voice.

7. There is an expansive literature on this struggle. For recent and leading work, see Judith Butler (2005), Markell (2003), Nancy (2002), Düttmann (2000), Tully (2000), and Honneth (1997). Also important are the readings offered by Bernstein (1984), Gadamer (1996), Fraser (1995), and Oliver (2001). One of the striking features of many contemporary accounts is how often their approach to the question of why human beings seek recognition echoes Hannah Arendt's claim as to why the necessity and necessarily transgressive quality of human action introduces a potentially productive negativity into the fabric of everyday life (1958).

8. Respectively, see Charles Taylor (1994, 33), Honneth (1997, 172), and Düttmann (2000, 63).

9. In particular, see Fraser (1995) and Honneth (1997).

10. A similar impulse appears in Ricoeur's attempt to cast recognition as a gift and Markell's differentiation between recognition and acknowledgement (2005, 33–38). For a contrasting view, see Düttmann (2000, 48–49). Related and equally important, this concern for identity has led to debate over whether human beings and particular communities enjoy a right to recognition, a juridical-institutional protection that may grant standing to human beings at the cost of promoting ethical interaction. In this regard, Sarah Burgess' investigation into the "demand" for recognition is much anticipated.

11. The literature on reconciliation is expansive and proceeds from a variety of religious and political perspectives. For several systematic treatments, see Schreiter (1992), Shriver (1995), and Vincent Taylor (1969).

12. For an account of the practical relationship between reconciliation and constitution-building, see Gross (2004, 47).

13. Working back through the idea of "exchange" held in the Greek terms for reconciliation, John de Gruchy has traced how Pauline doctrine includes a specific concern for the problem of the other. Equally important, de Gruchy's position illustrates both the tension and overlap between so-called political and religious renderings of reconciliation (2002, 51–56). Elsewhere, I have addressed the specific terms of Paul's call for reconciliation's "Word for words" (Doxtader 2001).

14. For an account of the latter, see Bar-Tal and Bennink (2004, 13). For a discussion of reconciliation's divine gift, see Tutu (1999).

15. For an overview of this debate over the nature and value of reparation and restorative justice see Doxtader and Villa-Vicencio (2004).

16. With thanks, I borrow this phrase from Charles Villa-Vicencio. For an extended account of why reconciliation may entail the displacement of identity, see both Doxtader (2003) and Schaap (2003).

17. For a discussion of this problem and how it is rooted in the difficult task of defining reconciliation, see Borer (2004).

18. For examples of this tendency, see Honneth (1997, 16), Markell (2003, 41), and Williams (1992, 239).

19. Patchen Markell's distinction between Hegel's "diagnostic" and "reconciliatory" voices is trivial evidence of the point. The substantive case appears in Williams's work on recognition, one that takes pains to include a consideration of how Hegel moved between reconciliation and the struggle for recognition (1992, 77, 147, 238). Also see Pippen (1989, 168).

20. This reading is influenced both by Williams's account of Hegel's early social theory and by the recent work by Giorgio Agamben on Pauline theology (2005, 55–57). For a detailed commentary on Hegel's young theology, see Harris (1972, 323–77).

21. This is Williams's (1992, 149) translation of the *Phenomenology*. Compare with Miller's translation (Hegel 1977, 408–9).

22. See Honneth (1997) for a full account of this developmental logic. For discussion of how recognition is figured through the dynamics of confession and forgiveness, see Williams (1992, 141) and Bernstein (1996).

23. In excess of the law of non-contradiction and the identitarian commitments of definition, this potential is a hinge, a faculty in which one comes "to be in relation to one's own incapacity" and where actuality does not transcend but abides with impossibility. For a detailed treatment of this sense of *dunamis, see* Agamben (1999, 183–84).

24. Taylor's position depends on a similar appeal to the dialogic, just as Honneth contends that the Hegelian legacy is a notion of recognition that realizes "a moral potential that is structurally inherent in communicative relations between subjects" (1997, 67) and Markell suggests that the politics of recognition—much like Schaap's understanding of reconciliation (2003, 14)—takes shape in a "specific way of making and justifying political and theoretical claims" (6).

25. What follows from this claim is a study that I cannot undertake here, a close scrutiny of whether and how Hegel includes speech within the development of self-consciousness.

26. This language appears in the post-amble of the 1993 Interim South African constitution and the preamble of the TRC's authorizing legislation.

27. The interruption in this passage—"where am I"—is interesting. It does not seem unreasonable to suggest that the expression occurred as Henry was attempting to find his place in the notes for his testimony. At a different level, the question expresses the ambiguity that characterized the space opened by the TRC, a forum that was in many instances defined as dedicated to helping South African recover a sense of place or standing.

28. In Henry's terms, the selection included by Krog was "duly edited to fit the narrative." An informal comparison of the TRC's hearing transcript and the passages included in Krog's chapter seems to confirm this assessment. See Krog (1998, 67–73). Beyond Krog's reading and far more troublesome for its proclamation—"Yazir Henry is a traitor"—is Henry's misrecognition in a recent travel guide's introduction to the TRC (Mitchell 2005, 67).

29. For the leading study of testimony presented to the TRC's Human Rights Violation Committee, see Ross (2003).

30. This language appears in the TRC's authorizing legislation. For many, the truth of Henry's testimony and critique is that the Commission was an abrogation of justice, a marked failure to bring gross violations of human rights of perpetrators to book or even to compel accounts of their role in an extended crime against humanity. Both a failure to disclose the truth of the past and a denigration of the need for systematic reparation, this shortcoming has been deemed to hold the seeds of future division, a Zimbabwe-style clash rooted in a sense of unfinished business and supported by those who were callously (re)traumatized by a Commission that some have characterized as the circus that came to town one week and disappeared the next. On the other side of the coin, the terms of Henry's position have been mustered as evidence for why the TRC mattered and how its detractors have misunderstood its mandate, process, and logistical constraints. One piece of a much larger transition puzzle, the Commission's charge to promote reconciliation was precisely that, a promotion, an attempt over the course of eighteen months to represent the range of apartheid's damage, balance a victim-centered process of healing with a controversial amnesty program, and define the task of reparation as an open-ended public good. In this sense, the TRC's symbolic importance ought not be dismissed as an abstraction, particularly as the Commission marked an attempt to invent and legitimize a vocabulary and normative framework for political debate over how South Africa might best move from past to future.

31. To this, it may important to add Henry's implicit claim that the TRC's concern to promote reconciliation through "a spirit that transcends conflict" may have rendered it somewhat averse to precisely those forms of clash that underwrite both reconciliation and recognition.

32. Moreover, they may have been present *before* the beginning, particularly if we do not assume that the TRC was created *ex nihilo* or that its work marked the start of interest in reconciliation. Indeed, both assumptions are deeply problematic. For instance, when it was discovered in 1989 that Nelson Mandela had taken it upon himself to write to P. W. Botha in the name of convening talks dedicated to a certain kind of reconciliation, the air in the ANC's Lusaka headquarters was thick with confusion and worry over whether the struggle's leading light had been broken and if he was preparing to sell out the cause. In the days after F. W de Klerk's 1990 decision to recognize the Congress as a legitimate political organization and release Mandela, the halls of Parliament were filled with accusations of treason that continue to echo in some quarters of South African politics. In 1994, as Mandela stood on the steps of the Union Building and was heard to announce during his inaugural address that "Laat ons die verlede vergeet! Wat verby is verby" (Let's forget the past! What's done is done"), the moment's felicity was tempered by concerns over whether the spirit of the new dispensation was coming at the expense of understanding history and the suffering of apartheid's victims.

33. The proceedings of the conferences were later published. See Boraine and Levy (1994).

34. For the fuller case, see du Toit (2000).

35. Quotations and extracts from the TRC's final report are henceforth cited by volume number and page. Thus, "(TRC-I 1998, 49)" refers to Volume 1, page 49. There is a tension here between this view of the mandate and the terms of the Promotion of National Unity and Reconciliation Act. Compare, for instance, this argument from the Commission with the terms of its legislative charge (TRC-I 1998, 55).

36. This position sits in stark contrast to Judith Butler's claims about narrative transparency (2005, 30–40).

37. With a meaning that is difficult to pinpoint, ubuntu variously connotes a group of people, a community, a shared political system or philosophy, and a collective way of life For treatments of ubuntu and its various philosophical, cultural, and political meanings, see Ramose (2002), Wiredu (1997), Shutte (2001), and Broodryk (2002).

38. This view appears to hold regardless of whether recognition entails an institutional acknowledgement of historical events or develops through an interpersonal process of mutual self-constitution. See the TRC Report (1998, V, 360).

39. Two points need to be made here. First, the reference here is obscure for those unfamiliar with the way in which some apartheid security officials reported that assassinations and torture sessions were occasions for parties. Second, the TRC itself may count as such a space, a forum that sought to refuse the historical precedent and presumption that holds the risk of rendering recognition token (TRC 1998, V, 392, 400).

40. This notion of an "undecidable" logic is developed by Norval (1996).

41. It is also the case the TRC defended the importance of identity, a claim that centered its findings on the needs of victims. In the Final Report, the tension between the two positions passes without comment.

42. With the notable exception of the Jeffery Benzien hearing, one of the common criticisms of the TRC's efforts was that it did not produce significant opportunities or incentives for "face to face" recognition (TRC 1998, V, 357, 378).

43. For an account of how this vision of amnesty remade if not dismantled the distinction between public and private, see Salazar (2002).

44. This case about the limits and distortion of law was made by two South African leaders, both of whom took a leading role in advocating for the TRC's creation. See Asmal (1992) and Omar (1995).

45. The literature on liberalism's ambivalent standing in South African politics is substantial and addresses the terms of both African and Afrikaner nationalism. See, for instance, Adam and Giliomee (1979). Hermann Giliomee, Johan Degenaar, and John Dugard have each addressed the issue in Jeffrey Butler (1987). Also important is Rich's study (1976).

46. In contrast, see Düttmann (2000, 50, 159) and Ricoeur (2005, 257). An interesting study remains to be done on whether the language of "separate development" in South Africa mimics the case for the origins of language advanced by Herder. In his account of recognition, Taylor relies heavily on the latter.

47. This is a sensitive issue. In the South African case, the matter has much to do with the complexity of colonialism and the fact that many Afrikaners have made the claim that their ancestors

were victims of British domination, a subjection that included imprisonment in concentration camps and that was left to the side by the TRC as the Commission was charged to understand apartheid-era violence between 1960 and 1993.

Works Cited

Adam, Heribert, and Hermann Giliomee. 1979. *Ethnic Power Mobilized: Can South Africa Change?* New Haven: Yale UP.

Adorno, Theodor. 1973. *Negative Dialectics*. Trans. E. B. Ashton. New York: Continuum.

Agamben, Giorgio. 1999. *Potentialities: Collected Essays in Philosophy.* Trans. Daniel Heller-Roazen. Palo Alto: Stanford UP.

———. 2005. *The Time that Remains: A Commentary on the Letter to the Romans.* Trans. Patricia Dailey. Palo Alto: Stanford UP.

Arendt, Hannah. 1958. *The Human Condition*. Chicago: U of Chicago P.

Asmal, Kader. 1992. "Victims, Survivors and Citizens—Human Rights, Reparations, and Reconciliation." Inaugural lecture. University of the Western Cape, South Africa.

Bar-Tal, Daniel, and Gemma Bennink. 2004. "The Nature of Reconciliation as an Outcome and as a Process." In *From Conflict Resolution to Reconciliation,* ed. Yaacov Bar-Siman-Tov, 11–38. Oxford: Oxford UP.

Benjamin, Walter. 1996. "The Critique of Violence." In *Walter Benjamin: Selected Writings, Volume 1, 1913–1926,* ed. M. Bullock, 236–52. Cambridge: Harvard UP.

Bernstein, J. M. 1984. "From Self-Consciousness to Community: Act and Recognition in the Master-Slave Relationship." In *The State and Civil Society*, ed. Z. A. Pelczynsk, 14–39. Cambridge: Cambridge UP.

———. 1996. "Confession and Forgiveness: Hegel's Poetics of Action." In *Beyond Representation: Philosophy and Poetic Imagination,* ed. R. Eldridge, 34–65. Cambridge: Cambridge UP.

Biko, Steve. 1978. *I Write What I Like.* London: Bowerdean.

Boraine, Alex, Janet Levy, and Ronel Scheffer, eds. 1994. *Dealing with the Past: Truth and Reconciliation in South Africa*. Cape Town: Institute for Democracy in South Africa.

———. 2000. "The Language of Potential." In *After the TRC: Reflections on Truth and Reconciliation in South Africa,* ed. Wilmot James and Linda van de Vijver, 73–80. Cape Town: David Philip.

Borer, Tristan Anne. 2004. "Reconciling South Africa or South Africans? Cautionary Notes from the TRC." *African Studies Quarterly* 8:1–22.

Borneman, John. 2002. "Reconciliation After Ethnic Cleansing: Listening, Retribution, and Affiliation." *Public Culture* 14:281–304.

Broodryk, Johann. 2002. *Ubuntu: Life Lessons From Africa.* Pretoria: Ubuntu School of Philosophy.

Butler, Jeffrey, ed. 1987. *Democratic Liberalism in South Africa: Its History and Prospect.* Middletown: Wesleyan UP.

Butler, Judith. 2005. *Giving an Account of Oneself.* New York: Fordham UP.

de Greiff, Pablo. 2005. "The Role of Apologies in National Reconciliation Processes: On Making Trustworthy Institutions Trusted." Unpublished Paper, International Centre for Transitional Justice.

de Gruchy, John. 2002. *Reconciliation: Restoring Justice.* Cape Town: David Philip.

Doxtader, Erik. 2001. "Reconciliation in a State of Emergency: The Middle Voice of 2 Corinthians." *Journal for the Study of Religion* 14:47–66.

———. 2003. "Reconciliation—A Rhetorical Concept/ion." *Quarterly Journal of Speech* 89:267–92.

Doxtader, Erik, and Charles Villa-Vicencio, eds. 2004. *To Repair the Irreparable: Reparation and Reconstruction in South Africa.* Cape Town: David Philip.

du Toit, Andre. 1994. "South African Response." In *Dealing with the Past: Truth and Reconciliation in South Africa,* ed. Alex Boraine, Alex, Janet Levy, and Ronel Scheffer, 117–36. Cape Town: Institute for Democracy in South Africa.

———. 1995. Testimony delivered to Parliament's Joint Committee on Justice with regards to the Promotion of National Unity and Reconciliation Bill, 6 February. Archives of Parliament, Cape Town, South Africa.

———. 2000. "The Moral Foundations of the South African TRC: Truth as Acknowledgement and Justice as Recognition." In *Truth v. Justice: The Morality of Truth Commissions,* ed. Robert Rotberg and Dennis Thompson, 122–40. Princeton: Princeton UP.

Düttmann, Alexander. 2000. *Between Cultures: Tensions in the Struggle for Recognition*. London: Verso.

Fanon, Frantz. 1967. *Black Skin, White Masks*. Trans. Charles Markmann. New York: Grove.

Fraser, Nancy. 1995. "From Redistribution to Recognition? Dilemmas of Justice in a Post-Socialist Age." *New Left Review* 21:68–93.

Gadamer, Hans Georg. 1996. "Hegel's Dialectic of Self-Consciousness." In *Hegel's Dialectic of Desire and Recognition,* ed. John O'Neill, 149–70. Albany: SUNY P.

Gross, Aeyal. 2004. "The Constitution, Reconciliation, and Transitional Justice: Lessons from South Africa and Israel." *Stanford Journal of International Law* 40:47–104.

Hardimon, Michael. 1994. *Hegel's Social Philosophy: The Project of Reconciliation*. Cambridge: Cambridge UP.

Harris, H. S. 1972. *Hegel's Development: Toward the Sunlight, 1770–1801*. Oxford: Clarendon.

Hegel, G. W. F. 1948. "The Spirit of Christianity and Its Fate." In *On Christianity: Early Theological Writing,* trans. T. M. Knox, 182–301. New York: Harper.

———. 1977. *Phenomenology of Spirit.* Trans. A. V. Miller. Oxford: Oxford UP.

Henry, Yazir. 1996. Testimony before the South African Truth and Reconciliation Commission, 6 August. Available at <http://www.doj.gov.za/trc/hrvtrans/helder/ct00405.htm>. Accessed 16 November 2006.

———. 2000. "Where Healing Begins." In *Looking Back, Reaching Forward: Reflections on the Truth and Reconciliation Commission of South Africa,* ed. C. Villa-Vicencio and W. Verwoerd, 166–73. Cape Town: University of Cape Town.

Herwitz, Daniel. 2003. *Race and Reconciliation: Essays from the New South Africa*. Minneapolis: U of Minnesota P.

Hoffman, Eva. 2002. "The Balm of Recognition: Rectifying Wrongs Through the Generations." In *Human Rights, Human Wrongs,* ed. Nicholas Owen, 278–303. New York: Oxford UP.

Honneth, Axel. 1997. *The Struggle for Recognition: The Moral Grammar of Social Conflicts*. Trans. Joel Anderson. Boston: MIT P.

Inwood, Michael. 1993. *A Hegel Dictionary.* Cambridge: Blackwell.

Krog, Antjie. 1998. *Country of My Skull: Guilt, Sorrow, and the Limits of Forgiveness in the New South Africa.* New York: Random House.

MacFarlane, John. 2000. "Aristotle's Definition of *Anagnorisis." American Journal of Philology* 121:367–83.

Markell, Patchen. 2003. *Bound by Recognition.* Princeton: Princeton UP.

Mitchell, Jason, ed. 2005. *Insight Guides: South Africa*. New York: APA Publications.

Nancy, Jean-Luc. 2002. *The Restlessness of the Negative*. Trans. Jason Smith and Steven Miller. Minneapolis: U of Minnesota P.

Norval, Aletta. 1996. *Deconstructing Apartheid Discourse*. London: Verso.

Oliver, Kelly. 2001. *Witnessing: Beyond Recognition.* Minneapolis: U of Minnesota P.

Omar, Dullah. 1995. "Introduction." In *Truth and Reconciliation Commission*. Rondebosch: Justice in Transition on behalf of the Ministry of Justice.

Pippen, Robert. 1989. *Hegel's Idealism: The Satisfactions of Self-Consciousness*. Cambridge: Cambridge UP.

———. 2000. "What is the Question for which Hegel's Theory of Recognition is the Answer?" *European Journal of Philosophy* 8:155–72.

Ramose, Mogobe. 2002. "The Philosophy of Ubuntu and Ubuntu as a Philosophy." In *Philosophy From Africa,* 2nd ed., ed. P. H. Coetzee and A. P. J. Roux, 230–38. Oxford: Oxford UP.

Republic of South Africa. 1995. *Promotion of National Unity and Reconciliation Act* (No. 34 of 1995). Available at <http://www.doj.gov.za/trc/legal/act9534.htm>. Accessed 16 November 2006.

———. 1993. Constitution of the Republic of South Africa (Act 200 of 1993). Available at: <http://www.oefre.unibe.ch/law/icl/sf10000_.html>. Accessed 16 November 2006.

Ross, Fiona. 2003. *Bearing Witness: Women and the Truth and Reconciliation Commission in South Africa*. London: Pluto.

Rich, Paul. 1976. "Liberalism and Ethnicity in South African Politics, 1921–1948." *African Studies* 35:229–51.

Ricoeur, Paul. 2005. *The Course of Recognition*. Cambridge: Harvard UP.

Salazar, Philippe-Joseph. 2002. *An African Athens: Rhetoric and the Shaping of Democracy in South Africa*. London: Lawrence Erlbaum.

Schaap, Andrew. 2003. "Reconciliation through a Struggle for Recognition?" Centre for Applied Philosophy Working Paper #12.

Schreiter, Robert. 1992. *Reconciliation: Ministry and Mission in a Changing Social Order*. Maryknoll, MD: Orbis.

Shriver, Donald. 1995. *An Ethic for Enemies: Forgiveness in Politics*. Oxford: Oxford UP.

Shutte, Augustine. 2001. *Ubuntu: An Ethic for a New South Africa*. Pietermaritzburg: Cluster Publications.

Taylor, Charles. 1994. "The Politics of Recognition." In *Multiculturalism*, ed. Amy Gutmann, 25-74. Princeton: Princeton UP.

Taylor, Vincent. 1969. *Forgiveness and Reconciliation: A Study in New Testament Theology*. London: Macmillan.

Truth and Reconciliation Commission. 1998. *Truth and Reconciliation Commission of South Africa Report, Volumes 1–5*. Cape Town: Juta.

Tully, James. 2000. "Struggles over Recognition and Redistribution." *Constellations* 7:469–82.

Tutu, Desmond. 1999. *No Future without Forgiveness*. London: Rider.

Villa-Vicencio, Charles. 1997. "Telling One Another Stories: Toward a Theology of Reconciliation." In *The Reconciliation of Peoples: Challenge to the Churches*, ed. Greg Baum and Harold Wells, 30–42. Maryknoll, MD: Orbis.

Williams, Robert. 1992. *Recognition: Fichte and Hegel on the Other*. Albany: SUNY P.

Wiredu, Kwasi. 1997. "Democracy and Consensus in African Traditional Politics: A Plea for Non-party Polity." In *Postcolonial African Philosophy: A Critical Reader*, ed. Emmanuel Chukwudi Eze. London: Blackwell.

Wood, Allen. 1990. *Hegel's Ethical Thought*. Cambridge: Cambridge UP.

No Time for Mourning: The Rhetorical Production of the Melancholic Citizen-Subject in the War on Terror

Barbara Biesecker

At the same time that the Bush Administration's declaration of the so-called war on terror and intervention in Iraq exacerbated tensions between its long-standing allies as well as enemies on the international front, it miraculously delivered the American people back to itself. Suddenly a whole host of high-profile domestic conflicts on whose outcome the very viability of the nation was said heretofore to depend were neutralized as the administration, with the help of the mass media, launched what many on the left might call its "shock and awe" campaign on the cultural home front. Most notably, perhaps, immediately after the attacks Republicans and Democrats gathered together for a robust round of "God Bless America" on the steps of the Capitol. As Tim Russert reported on that evening's NBC special news hour, "an extraordinary scene here in Washington. Twenty-four hours ago rancor, partisanship, not tonight. National unity, indeed a new tone in Washington" ("Attack" 2001). Shortly thereafter, conservatives openly censured Jerry Fallwell and Pat Robertson—two leading spokesmen of the right-wing's cultural revolution of the 1990s—for attributing the tragedy to Americans' own hedonistic lifestyles, and for months to come prime time public service announcements (the "I am an American" campaign, for example) as well as morning and evening prime-time news programs preached ethnic and racial tolerance and inclusion. Even Tom Brokaw, who in the late 1990s had made a cottage industry out of pitting the humble and selfless collective sacrifices of the World War II generation against the parochialism and self-serving identity politics of the next, publicly performed a complete about-face.[1] For the first time since The Good War, *E Pluribus Unum* had begun to feel less like "an [impossible] ideal" and more like "a description of American life" (O'Leary 1999, 6).

At this point, an obvious question presents itself: was Americans' post-9/11 patriotism an ultimately fleeting reaction to the terrorist attacks, or were we party to a *bona fide* collective conversion of political emotion? On May 30, 2003, *The Dallas Morning News* concluded that our spirited identification with the nation was no flash-in-the-pan phenomenon and that, quite to the contrary, "we [were] witnessing a sea change in our society." Citing a poll of 1,200 college undergraduates conducted by Harvard's Institute of Politics, the reporter took the transmogrification of love of country into blind faith in the military to be a particularly significant sign. In striking contrast with "what the same age cohort said near 30 years ago when—according to a Harris poll—only 20 percent of 18–29-year-olds said they had great confidence in the military," 75 percent of today's young respondents "trust the military to 'do the right thing' either 'all of the time' or 'most of the time'" ("New Generation Gap"). Similarly, a June 2003 Gallup poll indicated that despite continued strong U.N. opposition to the U.S.-led invasion of Iraq, mounting U.S. casualties (even after "major combat operations [had] ended"), and a skyrocketing federal deficit, national patriotic sentiment remained robust, with "seventy percent [of those persons surveyed] saying they are extremely proud to be Americans" (Bowman and O'Keefe 2005, 1). Even in January 2005—when Gallup last repeated the question and months after the Abu Ghraib prison scandal had broken—61 percent of all persons polled said they were "extremely proud" to be Americans, 22 percent said they were "very proud," and only 4 percent said they were "only a little" or "not at all proud" (1).

In view of its obvious vitality, it may at first seem strange to think of post-9/11 patriotism as a kind of melancholy or, more precisely, as one of a melancholic rhetoric's primary effects.[2] Although that is precisely what I intend to argue over the course of the essay, it is crucial that I note from the start that mine is hardly the first attempt to take leave of the analyst's couch and take measure of melancholy's role in collective and public life. As early as the late sixties, for example, Alexander and Margarete Mitcherlich turned to Freud's "Mourning and Melancholia" in order to analyze "the widespread failure in postwar Germany to confront the nation's Nazi past." In their *The Inability to Mourn,* a book that provoked heated but productive debate in West Germany, working through melancholia is posited as the requisite step toward "inventing a society that remembers, rather than unconsciously repeats, a murderous and authoritarian past" (Forter 2005, 135).

But if, like the Mitcherlichs, other theorists writing in the 1970s and 1980s found in Freud not only a theory of collective loss at times of national crisis but also—and more important—the outlines of a theory of practice for its overcoming, by the early 1990s a theoretical reversal or inversion had begun to take place. Radical theorists of race, ethnicity, postcoloniality, sexuality, and gender began to reconceptualize melancholy or melancholic subjectivity not as a pathological state that is to be worked through, but as the sign of a political, indeed hegemonic, prohibition to be worked against. In other words, for scholars such as Jahan Ramazani, Philip Novak, Michael Moon, José Muñoz, and Homi Bhabha the injunction to pass from melancholia to mourning is to be read as normalizing and, thus, disempowering for those of us threatened by racism, Eurocentrism, sexism, and homophobia.[3] As Muñoz puts it, for blacks and queers ... melancholia [is] not a pathology or a self-absorbed mood that inhibits activism, [but] a mechanism that helps us (re)construct identity and take our dead to the various battles we must wage in their names"(1997, 355–56).

In *The Psychic Life of Power,* Judith Butler extends this thinking on melancholia as the material trace of domination and exclusion into a theory of gender subjectivation and, albeit more intimated than fully developed, resistance.[4] Taking as her point of departure Freud's 1923 revision of his earlier account of mourning in which all mourning is melancholic since objects or ideals can be "relinquished" only by being ambivalently internalized, she argues that the condition of possibility for conventional gender identities (or the heterosexual matrix) is a "refused" identification with or repudiation of homosexuality. Furthermore, not only gender identity but also subjectivity as such is melancholic from the start:

> To make of melancholia a simple "refusal" to grieve its losses conjures a subject who might already be something without its losses, that is, one who voluntarily extends and retracts his or her will. Yet the subject who might grieve is implicated in a loss of autonomy that is mandated by linguistic and social life; it can never produce itself autonomously. From the start, this ego is other than itself; what melancholia shows is that only by absorbing the other as oneself does one become something at all. The social terms which make survival possible, which interpellate social existence, never reflect the autonomy of the one who comes to recognize him- or herself in them and, thus, stands a chance "to be" within language. Indeed, by forfeiting the notion of autonomy survival becomes possible. ... To accept the autonomy of the ego is to forget that trace; and to accept that trace is to embark upon a process of mourning that can never be complete, for no final severance could take place without dissolving the ego. (1997, 195–96)

It is crucial to notice, however, that although, according to Butler, the subject or ego is always already the effect of a psychic loss or foreclosure, the social terms that "institute the linguistic life of the 'one' who speaks" do not thoroughly regulate it. Because, as Freud long ago noted, melancholic incorporation entails a tropological "dissimulation" and "turning" rather than a simple acceptance or internalization, Butler writes that "interpellation works by failing, that is, it institutes its subject as an agent precisely to the extent that it fails to determine such a subject exhaustively in time" (197).

It is in Slavoj Žižek's body of work that one arguably finds the most elaborate engagement with melancholy's role in contemporary social, political, and cultural life. In "Melancholy and the Act," wherein he tackles the matter head on, Zizek unreservedly berates self-identified leftist cultural and social theorists for having rehabilitated a wholly inadequate theory of melancholy—what he calls "the hegemonic intellectual trend"—that aids and abets rather than contests global capitalism and its devastating social, political, and cultural effects. According to these theorists, he writes,

> mourning is a kind of betrayal, the second killing of the (lost) object, while the melancholic subject remains faithful to the lost object, refusing to renounce his or her attachment to it. This story [has been] given a multitude of twists, from the queer one, which holds that homosexuals are those who retain fidelity to the lost or repressed identification with the same-sex libidinal object, to the post-colonial/ethnic one, which holds that when ethnic groups enter capitalist processes of modernization and are under the threat that their specific legacy will be swallowed up by the new global culture, they should not renounce their tradition through mourning, but retain the melancholic attachment to their roots. (2000, 658)

Contrary to what a reader might expect Žižek to argue were he or she not already familiar with his work, the Slovenian Lacanian does not pressure the "politically correct" left to give up its investment in melancholy as an explanatory frame. Instead, he insists that Butler, Bhabha, and the like take it to the Lacanian/Kantian end of the line. On Žižek's view, their accounts fail theoretically, politically and ethically because they are not melancholic enough. In short, where they worry loss, he theorizes lack. Žižek explains:

> In Kant's terms, the melancholic is guilty of committing a kind of paralogism of the pure capacity to desire, which resides in the confusion between *loss* and *lack*: insofar as the object-cause of desire is originally, in a constitutive way, lacking, melancholy interprets this lack as loss, as if the lacking object was once possessed and then lost. (659–60)

Hence, by obfuscating the distinction between structural lack and historical loss, Butler's queer and Bhabha's postcolonial theory are, according to Žižek, politically naive, nostalgic, and reactionary.

Žižek's definition in this essay of the melancholic's so-called lost object as "nothing but the positivization of a void or lack, a purely anamorphic entity that does not exist in itself" is, of course, his theory of subjectivation and ideology writ small: always already at the core of subjectivity lies a constitutive void, the self is therefore fundamentally compensatory and ultimately delusional, and ideology is the symbolic space of self-enunciation at once inaugurated and governed by lack and always already lacking—a melancholic economy's spectral and structural effect. Contrary to what others have proscribed, the way out of the ideological enclosure is not to confront what we experience as reality but, instead, "to traverse the phantasy" that shores it up so as to come face to shadowy face with the fundamental lack, split, or antagonism around which our putative reality has been structured. In the words of Richard Boothby, whom Žižek himself approving cites, the task is "to be more profoundly claimed by the phantasy than ever, in the sense of being brought into an ever more intimate relation with the real core of the phantasy that transcends imaging" (2002, 18).

In *Welcome to the Desert of the Real,* Žižek once again sets into motion the logic of "going through the fantasy"—"not its symbolic interpretation but the experience of the fact that the fantasy-object [or symptom], by its fascinating presence, is merely filling out a lack, a void in the Other" (1989, 133)—in order to pronounce not only a sweeping diagnosis of Americans', indeed the West's, cathected relation to the terrorist attacks on the Twin Towers and Pentagon but also of the ever more bloody Israeli-Palestinian ideological deadlock. Here, I quote him twice, at some length:

> Who is really alive today? What if we are "really alive" only if we commit ourselves with an excessive intensity which puts us beyond "mere life"? What if, when we focus on mere survival, even if it is qualified as "having a good time", what we ultimately lose is life itself? What if the . . . suicide bomber on the point of blowing him- or herself (and others) up is, in an emphatic sense, "more alive" than the American soldier engaged in a war in front of a computer screen against an enemy hundreds of miles away, or a New York yuppie jogging along the Hudson river in order to keep his body in shape? Or, in psychoanalytic terms, what if a hysteric is truly alive in his or her permanent excessive questioning of his or her existence, while an obsessional is the very model of choosing a "life in death"? That is to say, is not the ultimate aim of his or her compulsive rituals to prevent the "thing" from happening—this "thing" being the excess of life itself? (2002, 88–89)

And:

> The problem with Ariel Sharon is not that he is overreacting, but that he is not doing enough, that he is not addressing the real problem—far from being a ruthless military executioner, Sharon is the model of a leader pursuing a confused politics of disoriented oscillation. The excessive Israeli military is ultimately an expression of impotence. (2002, 128)

To allow the "thing" to happen and to recognize that Sharon, his henchmen, and their military machine, like the emperor, have no clothes: In these and numerous other instances, Žižek points out the way in which the Real as the limit-point of all subject-formation and eluding all ideological fabrication "returns as the same through diverse historicizations/symbolizations" (1989, 50).

I cautiously accept Žižek's theorization of subjectivation, indeed of hegemony, as an always already failed compensatory and ideological effect and, hence, as "melancholic" through and through. Doing so, however, raises a host of difficult questions for me, not the least of which is the following: If the contingent and interminable process of collective subjectivation is set into motion and kept on the move by the irreducible gap between symbolization and the Real (for Žižek, the "fixed" coordinates of all historicization), to what are we to attribute the modulation or particularization of its forms? On my view, the short answer to that question is rhetoric—herein understood as a technology of (re)subjectivation whose constitutive but conjunctural effects contribute to the consolidation and stabilization of particular epistemological and political regimes.[5] The much longer version of the answer comes in the pages to follow, pages that—as I hinted nearly at the start—tender a reading of post-9/11 patriotism as the material upshot of a carefully crafted and meticulously managed melancholic rhetoric whose distinct features are: one, the discursive transfiguration of a historical and political catastrophe into the harbinger of an epochal Act "to come" and, hence, the ubiquitous deployment of the future anterior; two, the "perfecting"—in the Burkean sense—of the aesthetics of disappearance that structured Americans' perception of Gulf War One into the aesthetics of dematerialization that continues to structure our relationship to the ongoing "war on terror"; and, three, a visual ecology of repetition. The specific aim and accomplishment of this melancholic rhetoric, I suggest, is the formation of a public "political will" that, with considerable irony, cedes the power of the citizenry to the remilitarized state for the sake of protecting what *will have been* lost: namely, the democratic way of life.

The Phantasmatic Politics of the "As If"

> The only paradises are those we have lost.
> —Marcel Proust

Let it be said in this case that hindsight is twenty-twenty or that political reason is cunning since, by design or default, what is inscribed in the speech President Bush delivered only nine days after the attacks on the World Trade Center and

Pentagon are the logic and topoi that would govern the Administration's discourse and justify its "war on terror" from that point forward.[6]

Like so many other special addresses to a joint session of Congress and the American people, this one takes as its first task specific instruction in interpreting the collective historical text. In light of the recent events, the President focuses on only the past nine days and reads in them a warning: "Our nation has been put on notice" (2001). It is from this utterance that all else will follow. We are told that 9/11 should not be read as an event that carries the trace of history since "all of this was brought upon us in a single day—and night fell on a different world, a world where freedom itself is under attack." Instead, the events of 9/11 must be deciphered as the sign, indeed omen, of an incomparable, Absolute loss that will have been ours were we to refuse to answer to it:

> In our grief and anger we have found our mission and our moment. Freedom and fear are at war. The advance of human freedom—the great achievement of our time, and the great hope of every time—now depends on us. Our nation—this generation—will lift a dark threat of violence from our people and our future. We will rally the world to this cause by our efforts, by our courage. We will not tire, we will not falter, and we will not fail.

Here already is the shadowy outline of a melancholic rhetoric whose aim is to persuade us to act *as if* a certain loss had occurred even though it has in fact *not yet* been lost. How so?

In *Stanzas: Word and Phantasm in Western Culture,* Giorgio Agamben presents a short meditation on melancholia as a tropological effect. Turning once again to Freud's account of the genetic process of mourning, Agamben astutely notes how, for Freud, melancholia poses a theoretical embarrassment that takes the form of an internal contradiction:

> Although mourning follows a loss that has really occurred, in melancholia not only is it unclear what object has been lost, it is uncertain that one can speak of a loss at all. "It must be admitted," Freud writes, with a certain discomfort, "that a loss has indeed occurred without it being known what has been lost." Shortly thereafter, in the attempt to gloss over the contradiction posed by a loss without a lost object, Freud speaks of an "unknown loss" or of an "object-loss that escapes consciousness." In fact, the examination of the mechanism of melancholia . . . shows that the withdrawal of libido is the original datum, beyond which investigation can go no further; if we wish to maintain the analogy with mourning, we ought to say that melancholia offers the paradox of an intention to mourn that precedes and anticipates the loss of the object. (1993, 20)

On this reading, melancholy may not be understood simply as either a reaction to a historical loss or the playing out of a structural lack, since the loss is the ghostly predication of the subject who intends to mourn, of the subject's "imaginative capacity to make an object appear *as if* lost" (20, emphasis added). Yet the logic here is even more complex since melancholy simulates not only the loss but also the lost object itself. What melancholy stages, in other words, is the loss of an impossible object, ideal, or relation that the subject has never had. Importantly enough, this doubled fabrication of loss produces a decisive rhetorical gain since "what could never be possessed because it had never perhaps existed may be appropriated insofar as it is lost" (20).

I would like to suggest that the ambivalent possession of an impossible ideal is precisely what Bush's deceptively simple speech conjures over its course: Positioned by the discourse in the wake of its Absolute loss, the citizenry is incited to imaginatively possess and passionately protect "a democratic way of life" that can hardly be claimed as already its own. That is to say, bathed in the notional afterglow of the catastrophe to come, indices of actually existing democracy's failings—from the culture and history wars of the late 1980s and early 1990s that gave the lie to freedom of expression and freedom of speech to low voter-turnout and the thoroughly bungled presidential election of 2000 that, according to more than one journalist, threatened to devolve into a *bona fide* "constitutional crisis"—return in this speech, miraculously transformed by way of the future anterior, as signs of its success. Indeed, by "covering its object with the funereal trappings of mourning" (Agamben 1993, 20), Bush's melancholic rhetoric conjures an image of civic life that Americans cannot not want to claim as having been our own:

> Americans are asking, why do they hate us? They hate what we see right here in this chamber—a democratically elected government.... They hate our freedoms—our freedom of religion, our freedom of speech, our freedom to vote and assemble and disagree with each other.... These terrorists kill not merely to end lives, but to disrupt and end a way of life. (2001)

By virtue of the alchemy that is rhetoric, a "democratic way of life" that had been an object not only of "contemplation" but of persistent criticism and even rebuke in the recent past reappears as the idealized object of the melancholic citizen-subject's amorous embrace.

But if, as I have argued thus far, one of the crucial uses to which the future anterior has been put is the formation of a political syntax that promotes the production of the melancholic citizen-subject, another is the delimitation of a new political horizon and corresponding political rationality to which such a citizen may be productively articulated. About both, this must first be said: It is the fundamentally aporetic character of the Absolute loss that gives shape to this political imaginary and matrix of popular reasoning which informs it. Only under the pressure of the tightly controlled hallucination of a loss that is *at once* certain and indeterminate, *both* what always already is and what will have been, does it seem reasonable to declare a state of emergency that is indefinitely extended—temporally and spatially. As the President put it in the September 20th address and repeated on numerous occasions:

> This war will not be like the war against Iraq a decade ago, with a decisive liberation of territory and a swift conclusion.... Americans should not expect one battle, but a lengthy campaign, unlike any other we have ever seen.... Americans are asking: How will we fight and win this war? We will direct every resource at our command—every means of diplomacy, every tool of intelligence, every instrument of law enforcement, every financial influence, and every necessary weapon of war—to the disruption and to the defeat of the global terror network.

A "crusade" without reserve: a boundless state of exception in which what comes to light and will function as reason is, as Hannah Arendt observed long ago, the principle according to which anything is possible.[7] In this context, this rhetorically reconfigured scene, extraordinary acts will begin to take place, not the least of which have been the dramatic rejuvenation of the national security state via the constitution of the Department of Homeland Security and the Patriot Act, an unprecedented federal deficit and, last but not least, a decisive shift in American foreign policy to what is now commonly referred to as the Bush Doctrine, remarkable for its audacious positioning of the concept of pre-emptive military action at its very center. As Bush described it at his now famous Commencement Address at Westpoint on June 1, 2002:

> In defending the peace, we face a threat with no precedent.... For much of the last century, America's defense relied on the Cold War doctrines of deterrence and containment. In some cases, those strategies still apply, but new threats also require new thinking. Deterrence, the promise of massive retaliation against nations, means nothing against shadowy terrorist networks with no nation or citizens to defend.... We cannot defend America and our friends by hoping for the best.... If we wait for threats to fully materialize, we will have waited too long.... The war on terror will not be won on the defensive. We must take the battle to the enemy, disrupt its plans, and confront the worst threats before they emerge.

Out of this state of emergency has emerged a new kind of State.[8] If that is not a post-9/11 melancholic rhetoric's most spectacular achievement, it surely will be its most enduring effect.[9]

The Aesthetics of Dematerialization

I don't believe that there is any perception.
—Jacques Derrida (1970)[10]

It hardly need be said that one speech a collective disposition or political imaginary does not even begin to make. Thus, having examined the President's address in some detail, I want now to look briefly at a larger constellation of discourses—or, more precisely, representative bits and pieces thereof—through which the melancholic citizen-subject approached sense. To be sure, like the President's own, all of these discourses—from Colin Powell's 2003 statement before the U.N. Security Council to the U.S. Department of Homeland Security web site; from the testimonies of Donald Rumsfeld and John Ashcroft before various commissions to the mass media's daily coverage of September 11th, its aftermath, and the "war on terror"—adopt the temporal logic of the phantasmatic politics of the "As if." But they also do a good deal more.

As I have noted elsewhere (2003), it is often said that the start of the first Persian Gulf War marked the end of one era and the beginning of another. According to then President George H. W. Bush, Operation Desert Storm radically transformed the national political imaginary by finally putting to rest the ghost of Vietnam. According to General Schwarzkopf, leader of the U.N. alliance, it signified a dramatic revolution in the telos of military engagement along the lines laid down in the Weinberger Doctrine: "We are [no longer] in the business of killing" (Gesterson 1991, 51). And according to Jeffrey Records, a military analyst, it set a wholly new and impossible standard by which all subsequent U.S. military interventions would be measured: "If pre-Desert Storm U.S. military planning was haunted by the disastrous legacy of Vietnam, post-Desert Storm planning will be plagued by the specter of falling short of the splendid and relatively painless performance of U.S. forces in the Persian Gulf in 1991" (Dauber 2001, 158).

Notably, a host of cultural theorists and critics agreed that Gulf War One ushered in a new era. However, not persuaded that the operation was as "bloodless" as the administration and media would have the public believe, they argued that Operation Desert Storm delivered not a new kind of warfare but a new aesthetics of war whose strategically selected images and carefully crafted discourse together worked to literally "de-humanize" the cost of armed conflict. In a war between the United States, its allies, and Iraq that Anthony Giddens described as "the most heavily mediated, reflexively organized war in human history" (Shaw and Carr-Hill 1991, 2), the suffering and loss of life that is the inevitable price of combat was almost altogether absent. For the general public whose perception of the war was given shape by what did and did not appear on their television screens, these scholars rightly insisted, the first Gulf War was a war without bodies—a technological exercise executed not by men but by machines whose "surgical" "smart bombs" took out "units," not enemy soldiers, a "Nintendo War" during which, as Paul Virilio put it, "the aesthetics of disappearance" (1989, 11) carried the day.

To be sure, like those of the Gulf War that came before it, visual and verbal representations of the war on terror continued to entail the deliberate "absenting" of U.S. military personnel, enemy soldiers, and civilian casualties alike.[11] However, what was in one war an aesthetics of disappearance was transformed in the war on terror into an aesthetics of dematerialization—a stylization of war through which the specular was rendered spectral, uncertain, and indeterminate. If the thorough erasure of some bodies set representations and perceptions of the first Gulf War apart from its predecessors, I want to suggest that the signature stylistic gesture of the war on terror was to have put other bodies and materialities—from our adversaries to our infrastructure—*under erasure*. In other words, in the context of the new war on terror it is not only the case that some bodies are absent; it is also the case that other bodies and materialities are always *never simply present—in themselves and for us*.

Never simply present or, otherwise put, not-identical-to-themselves: from bin Laden's voice doubles to Saddam Hussain's body doubles, from Al Qaeda operatives who passed as commercial airline pilots to elite guards who "shed their uniforms and melt[ed] into the civilian population" (Bush 2004, "Iraq"), indeterminacies are what circulate here. Unlike all other wars in which the United States has been engaged, this time our "enemies do not mass armies on borders, or navies on high seas" but instead "blend in with the civilian population. They emerge to strike, and then they retreat back into the shadows" (Bush 2005, "Military Families"). Neither Iraq's "biological weapons factories on wheels and on rails" that "are designed to evade detection by inspectors" (Powell 2003) nor our own postal service that doubled in daylight as a delivery system for a deadly toxin is unambiguously itself. As then Secretary of Defense Donald Rumsfeld summarily explained to the members of the National Commission on Terrorist Attacks Upon the United States in a prepared statement that echoed the words delivered by other members of the Bush Administration on countless other occasions,

> This much is certain: on September 11th, our world changed—and while it may be tempting to think that once this crisis has passed and our nation has healed, things can go back to the way they were—we cannot go back.... The nature of the war we are fighting today, and the adversary we face, is unlike anything our nation has faced before.... Today, we face adversaries who hide in plain sight. (2004)

To this disruption of conventional specularity, figured most dramatically perhaps as the enemy who sees but cannot be seen, may be attributed the disorienting and anxiety-inducing effects of a post-9/11 melancholic rhetoric.

With this widely disseminated melancholic rhetoric whose central conceit helped to promote what Jacques Derrida (1994) elsewhere and for very different purposes called a state of "disjointure" or of being collectively put off center comes a hermeneutics of unusually intense and deep suspicion. Because nothing is simple or simply itself, the Bush Administration warns Americans—or, rather, all citizens of the world who stand against terrorism—that they can no longer afford to read at the level of the sign. Indeed, as Attorney General John Ashcroft insisted as recently as June 8, 2004, "This nation learned on the morning of September 11, 2001 [that] blue skies and quiet mornings should not be mistaken for peace." The potentially lethal exigencies of the "present" demand that we abandon familiar or, more precisely, naive modes of perception and understanding.[12] Our lives and our way of life depend upon our refusing the presumption that, in common parlance, "what one sees is what one gets." Again, quoting Rumsfeld's prepared testimony:

> We have entered a new security environment, arguably the most dangerous the world has known. And if we are to continue to live as free people, we cannot go back to thinking as we did on September 10th. For if we do—if we look at the problems of the 21st century through a 20th century prism—we will come to wrong conclusions and fail the American people. (2004)

Quite simply, the war on terror is rooted in learning how to read otherwise.

Not incidentally, on February 5, 2003, Secretary of State Colin Powell presented a commanding lesson in reading this dangerous new world in a new way. Indeed if, as ABC news anchorman Peter Jennings (2003) correctly noted that day, Powell's primary political task was "convincing a skeptical world ... that force [against Iraq] may be necessary," I suggest that his singular rhetorical objective was positioning audiences—not the least of whom, given the administration's unilateralist intentions, were viewers at home—attitudinally to accept the Bush Administration's hermeneutics of suspicion. Thus I want to challenge two popular explanations of the speech's overwhelming success: on the one hand, that the influence of the State's logos is best understood as an effect of Powell's ethos[13]; on the other hand, that the force of the address was a consequence of Powell's having cast his appeal in Bush's by then familiar—and, according to some, all the more edifying for their oversimplification—terms of "sacred duties and diabolical enemies."[14] I do not doubt that Colin Powell's credibility and charisma, as well as George Bush's "rhetoric of vilification" (Ivie [year], 162) were at play here. However, having said that much, I also submit that the power of the performance derived overwhelmingly from Powell's having pressed a good number of those seventy-six minutes of speech into the service of inciting viewers to belief in the administration's cryptology of terror by training them to doubt radically *some* experts' as well as their own perceptual experience.

Nearly from the start Powell's speech poses the possibility of accurate perception as an analytics of deception: "This Council placed the burden on Iraq to comply and disarm, and not on the inspectors to find that which Iraq has gone out of its way to conceal for so long. Inspectors are inspectors; *they are not detectives*" (2003, emphasis added). In one short declarative sentence and between two terms—inspecting and detecting—a new epistemological field that "allow[s] for the production of what counts for knowledge … and accord[s] salience to particular categories, divisions, classifications, relations and identities" (Rose 1999, 29) is opened up. Although I will say more below about how the institution of this space will function as ground for a variety of specific public programs that not only articulated melancholic citizen-subjects to the war on terror but positioned them as a certain kind of participant on the home front, suffice it to note at this point that the static satellite or surveillance photograph has a particular value here: to function rhetorically as visual "hard" evidence of something that is never simply present. Indeed, after Powell airs, translates, and analyzes two "intercepted telephone conversations," both of which, in offering audio "evidence" of Saddam's "policy of evasion and deception," will double as verbal anchors for the visuals to follow,[15] he prefaces the presentation of the salutary images in the following way:

> We also have satellite photos that indicate that banned materials have recently been moved from a number of Iraqi weapons of mass destruction facilities.
>
> Let me say a word about satellite images before I show a couple. The photos I am about to show you are sometimes hard for the average person to interpret, hard for me. The painstaking work of photo analysis takes experts with years and years of experience, poring for hours and hours over light tables. But as I show you these images, I will try to capture and explain what they mean, what they indicate, to our imagery specialists. (2003)

At this point the Secretary stages a series of (sometimes surprisingly attenuated) exercises in visual decipherment that—it is crucial to note—do not render the field's signs more transparent to the average observer but, instead, show them to be irreducibly opaque to the naked, unsuspecting, uninformed, and untrained eye. In the words of the Secretary himself, "Let's look at one":

> This one is about a weapons munition facility, a facility that holds ammunition at a place called Taji. This is one of about 65 such facilities in Iraq. We know that

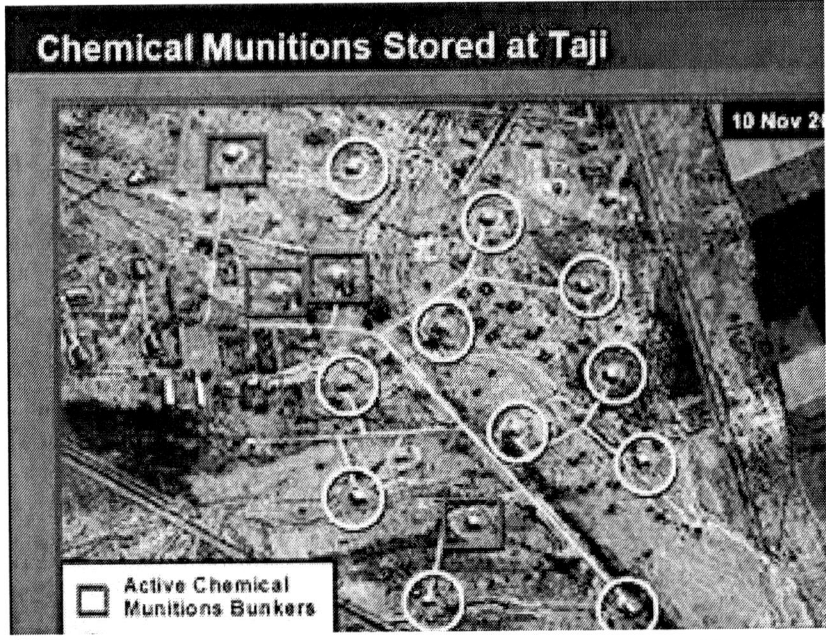

Figure 1. "Satellite Image One: Powell Presentation before the UN"

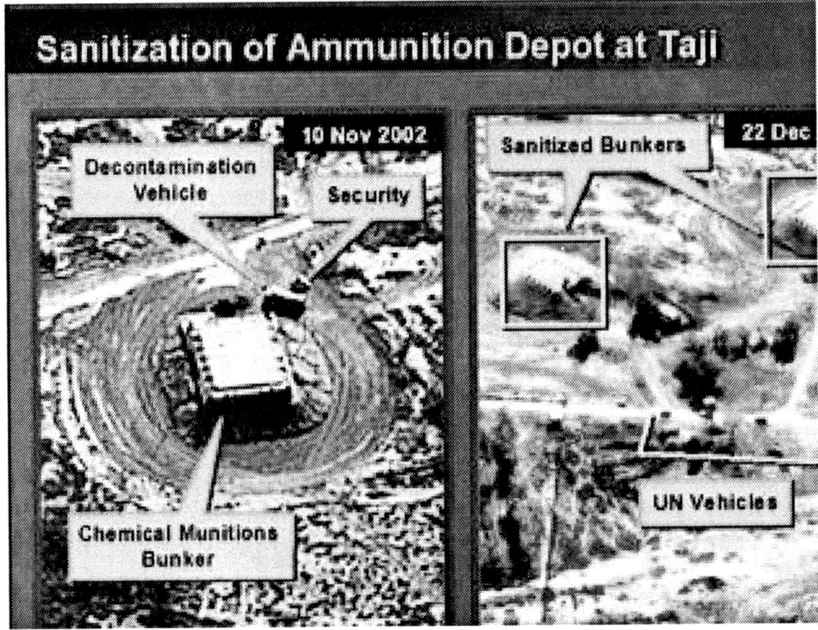

Figure 2. "Satellite Image Two: Powell Presentation before the UN"

> this one has housed chemical munitions. In fact, this is where the Iraqis recently came up with the additional four chemical weapons shells.
>
> How do I know that? How can I say that? Let me give you a closer look.
>
> Here you see 15 munitions bunkers in yellow and red outlines. The four that are in red squares represent active chemical munitions bunkers.
>
> Look at the image on the left. On the left is a close-up of one of the four chemical bunkers. The two arrows indicate the presence of sure signs that the bunkers are storing chemical munitions. The arrow at the top that says "security" points to a facility that is a signature item for this kind of bunker. Inside that facility are special guards and special equipment to monitor any leakage that might come out of the bunker. The truck you also see is a signature item. It's a decontamination vehicle in case something goes wrong. This is characteristic of those four bunkers. . . .
>
> Now look at the picture on the right. You are now looking at two of those sanitized bunkers. The signature vehicles are gone, the tents are gone. It's been cleaned up. And it was done on the 22nd of December as the U.N. inspection team is arriving, and you can see the inspection vehicles arriving in the lower portion of the picture on the right.
>
> The bunkers are clean when the inspectors get there. They found nothing.

Obviously, for the layperson visual clarity has not been restored. Without Powell's verbal cues, supplied by the "imagery specialists," one "look" offers no more illumination than any other; indeed, without our granting the specialists the benefit of their expertise things, as Kenneth Burke would put it, may be little more than the signs of words (1966). But as noted above, this exercise in seeing never promised its audience unmediated perceptual certainty. So what has been demonstrated here? What did this visual exercise as well as those that followed it accomplish rhetorically? Not only do they experientially make the case that *we* can never be certain of what we see. Even more, we are moved by exposure to our own blindness to believe that even—or especially—in circumstances in which we see nothing, something is likely taking place on the other side of a sign that *we* are incapable of reading on our own. Again, the Secretary:

> We know that Iraq has embedded key portions of its illicit chemical weapons infrastructure within its legitimate civilian industry. To all outward appearances, even to experts, the infrastructure looks like an ordinary civilian operation. Illicit and legitimate production can go on simultaneously or on a dime. This dual-use infrastructure can turn from clandestine to commercial and then back again.
>
> These inspections would be unlikely, any inspections at such facilities, would be unlikely to turn up anything prohibited, especially if there is any warning that the inspections are coming. Call it ingenious or evil genius, but the Iraqis deliberately designed their chemical weapons programs to be inspected. It is infrastructure with a built-in alibi.[16]

Of course, both before and after Powell delivered his speech, public culture had been saturated with the administration's hermeneutics of suspicion—from media coverage of the war on terror to the initiation of a host of national, state, and local programs that not only enacted its logic but, even more, induced citizens to internalize and work on its behalf. An example of the former: In August 2004, *Time* printed one of many "Special Reports" on the war on terror, this one targeting "Al-Qaeda in America." Prefaced by Stephen Ferry's two-page photographic image in which a casually clad lone young white woman, newborn in arms, looks away from a scene in which a loosely defined group of unsuspecting pedestrians take in a bit of ABC news beneath the network's larger than life illuminated news ticker on which appears "TERROR ALERT ELEVATED THIS WEEK," is "an exclusive look at what investigators have discovered about al-Qaeda's plans for its next big attack." In an article that reads like a piece of riveting detective fiction whose heroes for the most part are unidentified "intelligence and security officials," *Time* introduces readers to villains, like James Ujaama, "born James Earnest Thompson, [a] Seattle native indicted for plotting to establish a jihadi training camp in Bly, Ore[gon]"; Ali S.K. Al-Marri, "the Qatari student . . . arrested at his home in Peoria in December 2001 on suspicion of being a sleeper agent"; and Nuradin Abdi, "the Somali native . . . charged with conspiring to strike an unnamed Columbus-area mall" (Powell 2004, "Target," 34). From this report, like so many others, the obvious message readers are encouraged to take away is that an enemy as deceptive as it is deadly has infiltrated the homeland, indeed the heartland; nothing and no one anywhere is safe or above suspicion.[17]

As already noted, the administration's injunction to suspicion also materialized as a series of technologies of governance that incited citizens to "see" as/for the State. Perhaps the most innocuous instantiation has been the Department of Homeland Security's "Advisory System" that, at all but the lowest level "threat condition," not only warns the citizenry to various kinds of danger but also instructs individuals to "be alert to suspicious activity and report it to proper authorities" (Department of Homeland Security 2003).[18] The most notorious of these technologies, "Operation TIPS" (Terrorism Information and Prevention System), as well as the seemingly less invasive "Neighborhood Watch Programs," make reporting something that citizens see (but about which they are incapable of making sense) into a civic responsibility: Operation TIPS, the official website announced, "will be a national system for reporting suspicious, and potentially terrorist-related activity. The program will involve millions of American workers who, in the daily course of their work, are in a unique position to see potentially unusual or suspicious activity in public places" (2002).

About the Neighborhood Watch Programs, the Federal Emergency Management Agency had this to say:

> In the aftermath of September 11, 2001, the need for strengthening and securing our communities has become even more critical. President Bush has announced that, with the help of the National Sheriffs' Association, the Neighborhood Watch Program will be taking on a new significance. Community residents will be provided with information which will enable them to recognize signs of potential terrorist activity, and to know how to report that activity, making these residents a critical element in the detection, prevention and disruption of terrorism (2002).[19]

Overall, then, the key point is this: to an aesthetics of dematerialization and hermeneutics of suspicion has been articulated a melancholic citizen-subject who not only cedes all authority to the remilitarized state but also is induced to function on its behalf.

An Ecology of Repetition

> I want to be a machine.
> —Andy Warhol[20]

What now circulates among cultural theorists and critics as the conventional wisdom about the impact of the deluge of visual representations of 9/11 on the collective imaginary bears repeating and, I want to argue, rethinking. Many have noted that from the time the two commercial airliners plowed into the skyscrapers and for days, weeks, indeed months and years on end, people were besieged by stunningly similar—if not identical—moving and still images of the burning and collapsing Twin Towers. Analyses that sometimes more and sometimes less explicitly take their cues from a certain Freud understand people's repeated encounter with the attack—from the endless loop of reruns to still photos displayed in the print press's daily and bimonthly issues, special detachable photographic supplements, mid-week newsmagazine photographic editions, and "anniversary" pictorial spreads—as having put the nation on the road to recovery.[21] For example, in an essay that in many respects is exemplary and that aims to take measure of photographic journalism's therapeutic effect by rightly beginning on the obvious but no less fundamental point that the industry's obsessive use of these images had nothing to do with "newsworthiness" shortly after the attack, Barbie Zelizer makes a case for the curative capacity of photographic journalism: "Photography is well-suited to take individuals and collectives on the journey to a post-traumatic space.... They help dislodge people from the initial shock of trauma and coax them into a post-traumatic space, offering a vehicle by which they can see and continue to see until the shock and trauma associated with disbelieving can be worked through" (2002, 49). To be sure, this is one of the ways in which repetition can be understood to operate. Over the course of a series of visual encounters—a process that may justly be called mourning—the traumatic event or loss we have come to call "9/11" is progressively integrated into a psychic economy or symbolic order; the point of its integration marks the moment the subject is freed again to act, this time, Zelizer notes, in retaliation against a terrorist act that finds expression as public support for a war.[22]

With Zelizer and others I want to insist on the political significance of these repetitions, albeit with a difference. Guided by the threads of my analysis of this complex post-9/11 melancholic rhetoric thus far and, therefore, recalling the peculiar logic and combined effects of the phantasmatic politics of the "As if," the aesthetics of dematerialization, and its accompanying hermeneutics of suspicion, I want to insist that our repeated encounters with 9/11 were not restorative in the usual way. Instead of slowly inducing our release from the grip of the "lost" object, thereby positioning us in a masterful relation to the traumatic event, they helped to promote a collective and politically paralyzing fixation on the manufactured object—our democratic way of life—in melancholy. In other words, what the endless circulation of images of the attack on the Towers helped to ensure was that there would be no time for mourning.

Here I want to be clear that I am not arguing that the media, wittingly or not, effectively drained the collectivity of agency through the incessant circulation of visual representations of the lost object or the open wound.[23] To the contrary, from the start I have been arguing against the theory of representation (and not only of the collective psyche) that would allow this conclusion to be drawn and, thus, the crucial point to be missed completely: namely, that rhetorics are referential in the simplest sense, that is, that they are necessarily attached to referents or so-called real things in the world. Here, Derrida:

> We are talking about a trauma, and thus an event, whose temporarily proceeds neither from the now that is present nor from the present that is past but from an im-presentable to come (*á venir*). . . . There is traumatism with no possible work of mourning when the evil comes from the possibility to come of the worst, from the repetition to come—though worse. Traumatism is produced by the *future,* by the *to come,* by the threat of the worst *to come* (Habermas, Derrida, and Borradori 2003, 97).

In the thick context of, and having been explicitly articulated to, a widely disseminated post-9/11 melancholic rhetoric, images of the attacks of September repeatedly offered up by media do not re-present a trauma that has already taken (its) place but, instead, are persistent reminders of the Absolute catastrophe that will have been were we to refuse the "fitting response" in advance. Again, then, the paradoxical temporality and peculiar pull of a post-9/11 melancholic rhetoric: its "exigency" returns from the future.

* * *

Over the course of this essay I have tracked the way in which political and patriotic subjectivity has been reconfigured in the wake of 9/11. More specifically, I have argued that our new mode and heightened degree of post-9/11 national allegiance was and, in no small measure, continues to be the very real but nonetheless phantasmagorical effect of a widely disseminated melancholic rhetoric that incites the citizenry to cede its agency to the remilitarized state on behalf of a democratic way of life that *will have been* lost were we to refuse "to do everything in our power to prevent that day from coming" (Bush, "Assembly," 2002). Ultimately, the genius of this melancholic rhetoric is, of course, that a simple necessity seems necessarily, even naturally, to follow from it: a clarion call to preemptive arms.

Even if my analysis of this determined, determining, and dangerous rhetoric is on the mark, it may strike those who aspire to intervene in the political arena as coming too late. Indeed, although we may wish otherwise (and the numbers seem to be going up with each passing day), it is not possible to turn back the hands of time, intercept that clarion call, and, moved by a passion for the impossible, respond otherwise than by war to the terrorist attacks. An occasion, they might say, if ever there was one, for melancholic regret. So to what end, then, all this use of philosophy and theory for the study of rhetoric? My television is on in the background and tuned to the 24-hour news channel. As I hear vague rumblings about Iran's gearing up to manufacture nuclear weapons, I recall a passage from another piece of journalistic writing whose strange and slightly violent syntax reminds us that what is to come may be crafted in(to) a different tense:

> Neither monopoloy nor dispersion, therefore. This is, of course, an aporia, and we must not hide it from ourselves.... When the path is clear and given, when a certain knowledge opens up the way in advance, the decision is already made, it might as well be said that there is none to make: irresponsibly, and in good conscience, one

> simply applies or implements a program. Perhaps, and this would be the objection, one never escapes the program. In that case, one must acknowledge this and stop talking with authority about moral or political responsibility. The condition of possibility of this thing called responsibility is a certain *experience and experiment of the possibility of the impossible; the testing of the aporia* from which one may invent the only *possible invention, the impossible invention.* (Derrida 1992, 41)

Let us begin, again, to think what's next.

University of Iowa
Department of Communication Studies

Notes

1. For a detailed analysis of Brokaw's rhetoric, see Biesecker (2002).

2. This sentence is a near transcription of the sentence that opens Judith Butler's "Melancholy Gender/Refused Identification," the fifth chapter of *The Psychic Life of Power* (1997). My reasons for reiterating the sentence with a difference will be made clear below.

3. For a competing and compelling analysis of the relation between melancholy and political activism, see Crimp (1989).

4. "Subjectivation" is Butler's translation of the French *assujetissement* (1997, 11).

5. This definition of rhetoric is my attempt to step up to the crucial theoretical and critical challenge Butler poses and seeks to address in *Psychic Life of Power*: "Whether by interpellation, in Althusser's sense, or by discursive productivity, in Foucault's, the subject is initiated through a primary submission to power. Although Foucault identifies the ambivalence in this formulation, he does not elaborate on the specific mechanisms of how the subject is formed in submission. Not only does the entire domain of the psyche remain largely unremarked in his theory, but power in this double valence of subordinating and producing remains unexplored. Thus, if submission is a condition of subjection, it makes sense to ask: What is the psychic form that power takes? Such a project requires thinking the theory of power together with a theory of the psyche, a task that has been eschewed by writers in both Foucaultian and psychoanalytic orthodoxies" (1997, 2–3).

6. Bush's rhetoric has been read in very different ways by rhetorical critics. John Murphy's neo-Aristotelian analysis (astutely tethered to Bourdieu's conceptualization of social or cultural capital) of the President's polarizing rhetoric of "praise and blame" argues that its "Manichaen frame" "creat[ed] a kind of hermetically sealed system in which the world is as it is, people are as they are, and real Americans act accordingly" (2003, 626); D. M. Bostdorff argues on behalf of attributing the success of Bush's rhetoric to his and his speech writers' "reanimation of the appeals and forms of covenant renewal rhetoric" (2003, 298); and Joshua Gunn's psychoanalytically themed reading contends that Bush's "spiritually-themed speeches cast the President as a healing exorcist" and his "presidential speech craft" as part and parcel of a national "cleansing ritual" (2004, 4).

7. This analysis of the current state of exception in the United States is informed by Giorgio Agamben's theoretical elaboration of states of exception in *Means without End: Notes on Politics* and *Homo Sacer: Sovereign Power and Bare Life* (1998).

8. It is important to note the administration's unabashed attempt to "normalize" the current "state of emergency" in Section 103 of the Domestic Security Enhancement Act of 2003 (or Patriot Act II): "Under 50 U.S.C. §§ 1911, 1829 & 1844, the Attorney General may authorize, without the prior approval of the FISA Court, electronic surveillance, physical searches, or the use of pen registers for a period of 15 days following a congressional declaration of war. This wartime exception is unnecessarily narrow; it may be invoked only when Congress formally has declared war, a rare event in the nation's history and something that has not occurred in more than sixty years. This provision would expand FISA's wartime exception by allowing the wartime exception to be invoked after Congress authorizes the use of military force, or after the United States has suffered an attack creating a national emergency."

Furthermore, the resonances between this drafted legislation and Article 48 of the Weimar constitution are stunning: "The president of the Reich may, in the case of a grave disturbance or threat to public security and order, make the decisions necessary to reestablish public security, if necessary with the aid of the armed forces. To this end he may provisionally suspend the fundamental rights in articles [concerning personal liberty, the freedom of expression and assembly, and the inviolability of the home and of postal and telephone privacy]" (quoted in Agamben 1998, 167–68).

9. As is boasted on the U.S. Department of Homeland Security's website, this will have been the most massive reorganization (and consolidation) of the state (apparatus) "since 1947, when Harry S. Truman merged the various branches of the U.S. Armed Forces into the Department of Defense to better coordinate the nation's defense against military threats." See http://www.dhs.gov.

10. "Discussion," *The Structuralist Controversy* (1970, 272).

11. The Sinclair Broadcast Group's refusal to air a special 40-minute episode of "Nightline" during which the names of the U.S. war dead were read by Ted Koppel as their photographs appeared on the screen clearly demonstrates the general adherence by the media to the aesthetics of disappearance.

12. I put the "present" in scare quotes here in order to mark it as not simply the present or present perfect but a future anterior.

13. See, for example, Woodward (2004).

14. See Ivie (2005), especially chapter 5, "Idiom of Democracy," 148–87.

15. On the rhetoric of anchoring, see Roland Barthes' "The Rhetoric of the Image" 1977.

16. Only at this point is it possible to appreciate fully how "Saddam Hussein" functions rhetorically in this speech: not as the sure sign or singular embodiment of evil, as most critics would have it but, instead, as a Master or empty signifier that does not add any new positive content or material proof to the scene, but a quilting point that makes the scene make sense none the less. It is important (for my larger argument and theoretical project—see above) to underscore the irreducibly contextual character of the master signifier. Its rhetorical force is a conjunctural effect. At this point Saddam Hussein functions as the master signifier—the evil genius or mastermind—that makes it all make sense. Note that by the time of his capture (visual representations thereof) the point de caption has shifted and Saddam Hussein is transmogrified into what the Lacanian would call the *objet petit a* or little piece of shit. Such rhetorical transmogrifications are requisite to the continuation of the war and the indefinite extension of the State of Emergency.

17. One may even be sleeping with the enemy unawares. As reported in the *National Enquirer's* "I was a Terrorist's Lover": "A brilliant female med student lived intimately with one of the hijackers, but never knew she'd given her heart to a monster until after the terror attacks on America.... Turkish-born 'Fatima,' 26, was the sweet-heart of Ziad Jarrahi.... She says her 'kind and gentle' lover changed for the worse over the months she knew him... 'She said he liked to drink vodka, champagne, and wine,' a friend told the *Enquirer*.... 'But then last August the man Fatima fell in love with changed from Dr. Jekyll to Mr. Hyde'" (2001, 6).

18. As far as I am able to tell, since the attacks in 2001 the country has never been put at "green" alert, the only level at which we are advised to let our guard down.

19. For a very different and, on my view, overly generalized analysis of these programs, see Žižek (2004, 55–58).

20. Cited in Foster (1996, 130). Not incidentally, Warhol's words were a response to "Death in America," a 1963 art exhibit in Paris.

21. It is important to point out here that in a footnote Zelizer rightly levels the distinction between (and thus effects of) the still and moving images in *this particular case*, which is to say, representations of the attacks on the Twin Towers: "These moving images on loops repeat themselves so often that they come to have the quality of photography. They also appear in the same spaces as photographs, as in the online version of *The New York Times* or CD-ROM documentary compilations. Thus, while the temporal quality of still images and the repetition of moving images differs, the ordering of still images and repetition of moving images make them more alike" (2002, 50). The ensuing objections to the conclusions Zelizer draws with respect to the therapeutic power of the representations of 9/11 are intended to encourage the kind meticulous contextualization engaged at this point but abandoned when it comes to her treating the "Holocaust aesthetic" as a "template."

22. On the "minimalism" of the name, 9/11, and its significance or signification, see Jacques Derrida in Habermas, Derrida, and Borradori (2003).

23. Most critics read ground zero in this way: namely, as the nation's open wound. For a particularly fine example see Sturken (2002). Contrary to Sturken and others, I am arguing that the key is

to remind ourselves persistently that in the terms set by this melancholic rhetoric, the "event" has yet to take place.

Works Cited

Agamben, Giorgio. *Homo Sacer: Sovereign Power and Bare Life*. Stanford: Stanford UP, 1998.
———. *Means without End: Notes on Politics, Theory out of Bounds*, vol. 20. Minneapolis: University of Minnesota Press, 2000.
———. *Stanzas: Word and Phantasm in Western Culture, Theory and History of Literature*, vol. 69. Minneapolis: University of Minnesota Press, 1993.
Ashcroft, John. "The Department of Justice's Efforts to Combat Terrorism: Prepared Testimony of Attorney General John Ashcroft to Senate Judiciary Committee." http://www.usdoj.gov/ag/testimony/2004/060804agsenatejudiciarycommittee.htm (2004).
Barthes, Roland. "The Rhetoric of the Image." In *Image-Music-Text*. New York: Noonday, 1977. 32-37.
Biesecker, Barbara. "Remembering World War II: The Rhetoric and Politics of National Commemoration at the Turn of the 21st Century." *Quarterly Journal of Speech* 4 (2002): 393–409.
———. "Technologies of Truth and National Trauma." In *Proceedings of the Fifth Conference of the International Society for the Study of Argumentation*, ed. J. Anthony Blair Frans H. van Eemeren, Charles A Willard, and A. Francisca Snoeck Henkeman, 111–14. Amsterdam: Sic Sat, 2003.
Bostdorff, D. M. "George W. Bush's Post-September 11 Rhetoric of Covenant Renewal: Upholding the Faith of the Greatest Generation." *Quarterly Journal of Speech* 89, no. 4 (2003): 293–319.
Bowman, Karlyn, and Bryan O'Keefe. "Polls on Patriotism and Military Service." In AEI Studies in Public Opinion. http://www.aei.org/publications/pubID.22819/pub_detail.asp. 2005.
Burke, Kenneth. "What Are the Signs of What? (A Theory of 'Entitlement')." In *Language as Symbolic Action; Essays on Life, Literature, and Method*, 359–79. Berkeley and Los Angeles: U of California P, 1966.
Bush, George W. "Address to a Joint Session of Congress and the American People." http://www.whitehouse.gov/news/releases/2001/09. 2001.
———. "President Bush Delivers Remarks at Westpoint." CNN Live Event. Lexis-Nexis. June 1, 2002.
———. "President Addresses Military Families, Discusses War on Terror." http://www.whitehouse.gov. 2005.
———. "President's Remarks at the United Nations General Assembly." http://www.whitehouse.gov. 2002.
———. "Remarks by the President on Iraq and the War on Terror." http://www.whitehouse.gov. (2004).
Butler, Judith. *The Psychic Life of Power: Theories in Subjection*. Stanford: Stanford UP, 1997.
Crimp, Douglas. "Mourning and Militancy." *October* 51 (1989): 3–18.
Dauber, Cori. "The Shot Seen 'Round the World: The Impact of the Images of Mogadishu on American Military Operations." *Rhetoric and Public Affairs* 4, no. 4 (2001): 653–87.
Department of Homeland Security Homepage. http://www.whitehouse.gov/infocus/homeland/. (accessed July 7, 2003, 2003).
Derrida, Jacques. "Discussion." In *The Structuralist Controversy: The Languages of Criticism and the Sciences of Man*, Richard Macksey and Eugenio Donato, ed. Baltimore: Johns Hopkins UP, 1970, 265–72.
———. *Specters of Marx: The State of the Debt, the Work of Mourning, and the New International*. New York: Routledge, 1994, 265–72.
Derrida, Jacques. *The Other Heading: Reflections on Today's Europe, Studies in Continental Thought*. Bloomington: Indiana UP, 1992.
"Domestic Security Enhancement Act of 2003." http://www.pbs.org/now/politics/patriot2-hi.pdf. 2003.
Forter, Jeff. "Against Melancholia: Contemporary Mourning Theory, Fitzgerald's *The Great Gatsby*, and the Politics of Unfinished Grief." *differences* 14, no. 2 (2005): 134–70.

Foster, Hal. *The Return of the Real: The Avant-Garde at the End of the Century*. Cambridge, MA: MIT P, 1996.

Gilbert, Paul. *New Terror, New Wars*. Washington, D.C.: Georgetown UP, 2003.

Gunn, Joshua. "The Rhetoric of Exorcism: George W. Bush and the Return of Political Demonology." *Western Journal of Communication* 68, no. 1 (2004): 1–23.

Gusterson, Hugh. "Nuclear War, the Gulf War, and the Disappearing Body." *Journal of Urban and Cultural Studies* 2, no. 1 (1991): 41–55.

Habermas, Jürgen, Jacques Derrida, and Giovanna Borradori. *Philosophy in a Time of Terror: Dialogues with Jürgen Habermas and Jacques Derrida*. Chicago: U of Chicago P, 2003.

"I Was a Terrorist's Lover." *National Enquirer*, October 16, 2001, 6.

Ivie, Robert L. *Democracy and America's War on Terror, Rhetoric, Culture, and Social Critique*. Tuscaloosa: U of Alabama P, 2005.

Jennings, Peter. "ABC News Special Report." American Broadcasting Companies, Inc., February 5, 2003.

Muñoz, José. "Photographies of Mourning: Melancholia and Ambivalence in Van Der Zee, Mapplethorpe, and *Looking for Langston*." In *Race and the Subject of Masculinities*, ed. Harry and Michael Uebel Stecopoulos, 337–58. Durham: Duke UP, 1997.

Murphy, John. "'Our Mission and Our Moment': George W. Bush and September 11th." *Rhetoric and Public Affairs* 6, no. 4 (2003): 607–32.

"NBC News Special Report: Attack on America." National Broadcasing Corporation, September 11, 2001.

"Neighborhood Watch Programs." http://www.citizencorpts.gov/watch.html. Accessed July 19, 2002.

"New Generation Gap: Youths' Shift to Patriotism Is Refreshing." *The Dallas Morning News*, May 30, 2003. Lexis-Nexis, June 5, 2003.

O'Leary, Cecilia Elizabeth. *To Die For: The Paradox of American Patriotism*. Princeton: Princeton UP, 1999.

"Operation Tips: Terrorism Information and Prevention System." http://www.citizencorpts.gov/tips.html. Accessed July 19, 2002.

Powell, Bill. "Target: America; an Exclusive Look at What Investigators Have Discovered About Al-Qaeda's Plans for Its Next Big Attack." *Time*, August 16, 2004, 28–36.

Powell, Colin. "Iraq: Denial and Deception: U.S. Secretary of State Colin Powell Addresses the U.N. Security Council." http://www.whitehouse.gov/news/releases/2003/02/20030205-1.html. 2003.

Rose, Nikolas S. *Powers of Freedom: Reframing Political Thought*. Cambridge: Cambridge UP, 1999.

Rumsfeld, Donald H. "Testimony Prepared for Delivery to the National Commission on Terrorist Attacks Upon the United States." http:www.defenselink.mil/speeches/2004/sp20040323-secdef0923.html. 2004.

Shaw, Martin, and Roy Carr-Hill. "Public Opinion, Media and Violence: Attitudes to the Gulf War in a Local Population." *Gulf War Report Project. Report No. 1*. Hull: University of Hull, 1991.

Sturken, Marita. "Memorializing Absence." In *Understanding September 11*, ed. Paul Price, Craig Calhoun, Ashley Timmer, 374-84. New York: The New Press, 2002.

Virilio, Paul. *War and Cinema: The Logics of Perception*. London: Verso, 1989.

Woodward, Bob. *Plan of Attack*. New York: Simon & Schuster, 2004.

Zelizer, Barbie. "Photography, Journalism, and Trauma." In *Journalism after September 11*, ed. Barbie and Stuart Allan Zelizer, 48–68. London and New York: Routledge, 2002.

Zizek, Slavoj. "Melancholy and the Act." *Critical Inquiry* 26 (2000): 657–81.

———. *Iraq: The Borrowed Kettle*. New York: Verso, 2004.

———. *The Sublime Object of Ideology*. New York: Verso, 1989.

———. *Welcome to the Desert of the Real! Five Essays on 11 September and Related Dates*. New York: Verso, 2002.

Oral Rhetoric, Rhetoric, and Literature

Carroll C. Arnold

In 1960, Professor Donald R. Pearce edited and published a small volume entitled *The Senate Speeches of W. B. Yeats*.[1] Some editorial decisions Pearce made serve to focus attention on what the distinctive features of spoken, instigative discourse may be.[2]

Pearce included in his volume of "speeches" a body of extensively interrupted discourse on divorce, delivered in the Irish Senate. This material comprises remarks by Yeats and seven other senators plus a number of interruptive observations and rulings by the presiding officer of the Senate. The editor says he chose to present this discourse "practically in its entirety, partly as the best way of *incorporating necessary information*, and partly *to preserve the context* of excitement" surrounding what was "probably Yeats's forensic showpiece."[3] Elsewhere in his collection Pearce included what he titled, "Divorce: An Undelivered Speech."[4]

This editor's inclusion and treatment of materials satisfy common sense. Why? To ask the question is to draw attention to seldom discussed aspects of rhetorical speech: contextual information must be supplied if oral rhetoric (or its printed remains) is to be open to full understanding, and to think of an "undelivered speech" is not to be self-contradictory. I propose in this essay to explore why these common-sense judgments can be true and what the reasons may suggest concerning distinctions among oral rhetoric, rhetoric, and literature. In the process I hope to display some features of oral rhetoric which may partially account for the fact that editors like Pearce and ordinary users of English would find it unusual to refer to a man's "speeches" as his "tracts" and equally unusual to say that his "speeches" are, by definition if printed, "literature."

In furnishing contextual material for Yeats's remarks on divorce and in using the concept of "an undelivered speech" together with special contextual material, Professor Pearce acted as though some prose composed for oral delivery has attributes of a unique sort. He implied that these works by Yeats could not be rightly understood or rightly described by reference to the same data and terms that he would have used in presenting the other kinds of verbal works Yeats produced: essays, dramas, poems. In like ways most of us affirm in practical decisions that works we think of as "rhetorical" or "persuasive" are not fundamentally "literary" and that among "rhetorical" works those orally communicated or intended to be so communicated stand still farther apart because they were conceived for communication by means of the human behaviors we commonly call "speaking" and "listening." But, as I have said, the bases of these judgments are seldom discussed; therefore, in this essay I shall try to ask in several ways whether paragraphs like the following are the fruits of significant observations of the ways of men or are careless effusions. N. F. Newsome's "Preface" to a volume entitled Voices from Britain contains this paragraph:

> Here is an outstanding volume of history written in the spoken words of those who were living and making it. Nothing quite like this has appeared before. Great historic works by men who played a leading role in the events which they recorded, such as Churchill's World Crisis, are not the same as this book because they have been written afterwards with a retrospective eye. Collections of despatches, letters, or even speeches by eminent men are different because they have either been intended for the eyes or ears of only a comparatively few contemporaries or have been framed deliberately for posterity. Here we have the words which men and women of many nations chose for vast audiences of their contemporaries, words spoken from the heart and to the heart, expressing the feelings which the speakers were experiencing at the moment of delivery, and aimed at producing an immediate course of conduct among the listeners, which would itself make history.[5]

In making their distinctions Pearce and Newsome avoided such hard-to-anchor terms as "rhetorical" and "literary." In the inquiry I propose, I shall need the terms and must therefore define them. I shall not inquire directly into the reasonableness of our common distinction between discourse that is "rhetorical" and discourse that is "literary," but I shall assume that some distinction of the sort can be made. I shall take it as given that whatever "rhetoric" and "literature" may be, they are not *ipso facto* identical and that "rhetoric," whether written or oral, is, as Lloyd F. Bitzer has said, "pragmatic; it comes into existence for the sake of something beyond itself; it functions ultimately to produce action or change in the world; it performs some task. In short, rhetoric is a mode of altering reality, not by the direct application of energy to objects, but by the creation of discourse which changes reality through the mediation of thought and action."[6] Within this understanding of "rhetoric" I wish chiefly to inquire whether rhetoric presented orally differs sufficiently from other rhetoric to justify the differentiations implied in editorial and ordinary practices.

I

Rhetorical discourse that was once oral or was intended for oral presentation constitutes troublesome material for literary historians even when all that remains is the printed matter. Categories like poetry, drama, novel, essay—even journalism—represent conceptually stable classes of verbal achievements which are useful to historians of the verbal arts, but "speech" has in modem times proved far less useful as a characterizing or critical construct. It is true that literary histories and theoretical works mention "oral literature," "speeches," "orations," and "public addresses," but these terms are usually introduced without any intention of specifying literary, philosophical, or other generic features of the verbal works. For the most part such terms propose only that the works referred to existed at some time in an acoustic medium.

I suggest that the difficulty of the literary historian and the practices of editors of speeches are rooted in the public and private meanings with which orality[7] stamps spoken rhetoric. Some implications of the rhetorical theory of an older, essentially oral, civilization give credibility to the suggestion.

The body of theory purporting to explain the features of rhetorical speeches has a long and uneven history. It originated in the classical era of the western world under the inclusive name "rhetoric." It was initially a theory of public speech, though from its beginnings it also had important applications to written discourse. I shall not undertake to outline the theory; I wish only to point out that whenever this rhetorical theory focused directly and broadly on oral rhetoric, it dwelt especially on the practical consequences—the meanings to persons involved—of the human relations implicit in and generated by orality. It commented -only secondarily, if at all, on the aesthetic attributes of that which was said.[8] It also assumed that no "speech," no rhetorical speaking, could be thoroughly understood apart from its original context.

Ancient theory at its best emphasized that the possibilities of interaction[9] between a maker of spoken rhetoric and time-and-place-bound respondents must principally control that maker's creative options, and that the interactions actually generated by speaking would determine the social consequences of the discoursing. The theories of the oral world stressed what the shadow of the printing press often obscures for moderns: where orality is the mode of rhetorical discourse, exposure of the self in a personalized relationship with another specially modifies the creative and responsive experiences of both makers and listeners. Even in preparation, the theory went, prevision of interaction with particular listeners must direct the intending speaker's choices.

The best writers on rhetoric in the classical era were at pains to analyze the interplaying forces emanating from the person of the communicator, from his intentions, from the substance of his discourse, and, especially, from the thoughts and feelings generated by respondents' consciousness of the circumstances under which they engaged with their communicator. These writers implied that the intellectual, verbal, and perceiving processes of all engaged in oral, rhetorical communication would be uniquely aligned just because the participants' relationship was exposed, personal, and interactive rather than separative, impersonal, and remote. Plato's reasons for preferring speech over writing express this view directly.[10] Isocrates protested that the sophists of his day were mistaken in applying to the art of speaking rhetorically "the analogy of an art with hard and fast rules." To their doctrines he replied:

> what has been said by one speaker is not equally useful for the speaker who comes after him.... But the greatest proof of the difference between these two arts is that oratory is good only if it has the qualities of *fitness for the occasion,* propriety of style, and originality of treatment, while in the case of letters there is no such need whatsoever.[11]

As is so often the case, Aristotle illustrates the ancient view incisively:

> Compared with those of others, the speeches of professional writers sound thin in actual contests. Those of the orators, on the other hand, are good to hear spoken, but look amateurish enough when they pass into the hands of a reader. This is just because they are so well suited for an actual tussle, and therefore contain many dramatic touches, which, being robbed of all dramatic rendering, fail to do their own proper work, and consequently look silly. Thus strings of unconnected words, and constant repetitions of words and phrases, are very properly condemned in written speeches: but not in spoken speeches —speakers use them freely, for they have a dramatic effect.[12]

Aristotle was here thinking of how personalized interaction affects generation and perception of style, but in all his discussions of the spoken word he stressed the special psychological and motivational concomitants of orality which must qualify experience. This pervasive awareness of the consequences of orality is found even when he discusses interrogation in dialectic:

> He who is about to ask questions must, first of all, choose the ground from which he must make his attack.... As far as the choice of ground goes, the philosopher and the dialectician are making a similar inquiry, but the subsequent arrangement of material and the framing of questions are the peculiar province of the dialectician;

> for such a proceeding always involves a relation with another party. ... the philosopher and individual seeker does not care if ... the answerer refuses to admit them as premises] because they are too close to the point of departure and he foresees what will result from his admission....[13]

As has been pointed out, we, too, often recognize in ordinary practice that there is special significance in orality, but we are less consistent than some of the ancients in recognizing the extent to which orality and the conditions surrounding it create meanings of unique sorts. And yet coruscating meanings of orality are always present in rhetoric that is oral.

"Speaking," "spoke," or "speech" can, and often do, function for us as terms stipulating something more subtle than that an acoustic transmission occurred, but we do not always regard the full human experience to which the terms denotatively refer. It is not at all unusual to find otherwise careful philosophers and critics using variants of "speak" as though the experiences of writing-reading and speaking-listening differed in no fundamental ways. On the other hand, it is an interesting test to try to use the words, "He spoke to me," without implying that a special degree of intimacy and direct relationship was established between the "he" and the "me." It is all but impossible to communicate exclusively immaterial, disembodied, or extramundane experience through the word "speak" or other terms that connote the *action* of speaking. I suggest that for most readers a greater degree of intimacy and interaction, hence danger, is connoted by the King James Version's "And they heard the voice of the Lord God walking in the garden. . . . " than by the Revised Standard Version's "And they heard the sound of the Lord God walking in the garden. ..." And G. Lowes Dickinson's comment on Greek omens and oracles illustrates how human experience with gods who "speak" as well as prefigure may be culturally significant data. Says Dickinson:

> And if anyone were dissatisfied with this method of interpretation by signs [omens], he had a directer means of approaching the gods. He could visit one of the oracles and consult the deity at first hand about his most trivial and personal family affairs.[14]

Through oracles the gods spoke and entered mediately but intimately into human events and experience; they did not merely signify.

My point here is simply that common usage, even across cultures and in relation to deities, illustrates that orality—the act or the anticipated act of speaking to alter another's perceptions—is itself meaningful. The fact of orality means some degree of interdependence prevails or is going to prevail between speaker and others, for mutually influential interaction or the expectation of it is inescapable in speaking and being spoken to.

The fact of orality also generates whatever meanings any participant in orality has learned to attach to associations with other humans and to the processes of sustaining them by means of speech and listening. Quite apart from the persons involved, these learned meanings of speaking and listening may be supportive or destructive of wishes to influence or be influenced through speech; in any case the meanings of orality in consequence of the attitudes projected upon it as an action are seldom insubstantial. During the experience of oral communication intricate but measurable psychological, linguistic, and even physiological changes occur in human beings (as speakers *and* as listeners) and a number of such changes seem defined by the conditions orality peculiarly invokes.[15] Speaking and listening *as actions* thus have positive, negative, or indifferent values in and of themselves.

Turning to what most men have observed in themselves, one can say further that orality, in and of itself, alters both the readinesses and the receptivities of those involved in it. Whether the relationships of orality are previsioned or experienced in actuality, speaker and listener revise their views of self; experience becomes markedly other-directed; personality is recognized as an inevitable, legitimate, energizing element among affective forces; special communicative resources are seen to exist and to require use and control; special hazards are recognized, requiring to be mastered sufficiently to meet conventional standards of the oral mode. These, too, constitute meanings of rhetorical speech as action. The meanings are seldom verbalized, but they nonetheless form a part of, or modify, any message given or perceived when there is speech to alter another's perceptions.

Speech as action and rhetorical speech as rhetorical action have still other meanings which need not be discussed here since at this point I seek only to illustrate the fact that orality, as I have defined it, involves speakers and those spoken to in ways and with meanings that are not at all comprehended within the familiar but simplistic formulation: the media were acoustic and, perhaps, visual. I have sought to show that significant and special meanings are communicated by the *use of* that acoustic-visual medium we call speech.

II

The meanings that flow from the *use of* speech for rhetorical purposes are reflected in speakers' creative experience in anticipation of communicating orally and during the action thereof. Doubtless creative choices are affected in numerous ways. One of the most obvious sources of such influence on creativity is reflected by the question speakers have raised across more than twenty centuries: Will I be able to command *myself,* including my thoughts, under the conditions of orality? The ancients' concern with their rhetorical "canon" *memoria* and modern talk of "stage fright" and "speech reticence" both reflect awareness that a unique set of problems affects the making of rhetorical communications that are oral.

Quintilian pointed to the special strains of speaking as experience, saying that in each instant of speaking rhetorical speakers must at one and the same time recall their plans for communication, preserve awareness of how far the plans have been achieved and what remains to be done, look ahead to what is required in instants to come, and do all of this while maintaining precisely the intellectual, personal, and emotional relationship with listeners which immediate and longer-ranged purposes require.[16] Whatever we may think of Quintilian's psychological concept of memory, he fastened on one of an oral communicator's peculiar conditions of creativity: intellectual, emotional, and overt behavioral processes must be managed as part of a plan during personal interaction with those on whose judgments the speaker's own purposes depend.[17] In this sense rhetoric that is oral is always rhetoric-in-stress. Creation of non-oral discourse involves psychological stress, too, but not of these kinds.

Displayed choice and self-command during the making of oral rhetoric become part of the communicated rhetoric, as Aristotle was fist to note. Each behavior 'presents public evidence of the speaker's principles of choice, his failure to choose when choice was possible, or his lack of principles by which to choose what to do and say in his circumstances. All discernible features of planning for speech and of the speaking itself and all discernible omissions declare, clarify, obscure, or otherwise signal to those who see and/or hear, a speaker's intelligence, his intentions toward those to whom he is relating himself, his integrity, his capacity *to* relate himself to others, or his want of these.

Aristotle was tempted to believe indications of *ethos* exhibited during rhetorical speech formed the most powerful influence in spoken rhetoric. Possibly he over-estimated this influence; some modern studies hint that there are times when reputation and exhibited choices have only short-ranged power over listeners' attitudes.[18] But there is no doubting that each visible or audible reflection of choice can conclusively modify the meanings of things said, given a suitable set of circumstances. Even a disembodied voice will contribute its special stratum of personalized meaning.

To the extent that they are sensitive to such potential nuances of rhetoric when presented orally, speakers structure their verbal creations in special ways the better to meet the opportunities and risks that are inevitable when their rhetoric is to be oral. Hence rhetoric created for oral presentation is likely to reflect its maker's plans for investing (and protecting) his physical and psychological being in the final emergence of the communication. Words from Yeats's "undelivered speech" illustrate:

> I know that at the present stage of the discussion a large part of the Irish public, perhaps a majority, supports him [President Cosgrave], and I do not doubt the sincerity of that support—the sincerity that has heard only one side is invariably without flaw—and I have no doubt even that if he and they possessed the power they would legislate with the same confidence for Turks, Buddhists and followers of Confucius. It is an impressive spectacle, so quixotically impressive, indeed, that one has to seek its like in Mediaeval Spain. I wonder, however, if President Cosgrave and his supporters have calculated the cost—but no, I am wrong to wonder that, for such enthusiasm does not calculate the cost.[19]

Even in cold print Yeats's "undelivered speech" is a vehicle evidently created for use in personalized, not impersonal, influence. The living non-Catholic confronting the Catholic majority in a losing senatorial cause has been afforded "working room" by the choice of thoughts, of their sequence, and of the words and figures by which the flow of thought is symbolized. The extension of both body and mind toward interaction with other bodies and minds is provided for. Because we can see that this prose was created to give playing room to Yeats's reputation, personality, voice, and action, we sense with Pearce that this is, indeed, an undelivered *speech* and not at all an essay or editorial conceived for print.[20]

Most risks and special opportunities peculiar to rhetoric under conditions of orality derive from the fact that rhetorical speech acts are confrontations[21] of active beings; they are not confrontations of impersonally symbolized concepts (e.g., the symbolizings here presented in this journal) and vaguely specifiable human beings (e.g., the unknown readers of this essay). The distinction is important because confrontations of *persons* extort and define commitments. In the confrontations of oral rhetoric one must *stand with* his symbolic acts. His personal presence (even if only by voice) is itself symbolic, rhetorical action. His verbal and physical behaviors merge to form a flow of symbolic activity representing to the listening other the rhetorical speaker's entire physical and psychological organization—his perceptions of the ways things are and the ways they ought to be and his responses thereto. All this is carried to the listening others for interpretation and judgment. More than signification, verbal and gestural, occurs. A self that is not an abstraction but has a body supportively authorizes each signification.

Examining the last sentence quoted above from Yeats can illustrate the extent to which orality forces commitment. The debate for which Yeats prepared his speech did not take place. He sent "my notes" to *The Irish Statesman*, which published them. Neither then nor now could any reader know whether the aposiopesis of the last sentence quoted here was a literary man's display of verbal skill, a debater's way of placing an opponent in an awkward dilemma, or a break of thought faithfully representing emotional frustration in the self of Yeats. Had Yeats spoken, he must have committed his entire being to one of these interpretations or some other. The extensive commitments extracted by orality multiply possible communicables but thereby superpose special dimensions of risk upon every action consciously or unconsciously directed to the eye and ear of an other.

More than this, by choosing speech as his mode, a maker of oral rhetoric commits himself to "make something" of a human relationship. He, as person, and his symbolized claims must stand or fall by the qualities of the relationships he can create, sustain, and direct. The interplay among rhetorical speaker, listener, and rhetorical discourse is therefore much more complex than is conceivable within the now popular sender-channel-receiver-feedback communication models derived from principles of electrical circuitry. One who speaks rhetorically chooses to inaugurate and to try to sustain until attainment of a purpose a series of events in human relations. He does so by means of symbolic acts which assert what and how listeners ought to *be* in successive instants. He does this in hope that his listeners will find

> in the perceivable behaviors of speaking whatever is necessary to lead them to make closures on such internally created messages as will have consequences for them which resemble the consequences the speaker conceived as his original reasons for instigating. Whether listeners' (or readers') closures have consequences like those their communicators previsioned is precisely what is at issue in all rhetorical communication; with reference to the mode of communication, what respondents "have to go on" is a major source of philosophical and psychological differences among communicative experiences.

It appears to me that a basic characteristic of rhetorical engagement or relationship under conditions of orality is that each party retains his dominion over self but commits himself to ally (often fitfully) with the other in closure-encouraging, closure-making activity. Because the alliance is sustained orally, the burden of sustaining it to the listeners' satisfaction falls upon the person-as-action of the speaker.

As instigator, a rhetorical speaker assumes (and if listened to, is granted) the right and the burden of sustaining and directing the course of the communicative alliance by fusing his person and personality with a conceptual message. There is, however, the possibility that the thinking-feeling alliance essential to his purposes may become captious or disintegrate, leaving him, as it were, talking to himself. What we casually call "loss of attention" is, from the speaker's viewpoint, a public destruction of a relationship he was publicly committed to sustain and on which he risked aspirations that went quite beyond a wish for listeners' adherence to what he said; they grasped at public endorsement of his state of being, *now*.

To put the matter differently, any speaker with rhetorical intent acts, first projectively and then actually, as his own protagonist in an interaction with fellow human beings who, on their parts, see *themselves* as both chief protagonists and directors in the relationship. The conditions being those of orality, something resembling the speaker's script is to be played ensemble, despite the fact that no one engaged in the personalized, rhetorical situation can be cast as a minor actor within *his* dramatic world. In speech the physical person and the existential self are invested—in what is prepared to be spoken, in what is spoken, and in the instant-by-instant *being* of speaking. Listeners expect it to be so and, if they listen, they ready themselves to close on instigated but private messages, all the while regarding the speaker as an "other" who seeks a role within their worlds.

The sovereign parties in rhetorical alliance have different jurisdictions, and we shall misunderstand any rhetorical interaction and suasion if we suppose one party passive, at the mercy of, or the "victim" of the other. Professor Mendel F. Cohen has pointed out that all didactic communication (which is rhetoric under the definition I am using) confesses that someone else's behavior can alone fulfill the communicator's goals, but his analysis helps one to see that the "confession" is purposive.

An individual's own desires, values, and interests will determine whether such facts [that respondents have their own ends] are reasons for *him* to advise P [where P is respondent] at all, and if so whether they are reasons for him to advise P to do T or something else. For someone who desires to see P attain his ends or feels obligated to be of assistance to P, they will be reasons to advise P to do T. For someone who believes P's ends are improper or who hopes to benefit from the frustration of P's purposes, they will be reasons to advise P to do something other than T. And for someone who is completely indifferent to P, these facts will not constitute reasons for advising P at all.[22]

Any act of discoursing rhetorically implicitly declares that either the first or the second of Cohen's conditions exists. The communicator is *not* indifferent to his respondent's goals; for his own purposes, he has chosen to be dependent upon P's pursuit of his own ends. In oral rhetoric the choice of speech as a means of communication further declares the speaker's wish that P shall, in *this* time and place and through the moments of *this* personalized relationship, close on instigated but private messages relative to P's own purposes. If all goes according to the speaker's wish, P's closures will have consequences at once serviceable to P's ends and consonant with the closures the speaker envisioned as serviceable to his ends. If rhetoric is oral, speakers thus stake their senses of personal, social, and physical well being upon their ability to instigate, sustain, and direct relationships with listeners in such ways as shall seem to serve the ends of both. The maker of rhetoric has chosen as his instrument of influence a procedure in which, at inevitable risk of synchronal, manifest defeat, the conjoined forces of symbolization, including the symbolic significations of his state of being, are extended into the worlds of others in search of mediated change.

III

On the basis of what has been said, I suggest that at least the following understandings and concessions are constituents of all interactions in which rhetorical speakers and listeners participate.[23]

A. A speaker and some listeners are *knowingly* engaged in a mutual, working relationship of considerable intellectual and psychological interdependence. I have discussed this kind of knowledge in the speaker; it is also the knowledge of every rational and attentive listener who knows the speaker knows he is listening. Any listener who believes himself part of the audience the speaker means to address presumes that the relationship he enters by attending is one offered to him with a view to changing his perceptions; he knows his continued participation in the relationship is largely voluntary, but he also knows that to whatever degree he allows the relationship to continue, he concedes to his speaker the privilege of *trying* to direct his perceptions of reality.

Such acknowledgments do not, of course, comprehend all rhetorical forces that can be generated by oral rhetoric. Unknown to the speaker, he may be overheard or otherwise influence. But unknown vectors of influence cannot define the conditions of communication for the communicator. On the other side, a listener may regard himself as beyond the instigative intentions of a rhetorical speaker even though an acoustic bond associates them. But our central questions in this essay concern whether there are forces that consistently shape rhetoric that is oral, and such conditions as I have just mentioned do not invalidate the view that a basic feature of oral rhetoric is that it will reflect and be perceived as reflecting acknowledged, mutual relations of solicitation, dependence, collaboration, and concession between an acting speaker and some active listeners who know and are known lo know they are exposing themselves to the possibility of change.

B. Speaker and listener know, or think they know, that each will behave according to his own purposes and has the right so to behave.[24] Because of this knowledge, speakers will sometimes seek to conceal their aims and grounds for choice but on other occasions will make their intentions and principles of choice unmistakably clear.[25] For the same reason listeners will be sometimes exceedingly accepting (when identifying their own with the speaker's aims and principles of choice) and sometimes suspiciously defensive (when, as Johnstone suggests, they view their speakers as having possibly ''harmful properties"). Thus, in oral rhetoric each partner is striving in each successive moment to adjust his behavior to what he presumes, on the basis of what he has seen and heard so fur, are the purposes and principles of the other. Purposiveness is therefore always present in the relationship, but the purposes at work may or may not be like; they may be coalescent or polar, fixed or provisional, isochronal or anachronous, and they may be reflected in or determined by either verbal or physical behavior. In these senses purpose is protean content of oral rhetoric because the behaviors that sustain the human relationship emerge as association progresses. Similar kinds and qualities of fluctuating purposiveness, especially in the communicator, are all but inconceivable in systematic discourse that is not oral.

C. Speaker and listener are knowingly engaged in a relationship wherein the listener's immediate definitions of "sufficient reasons" are the coin of exchange. Having chosen to exert influence through speech, the speaker entered, as it were, into a special bargain with his sovereign listeners. He accepted as determining—for each moment of relationship—his listeners' standards of "sufficiency." Moreover, "sufficiency" is in these circumstances not exclusively logical, or derived from the denotations of what is spoken; it may not even be directly the product of verbal behavior. Consciously or subconsciously, speaker and listener know that "sufficient reasons" may be emotional, charismatic, or logical, or any of these, functioning in any degree of combination to justify adherence[26] to the positions and attitudes represented by the speaker. It is common to find this condition under which oral rhetoric must function deplored in the literature of philosophy, rhetoric, politics, and religion. But the condition obtains, as both reason and the complaints testify.

IV

On the reasoning offered here oral rhetoric can only be understood as someone's attempt at intricately adapting ideas, symbolic action, time, and personality in hopes of winning adherence from a specifiable segment of humanity to which all rights of final judgment have been conceded for the duration of engagement with it. Put another way, a unit of rhetorical discourse that is or is intended to be oral is an instigative portion—only a portion—of conception and attitude inducing interaction with a particular body of listeners, in whom, and only in whom, the final, altering rhetoric can be generated and the purposes of the speaker realized.

Such a description yields some answers to the three lines of questioning with which this essay began. The questions were: Why must discourses that were once oral or intended to be oral be preserved in context, as other verbal works need not? Why is it no self-contradiction to think of "undelivered speeches"? Why has "speeches" proved so unsatisfactory a critical and historical construct in modern literary history and theory? A general answer to all three questions is: no other literary or quasi-literary enterprise has precisely the set of features peculiar to oral rhetoric and no other discourse comes into existence through a like pattern of opportunities, constraints, risks, meanings, and tacit understandings.

In specific response to the last of the three questions it is useful to observe again that in rhetorical engagements by orality, aesthetic functions and values are of but secondary significance; practical judgments about the relevance of another's *purposes* are determining.

This distinction is not always remembered by literary historians and critics or even by rhetoricians, but the distinction seems fundamental. Nor is it less so if, as Wellek and Warren express it, a unit of rhetoric poses "problems of aesthetic analysis, of stylistics and composition, similar or identical to those presented by literature. .. ."[27] The discourse still could not have been conceived as oral rhetoric or have existed as rhetoric in the conditions of orality by *virtue of* its aesthetic values. To the degree that interactions under the conditions of orality are controlled by aesthetic perceptions and valuations, the interactions culminate in closures largely, if not wholly, definitional and criterial—either of which remains at least one step away from a closure or action perceivable or useful, hence satisfying, within the speaker's world.

Even attempts to see oral rhetoric and non-oral rhetoric as a single class of at least quasi-literary works have proved little more satisfying than attempts to see literature and rhetoric as whole and part. We are now in a position to see why.

At the turn of this century, George Pierce Baker, Charles Sears Baldwin, and others pointed to the special problems of adaptation which are shared by letter writers, editorial writers, a few other makers of "public address," and rhetorical speakers.[28] The attempt was to assimilate oral rhetoric within a literary category designated "public address." The limited relevance of aesthetic considerations to rhetoric in general proved a principal obstacle.[29] But even so functional a concept as "public address" furnished no basis for integratively conceiving writer-reader and speaker-listener relationships and their consequences to creativity. Not even the writer of a personal letter must stare his failure in the eye, and readjust, or fail to readjust and so fail again, when in some moment he misses the private mood of his correspondent. Such prospects do not qualify his moments of composition as they must the composition of rhetorical speakers-to-be.

Two broad but particularizing features give spoken rhetoric characteristics distinctive from those of "literature" in general and even from those of written rhetoric: the commingled functions of messenger and message and the constraints and opportunities of being locked in personalized association with a particular audience. These differentiating features arise from, and their differentiating influences are at least partly determined by, dimensions of risk to the self which a relationship sustained by orality thrusts upon speaker and listener.

Responding to the second question originally posed, one sees that it is no contradiction of terms or concepts to think of "undelivered speeches." It is entirely possible to create a verbal schema with which forces of the maker's (or another's) person and self-revelation are later to be intertwined according to plans transcending the words composed. And we may turn the coin. It is no contradiction to think of orally presented non-speech—even of rhetoric orally presented which is not "oral rhetoric." All have submitted to both. They rise unsocially from pages or spring as soliloquies from private thought and feeling. They consult and adapt scarcely at all to actual listeners' immediate bases of judgment. Utterance cannot make them "oral rhetoric" for they are not on-going adjustments of design and resources created for and in response to moments of solicitous, personalized interaction.

With the question of contradiction resolved, it becomes still clearer why speaking and speeches comprise generally unprofitable targets for literary criticism that seeks to illumine the aesthetic qualities of the works it inspects. Oral rhetoric is "strong" or "weak" in reference to particular circumstances for which it was conceived and in which it matured. The relevance of a unit of oral rhetoric to circumstances not foreseen during its creation or adjusted to during its presentation is gratuitous. Accordingly, oral rhetoric becomes "literature" in the usual sense only by the accidents of subsequent circumstances. If conditions like those that generated it recur and reinstate its relevance to the social experience of men, rhetorical discourse that was once oral may be *given* the status of "literature" as that term is commonly used today. But it is the renewal of conditions of response, rather than the work itself, that confers upon once oral rhetoric the universality of appeal that modern literary history and theory ordinarily consider the mark of "literature."[30]

And Professor Pearce's need to furnish context for "a speech" is accounted for by all the considerations reviewed here. Oral rhetoric is time-bound, occasion-bound, and bound to a particular human relationship previsioned, instigated, and sustained within a particular set of circumstances that pass into history as utterance ends. For the most part essays, dramas, poems, novels, and other "literary" forms are explicable apart from the circumstances of their creation, but the real or imagined circumstances of creation are the explanations of instigative messages that are oral. If a "speech" is truly rhetorical, it is the product of circumstantial engagement, imagined or imagined and actual.

V

I have hoped to show in preliminary fashion that oral rhetoric differs fundamentally from that which we normally call "literature" and differs significantly from other rhetoric that is not oral. The differences emerge in consequence of the unique human relationships that constitute the conditions of orality. I have argued that to personalize rhetorical instigation by means of orality is to engage humanly, particularly, interactively, in a special kind of context, with unique commitments of the self and, therefore, with unique risks to the selves of both speakers and listeners.

Doubtless there is much more to be discovered concerning the act of speaking rhetorically and its consequences to rhetorical discourse that is oral; many aspects of speech as action and of rhetorical engagement are yet to be probed. It is, to take but one case, a prominent limitation of this inquiry that implications and consequences of listeners' rhetorical engagements have been only superficially considered.

Department of Speech
The Pennsylvania State University

Notes

1. Bloomington: Indiana UP, 1960.

2. I believe Donald C. Bryant was first to use the term "instigative" to suggest both the intention of rhetorical communicators and the fact that completion of any rhetorical message occurs within those who have received it. See Donald C. Bryant, "Rhetoric: Its Functions and Its Scope," *Quarterly Journal of* Speech 39 (December 1953): 401–24.

3. Pearce, 6. My italics.

4. Ibid., 156–60.

5. *Voices from Britain*, ed. Henning Krabbe (London, 1947), 67. I choose to illustrate with Pearce's and Newsome's treatments of oral rhetoric because each writer makes his distinctions on practical rather than theoretical grounds. Each is chiefly interested in the historical and biographical significance of the discourse he discusses.

6. Lloyd F. Bitzer, "The Rhetorical Situation," *Philosophy and Rhetoric* 1 (January 1968): 3–4.

7. I shall use the term *orality* to mean: speaking to another with intent to alter his perceptions. I shall substitute this term for "speaking" and "speech" simply because the commoner words are constantly used even in philosophical literature without reference to such implications of speech-as-action as I wish here to discuss.

8. I think it relevant to observe that the ancient eras in which aesthetic considerations dominated over pragmatic considerations in judgments of oral rhetoric are historically designated the first and second "sophistics."

9. Consider Aristotle's observation, "It is not true, as some writers assume in their treatises on rhetoric, that the personal goodness *[ethos]* revealed by the speaker contributes nothing to his power of persuasion." [*Rhetoric,* 1356. trans. Rhys Roberts] Again, " the prudent and cautious speaker is controlled by the reception given by his audience—what it rejects has to be modified." [Cicero, *De Partitione Oratoria,* IV. 15. trans. H. Rackham.]

10. *Phaedrus,* St. 275–277.

11. "Against the Sophists," *Isocrates,* George Norlin trans., 3 vols. (Cambridge, MA: Harvard UP, 1956), 11, 171, secs. 9–13. My italics. Norlin calls special attention to Isocrates' emphasis elsewhere on "fitness for the occasion" as a controlling consideration in the creation of oral rhetoric.

12. *Rhetoric,* 1413b, trans. Rhys Roberts (New York: The Modern Library, 1954), 197.

13. *Topica,* 15Sb, trans. E. S. Forster (Cambridge, MA: Harvard UP, 1960), 675.

14. The *Greek View of Life* (Ann Arbor: U of Michigan P, 1958), 20.

15. Experimental research supports this statement for both speakers and listeners, though the precise natures of the changes and their exact causes are only spottily understood. For a partial review of the research, see Wayne N. Thompson, *Quantitative Research in Public Address and Communication* (New York: Random House, 1967), especially 72–92, 162–63, and 167–74.

16. *Znstitutio Oratoria,* XI. ii. 3.

17. It is significant that with absorption of most rhetorical theory into the theory of written composition and criticism, *memoria* disappeared from the language and considerations of rhetoric, except among those teachers and theorists specifically concerned with oral rhetoric.

18. Findings on this point remain confusing, especially because the influences of exhibited choices *during speech* have been much less studied than the influences of reputation. What does emerge from the welter of experimental studies of *ethos* is that these forces *can* influence powerfully and that their influence seems to vary from situation to situation. Especially suggestive reports include: Carl I. Hovland, Irving L. Janis, and Harold H. Kelley, *Communication and Persuusion* (New Haven: Yale UP, 1953), chap. 2; John Waite Bowen, "The Influence of Delivery on Attitudes toward Concepts and Speakers," *Speech Monographs* 25 (June 1965): 154–58; James C. McCroskey and Robert E. Dunham, "Ethos: A Confounding Element in Communication Research," *Speech Monographs* 32 (November 1966): 456–63; Paul D. HoltPnan, "Confirmation of Ethos as a Confounding Element in Communication Research," *Speech Monographs* 33 (November 1966): 464–66; Robert D. Brooks and Thomas M. Scheidel, "Speech as Process: A *Case* Study," *Speech Monographs* 35 (March 1968): 1–7.

19. Pearce, 156–57.

20. How different from other composition the process of preparing oral rhetoric may be is suggested (without comment on its uniqueness) by Pearce: "According to Mrs. Yeats . . . he [Yeats] usually

enjoyed an afternoon putting a speech together. Once she invoked for me a charming picture. Yeats would stride, tall and silverhaired, up and down the length of his study, shaping and rehearsing a passage, dictating it to her when it satisfied his ear, now and then breaking into laughter over some witty phrase, or mischievous illustration of a point." Pearce, 20.

21. I shall use this term in its simplest meaning: coming into direct, acknowledged relation with another, as in standing before him.

22. "'Is' and 'Should': An Unbridged Gap," *Philosophical Review* 74 (April 1965): 227. While Cohen is not concerned exclusively with either rhetorical or oral discourse, his observations apply to rhetoric in that they apply to didactic communication of all sorts and to such orality as springs from didactic intentions.

23. Some of what follows was suggested to me upon reading J. L. Austin, *How to Do Things with Words,* ed. J. 0. Unnson (New York: Oxford University Press, 1965), 108–19, and P. F. Strawson, "Intention and Convention in Speech Acts," *Philosophical Review* 73 (October 1964): 439 40. Strawson seems to me to have elucidated little regarded, implicit understandings of persuasive situations when he observed: "We might approximate more closely to the communicative situation ... by supposing it not only was clear to both A[udience] and S[peaker] that A was watching S at work, but also clear to them both that it *was* clear to them both." At some level, though not necessarily at all levels, of orality this kind of mutual awareness of communicative intentions *seems* to me imperative or no rhetorical communication can occur.

24. I cannot entirely agree with Professor Henry W. Johnstone's statement that in persuasion "the wish of an audience to reserve the right to disagree with the speaker addressing it may be viewed as a desire on its part to come to its own conclusions.... One may think of this reaction as a process through which an audience in turn comes to regard the speaker addressing it as an object whose harmful properties are well known but *can* be rendered ineffective by means of equally well-known precautions." *Philosophy* and *Argument* (University Park: The Pennsylvania State University Press, 1959), 53. It seems to me this observation is unduly two-valued, missing the fact that we sometimes yield to social control, shedding consciousness of speakers' "harmful properties" when persuasion appears to promise resolution of our anxieties or when it intensifies our existing beliefs. Under conditions of orality, when the forces of personality and exhibited choice are legitimized, such willing suspension of doubt seems even more possible. On the other hand, awareness that rhetoric is instigative can at other times produce just the defensiveness Johnstone points to. This is precisely the reason no competent analyst of rhetorical discourse dares disregard the fact that purposiveness is a recognized feature of persuasion and is endorsed or regarded as potentially harmful by all respondents engaged in confrontational rhetoric. Neither may the analyst safely disregard the fact that those who speak rhetorically are, if sensitive, aware that their listeners may and probably do have purposes different from their speakers'—an understanding clarified by Cohen's analysis.

25. Robert L. Scott's "A Rhetoric of Facts: Arthur Luson's Stance as a Persuader," *Speech Monographs* 35 (June 1968): 109–21, interestingly discusses some of the ways in which the supposition that, rhetoric can be invariably candid and invariably objective must break down as a premise on which to erect a theory of persuasion or of rhetoric.

26. It seems useful to follow Chah Perelman and L. Olbrechts-Tyteca in using the tentative terms *adherence* and *adhesion* to describe the acceptance that is at stake in rhetorical engagements. *Belief, agreement, acceptance,* and like terms connote complete and sustained concession such as is seldom characteristic of responses to rhetoric whether oral or other. Total commitment with sacrifice of all reservations is seldom hoped for or granted on matters normally treated rhetorically. Fixed adherence may be the rhetorician's wish, but, if he is realistic, he will seldom expect to win it where it did not exist before rhetorical engagement. *See Traité de l'Argumentation,* 2 vols. (Paris: Presses Universitaires de France, 1958), 1:5 for discussion of this point.

27. René Wellek and Austin Warren, *Theory of Literature*, 2nd ed. (New York: Harcourt, Brace & World, 1956), 15.

28. Baker's introduction to his *The Form of Public Address* (New York: Henry Holt and Company, 1904) fairly represents this attempt to integrate all rhetorical discourses or "addresses" within a single "literary" form and, thereby, to treat written and oral rhetoric as without fundamental differences.

29. Baker himself was ambivalent. Note the general equality and sometimes the primacy of aesthetic considerations apparent in the criteria of criticism proposed in the following: "Ideal public address means, then, significant thought presented with all the clearness that perfect structure can give, all the force that skillful sifting of material can produce, all the persuasiveness that perfect

understanding of the relation of the audience to speaker and subject can give, with vivid narration and description, a graceful style, and an attractive personality" [xix.] For Baker, Sears, and their colleagues, the criteria of *significance, vividness, perfection, grace,* and *attractiveness* tested universality and permanence of appeal as often as pragmatic relevance to particular listeners and readers. When he was clearest, Augustine's criteria for judging rhetorical discourse were in sharp contrast: "He who teaches should avoid all words which do not teach. And if he can find ... correct words which are understood he should select those; but if he cannot find them, either because they do not occur to him or because they do not exist, he should use words less correct, providing that the thing taught is taught and learned without distortion when they are used." *On Christian Doctrine,* trans. D. W. Robertson Jr., (New York: The Liberal Arts Press, 1958), Book IV. 24, p. 134.

30. What I have said here is, I believe, but an application to oral rhetoric of observations made by Bitzer, especially 10 and 12–13.